WOODWARD
AND
BERNSTEIN

WOODWARD
AND
BERNSTEIN

LIFE IN THE SHADOW
OF WATERGATE

ALICIA SHEPARD

John Wiley and Sons, Inc.

Published by John Wiley & Sons, Inc., Hoboken, New Jersey
Published simultaneously in Canada

For general information about our other products and services, please contact our Customer Care Department within the United States at (800) 762-2974, outside the United States at (317) 572-3993 or fax (317) 572-4002.

Wiley also publishes its books in a variety of electronic formats. Some content that appears in print may not be available in electronic books. For more information about Wiley products, visit our web site at www.wiley.com.

Library of Congress Cataloging-in-Publication Data:
Shepard, Alicia C., date.
    Woodward and Bernstein : life in the shadow of Watergate / Alicia
Shepard.
        p. cm.
    Includes bibliographical references and index.
    ISBN-13 978-0-471-73761-2 (cloth)
    ISBN-10 0-471-73761-5 (cloth)
        1. Woodward, Bob. 2. Bernstein, Carl, 1944– 3. Journalists—
United States—Biography. 4. Watergate Affair, 1972–1974—Press
coverage. 5. Washington Post, Times Herald. I. Title.
    PN4874.W6937S54 2007
    070.92'273—dc22
        [B]   2006012520

Printed in the United States of America

10 9 8 7 6 5 4 3 2 1

For Cutter and Lydia, who inspire me
and were always at the other end of the phone

Contents

Preface

In May 2002, Steve Mielke, an archivist at the University of Texas, got a curious phone call from his boss, Thomas F. Staley. Staley ran the university's Harry Ransom Center, and he wanted to see Mielke right away but wouldn't say why.

He probably wanted to talk about a new literary collection, thought Mielke. Mielke had catalogued the papers of playwright Tennessee Williams. Maybe it was another prized literary collection. Since 1988, Staley has been the head of the venerable Ransom Center, an American cultural archive in size and scope second only to the Library of Congress and the New York Public Library. The Ransom Center houses the world's first photograph (circa 1826) and one of the five surviving U.S. copies of the Gutenberg Bible. And thanks to Staley, the final proofs for James Joyce's *Ulysses* rest here. Staley's enthusiasm for what he does is palpable. When Mielke met him that day it was no different.

Mielke listened intently. Glenn Horowitz, a rare book dealer from New York City, had contacted Staley about buying a historical collection. These papers would be an unusual purchase for the Ransom Center, but a valuable addition and an enormous publicity boon. The owners wanted $5 million. Staley asked his archivist to go to New York City and Washington to evaluate the papers.

Mielke, intrigued, quickly agreed, but there was a caveat: he could tell no one. Secrecy was in order because of the nature of the papers. They would be called by a code name: Wormwood. Staley was just beginning negotiations and did not want his staff or any outsiders to know the famous papers were even for sale. They had never been offered for purchase before. If the Ransom Center got the papers, they would have to be locked up for security reasons while Mielke organized them. Inside the files were names of government officials whose connection to a historically important time had never been revealed. Only Mielke and Staley would have a key. The owners insisted. The owners! That was something else unusual about this deal. They were still alive. Mielke had only worked on collections belonging to dead authors. It could be helpful to be able to call them with questions or if something were missing. Another attractive aspect was that this collection, unlike many others, had an indisputable beginning. It started on June 17, 1972, with a *Washington Post* reporter's notebook.

The first thing Mielke did was start reading *All the President's Men*. Plane reservations were made, and he flew to New York to meet with Carl Bernstein and then a few weeks later to Washington to see Bob Woodward. Carl Bernstein and Bob Woodward— two of the most celebrated journalists in the world. Their names could be *Jeopardy* clues. In fact, the two men are American folk heroes for the role they played in uncovering what is often called the worst political scandal in U.S. history. Now they wanted to sell their Watergate papers, including everything they wrote and kept from June 1972 through the end of 1976. Altogether there were seventy-five boxes filled with 250 reporter pads, interviews, book galleys, typed notes, letters, and memorabilia, covering nearly 40 feet of shelf space. Neither man had thrown away anything.

Selling the papers had been Bernstein's idea. "I think that Carl needed the dough," said Benjamin Bradlee, executive editor of the *Post* during Watergate. Though Woodward and Bernstein together achieved something extraordinary in covering Watergate, it was Woodward who was able to parlay it into a lifelong career writing stories and books that have earned him fame, respect, and millions. Bernstein, on the other hand, has had a sporadic career that pales next to his prolific former partner's. Still, he has managed to turn his Watergate experiences into a steady income stream by giving speeches, writing two books and dozens of magazine pieces, and working in television. And yet, money has always been a problem. "By anybody else's standard, this would be a hell of a career," said respected journalist Haynes Johnson, who has known Bernstein since he was a teenage copyboy at the *Washington Star*.

"But he's always compared to Woodward. It shouldn't be that way."

But it is. Now, if Woodward would agree, the pair could sell their papers for a huge profit. Bernstein's papers were worth little alone. Horowitz and Bernstein went to Washington to see if they could convince Woodward. "Bob was reluctant—reluctant was a good word," said Horowitz. After Woodward was assured that he and Bernstein could protect their still living confidential sources until they died, he was game. He, however, did not need the money. Once again, as has happened several times throughout their lives, Woodward, who colleagues say is always generous with his time and money, was willing to help out his old partner.

Mielke liked what he saw, and soon Horowitz had successfully brokered a deal that was offered only to the University of Texas. The pair would get $5 million and give the university $500,000 to care for the papers and hold symposiums. The $5 million price tag, which private donors covered, made it one of the largest purchases of its kind in U.S. history, especially for the works of living writers. At a dinner before the sale was announced in April 2003, Harry Middleton, former director of the Lyndon Johnson presidential library based on the Texas campus, turned to Bernstein, now gray, and Woodward, graying at the temples, both noticeably thicker than when they helped topple a president three decades ago. Neither man was yet sixty, but they were damn close. "He looked at Bob and Carl and said that they must now understand, as they enter their seventh decade, that they are as much a part of the story of Watergate and historical record as any of the people they reported on," said Horowitz. "In many ways, that was a humbling moment for them. They had entered a different sphere of the public consciousness."

Bob Woodward, now sixty-three, and Carl Bernstein, sixty-two, are often introduced as the two men who profoundly and permanently changed journalism. Not only did Woodward and Bernstein play a pivotal role in President Richard M. Nixon's August 9, 1974, resignation, but their Watergate reporting and what immediately followed shaped the next thirty years of journalism. In today's media-saturated society, with the confusion of a million different ways of getting information, it's instructive to recall the narrow media universe of the early 1970s. Then, Americans relied largely on newspapers and the three major TV networks for their news. During Watergate, people rushed to the curbs to pick up papers for the latest development. During the Watergate hearings in 1973, Americans were glued to their TVs. But in the early days, the public turned to the *Washington Post* and a few other newspapers. Gradually they got to know the names Bob Woodward and Carl Bernstein.

Today the men are cultural icons. What other journalists could sell the thirty-year-old contents of their newsroom desks for $5 million? They are in the same pantheon with Ida Tarbell, Lincoln Steffens, Walter Lippmann, Edward R. Murrow, Walter Cronkite, and H. L. Mencken.

As important as Watergate was in political history, it was equally so in journalistic history. The beauty of Woodward and Bernstein's story is that also tells the larger narrative of what has transpired in journalism since Watergate. Watergate marked the birth of a different kind of reporting—more aggressive, less respectful of the establishment.

In telling the narrative of their lives, this book looks at how these two men influenced the modern history of journalism by exploring the advent of celebrity journalism, the controversial use of anonymous sources, the media's relationship with the public and the executive branch, the importance of the reporter-editor bond, and the role of investigative reporting. A year after Nixon resigned, journalists founded the nonprofit Investigative Reporters and Editors organization that today has about five thousand members. It was Woodward and Bernstein, the first Average Joe reporters to become full-blown celebrities, who became the story itself, and who became in some cases more famous than the people they were writing about. They popularized and made the use of anonymous sources an acceptable journalistic practice, although even today it is still the profession's trouble spot. And their reporting also produced one of the greatest and longest-lasting modern mysteries: Who is Deep Throat?

"As far as I'm concerned Woodward and Bernstein inspired a generation of journalists," said Alex Jones, head of the Joan Shorenstein Center on the Press, Politics, and Public Policy. Today many of those journalists are working at the nation's best newspapers, magazines, and TV and radio outlets, or running journalism schools. Over and over in reporting this book, I heard men and women say they had gone into journalism solely because of what Woodward and Bernstein had accomplished. There's nary a journalism class that does not tell the tale of what many call journalism's finest hour or show the movie *All the President's Men.*

I recently taught two classes on Watergate and the press to mostly undergraduates. All but a handful had already seen the movie, even though it came out when their parents were in their twenties. They had all heard of Deep Throat, and many were dismayed to see him on CNN in April 2006 as Larry King grilled a confused ninety-two-year-old man who barely remembered what Nixon did. He looked nothing like the image the movie had drilled into their consciousness, just as people are sometimes confused to find that Woodward looks nothing like Robert Redford. The names Woodward and Bernstein are so ingrained that sometimes people don't know which one is which. Bernstein will be walking down a New York City street and someone will see him and say, "Bob!" A newspaper recently ran a correction when it included Bernstein in a celebrity birthday round-up for February 14, but used Woodward's picture.

Not only did Woodward inspire a generation, they created a new vocabulary. "The terminology made popular by Woodward and Bernstein is now part of the journalistic vernacular," wrote Will Manley for the American Library Association in October 2002. "A reliable source, investigative reporting, deep background, off the record, stonewall, can you confirm or deny, and Deep Throat are all expressions that are peppered in the give and take between reporters and government officials. To truly alter the way our everyday world works, a book must first come along at the right place and time, but timing is only one-half the equation. The book must appeal to something deep within the human heart."

Woodward and Bernstein's saga captured the imagination of scores of Americans, judging by two feet of fan mail now in their Watergate archives. But the two reporters did *not* single-handedly bring down the president, though the media and public have solidly bought that myth and continue to perpetuate it. "They were not responsible for Nixon leaving office, but they had a hand in it," said Jones. "That's not to minimize what they did. But they get too much credit." They would agree, and have said so many times. The courts, the Congress, the grand jury, and the FBI all played key roles. In reality, had former Nixon aide Alexander Butterfield not told Senate investigators on Friday, July 13, 1973, that Nixon kept a secret taping system, Nixon might never have resigned.

Woodward and Bernstein get a disproportionate amount of credit—much to the frustration of several historians, and the authors themselves—simply by virtue of having published a wildly popular book that was transformed into a well-made, blockbuster movie that has endured. Many have misread their fascinating story as being the *only* story. Further fueling their fame was that they unwittingly turned a single secret source into a legend with the naughty nickname Deep Throat. Had they not written *All the President's Men*, had it not become a major motion picture, had their mysterious source been named My Friend, as Woodward first called him, and had Deep Throat's identity not remained unknown for three decades, it is possible I would not be writing this book. But all that did happen, and Woodward and Bernstein did indisputably play a role in Nixon's downfall, particularly by keeping the story alive in the early days of Watergate.

Three decades after Watergate, their names, especially Woodward's, are still synonymous with the gold standard in investigative, in-depth reporting. They still play a major role in journalistic and U.S. history. No matter what the scandal du jour, columnists and commentators continue to invoke their names when talking about some transgression or plead for another pair of Woodward and Bernsteins.

Today, Woodward, the lightning rod of the pair, enjoys extraordinary entrée to the George W. Bush White House, and critics accuse him of writing to protect the very access that he eschewed so long ago. He is not a muckraker, as he was called back then; he is a chronicler. In writing this book, it became clear that Woodward has become far more controversial than he ever was during Watergate. There are two main camps of Woodward opinions out there. One camp, highly critical and much more vocal, has accused him of all sorts of journalistic crimes, including calling him a mouthpiece for the Bush administration. The author Joan Didion, for one, referred to his work as "political pornography." The other is a much larger camp, if sales are any indication, who respect his reporting and feel, despite flaws, that Woodward provides readers an exceptional contemporary insight—the best they'll ever get—into the dealings of high-ranking officials and their peers.

Whether it's the present or the past, Woodward and Bernstein remain fixed in the public's mind. But there's so much more to their story beyond the tale they shared in *All the President's Men*. So much more happened to them after Nixon resigned and they skyrocketed to fame and glory. Few people know much about their relationship after Watergate, their loyalty to each other, how fame affected them, and the different trajectories their lives followed. Theirs is a fascinating, historically significant story of two men who could not be more different. Today, for example, Bernstein publicly demands a Watergate-like investigation of the Bush administration, and Woodward keeps his opinions private.

"There are special things only the two of us understand, from the work we did together to the way each of us looks at journalism," Bernstein told me in 2003. "There are things we say to each other that we'd never say to anyone else. It was true during the reporting of Watergate, and it's true now. No, we would not have been friends otherwise. We were not inclined to like each other before, and within weeks we came to develop this incredible respect for each other. Now, it's a great friendship."

They are separate people, driven by separate demons. There will always be comparisons, but they are not, despite public pressures, in some kind of race. They do different things. They have different lives. But once they were in a race together to get to the bottom of a White House mystery that would change their lives forever.

1

The Up and Comers

On the average there are roughly fifty burglaries daily in the District of Columbia. Some are reported at length in our news-paper. Most are reported in smallish type in a crime column. Obviously, this burglary was different.

—*Washington Post* managing editor Howard Simons in 1973

In June 1972, Leonard Downie Jr. was living in London on a fellowship with the London School of Economics. He was a long way from his job at the *Washington Post*, a paper he'd joined as a summer intern in 1964. Downie had worked his way up as a hotshot metro reporter covering local police and courts, and in the process had become one of the top investigative reporters in Washington. As was his habit, he routinely read the *International Herald Tribune* to keep up with what was happening back in the United States.

One day, he picked up the paper and read a story about an odd burglary inside the Democratic National Committee headquarters at the Watergate hotel complex. Five men in business suits wearing surgical gloves had been arrested on June 17, 1972, with nearly $2,300 in cash—most of it in sequentially numbered $100 bills—and carrying sophisticated bugging equipment. Downie found the story totally intriguing. One of the five men was James W. McCord Jr., who not only worked for the CIA but handled security for President Richard Nixon's re-election effort. Downie was dying to know more. The story he read on June 19, 1972, was written by Carl Bernstein and Bob Woodward. Downie was familiar with Bernstein's name but had no idea who the other reporter was.

"I'd never heard of Woodward," said Downie, who would become executive editor of the *Washington Post* almost two decades later in 1991. He wondered who Woodward was and what he was covering and whether they would work together when Downie returned to the *Post* in July.

Downie didn't know him because Woodward, twenty-nine, had joined the paper only nine months earlier, in September 1971. Woodward had not been a reporter for very long, but with a desire to write, unparalleled curiosity, and an insatiable need to uncover secrets, what other career would suit him?

Woodward had found his way to the *Post* from his hometown of Wheaton, Illinois. Wheaton is home to Wheaton College, a private, conservative Christian college, often called "the Harvard of Christian schools." With two thousand students, the college provided a steady stream of babysitters for the Woodward family.

Today it is home to the Billy Graham Center Archives, and it exerts a strong religious influence on the community. The college had set the morality bar high for the townspeople. Woodward's parents and their friends drank and smoked—a Wheaton College taboo—and often family members had to clean up evidence of sin before the babysitter arrived, as Woodward told author David Halberstam in the mid-1970s. Over the years, many a young religious zealot tried to convert the adolescent Bob Woodward. "Have you taken Christ?" they asked.

"Yes, I have," he told them, when he was about seven or eight. Over the years, he tried several times to become a born-again Christian, but it never took.

"It was a significant introduction into fraudulent behavior," he told Halberstam.

When Woodward was twelve, his parents' marriage crumbled, and along with it his childhood sense of security. Not only were his mother and father no longer married and living in the same house with him, his brother, David, and his sister, Anne, but his mother moved out. The children, in a decision uncommon in the 1950s, stayed with their father. The breakup of his family was terribly traumatic for Woodward, especially because, as he told Halberstam, the way he discovered his parents' impending divorce was by snooping through the mail. (He later learned while rifling through his father's pockets that his father intended to remarry. Alice Woodward was part of Bob's life for the next forty-one years.)

"He undoubtedly felt like he had been pushed aside," his father said in a 1996 *GQ* profile. "At the time of the divorce, I was really getting involved in the practice of law. Bob had no close relationship with somebody in the home as a parent."

His parents' painful divorce and later working as a janitor cleaning his father's law office at $11.75 a week are keys to Woodward's development as a reporter. The inquisitive Woodward could not help snooping through the treasure trove of documents that just might reveal Wheaton's secrets. "I was raised in a small town in the Midwest, and one of the things I learned very early was that everybody in the town had a secret," Woodward told movie director Alan J. Pakula in 1975. "My mother had a secret. Or a series of secrets. I had secrets. My friends had secrets. And most of the time nobody ever found out about those secret things." Woodward didn't know it at the time, but he possessed the kind of insatiable curiosity that defines reporters. They don't go into journalism for the money, though they feel blessed to be paid for doing what they love. But the bottom line is that they just *have* to know.

Woodward would be at his father's office at 10 p.m. when no one else was there. "You'd go around cleaning up ashtrays and trash cans and sweeping," he told me. "What's that on the desk? Oh that's interesting. You start looking at what's on the desk, then in the drawers, then in the files, then eventually to what they call the disposed files—in other words, old cases in the attic. Look, I'm a teenager. It just seemed obvious. There was no doubt or hesitation because again it's a private transaction. No one knows you are doing this. Maybe it's a waste of time. Maybe it's not. But you are going to learn something."

Alone at night, the young Woodward scoured divorce cases, IRS files, trial transcripts, and fraud cases. These all fascinated him, though he often discovered that hypocrisy pervaded people's actions. In one case, a high official in the school system was making advances on a student. The district attorney wired the girl to meet with the official, and Woodward found the transcript in the files.

"It was the first time you see the evidentiary purity of a tape recording," Woodward said.

As a junior at Wheaton Community High School, Woodward ran for student body president, but didn't win because many of his peers found him to be aloof and distant. Scott Armstrong, a Wheaton friend of Woodward's younger stepsister, Sue Keller, comanaged the freshman class campaign for Woodward with Keller. "I was the only person who delivered their class for him," said Armstrong, who was thirteen when he and Woodward first met. "I actually delivered a lot of people, but maybe it's more attributable to his stepsister."

After his father remarried, the family grew to six children—three of Alice's, three of Al's—and then became seven when Alice and Al had a daughter, Wendy. "They, the Woodwards, steps and others, all lived happily on Prairie Avenue," said Armstrong. "It was a mingled family. It was a large family, and his father was a terrific, intelligent lawyer, a city-father type, and his stepmother was a very energetic, make-everything-happen, Martha-Stewart-before-Martha-Stewart kind of woman, very capable and competent. His mother lived in a nearby community."

It may have seemed like a happy family to Armstrong, but that was the surface snapshot. Woodward's parents' divorce had had a profound effect on him, especially, as he told Pakula, since his mother had also had several nervous breakdowns while he was growing up. He has often told the story of counting Christmas presents after he realized that his father was being far more generous to his step siblings than to his own children. "Woodward counted the number of presents his stepmother bought for him and his younger brother and sister and compared them against the number of presents she bought her own kids," noted Pakula, after Woodward told him the story in 1975. "He had made a list of both sets of presents—priced them in stores. She had spent much more money on her own kids. He told his father it was unfair. When he called his father, he [Woodward] was hysterical. His father gave him the difference and told him to buy gifts for the kids. His father would not have discussed it with his stepmother, didn't want conflict. That kind of list, making investigations, thoroughness, obsession with unfairness has a lot to do with how he functions as an investigative reporter." Woodward told Pakula that he "kind of liked making investigations and was obsessive about unfairness."

Woodward had been groomed to follow in his father's footsteps. Known as Woody to close friends and Al to others, his father was a prominent lifelong Republican lawyer in town and later an Illinois Appellate Court judge. According to Pakula's notes, Al Woodward was a stoic workaholic who left his son alone. "Father Faulknerian character in the Midwest. Meticulous," wrote Pakula in his notes. "Do anything for anyone—simplistic—not intellectual. Family person. Father's reason for taking custody of family: 'mother was incapable of taking care of us. It was not that he had any need to raise family.'"

Around town, Bob was known as "Al's boy." For most of his life, he had followed a prescribed track that would lead him toward a law career. He'd played football in high school to please his father, although mostly he'd warmed the bench. His father had been captain of the Oberlin College football team, however, and playing high school ball was considered the manly thing to do. Woodward's approach to football was a harbinger of his future. His coaches were impressed not by his natural talent but by his indefatigable work ethic. Years later, Woodward's same intense dedication to reporting, despite his being a clumsy writer, would wow his editors.

"I think I played in two games in three years," Woodward told the *Chicago Tribune* in 1991. "Back then, Wheaton was dominated by two auras. One was that of Red Grange, who played football there. And the football stadium was called Grange Field. You played football if you possibly could. It was the thing to do. It was better to go out and sit on the bench than not go out. The second aura was that of Billy Graham."

In 1961, the year Woodward graduated from high school, he won a Naval Reserve Officers' Training Corps (NROTC) scholarship to Yale University. It helped to offset the cost of the pricey Ivy League college. But the scholarship meant that he would owe the navy four years of his life after graduation.

"I had a girlfriend that moved to New Jersey and that's why I went to Yale," Woodward told the *Houston Chronicle* in 1974. The girlfriend was Kathleen Middlekauff. She had grown up in Wheaton and had been Woodward's high school girlfriend, and she eventually married him in 1966, becoming Kathleen Woodward. She still uses that name today, although they divorced in 1970.

Moving halfway across the country into Yale's liberal elitism had a big effect on the conservative Midwesterner, who at his 1961 high school graduation had spoken words borrowed straight from Arizona Republican senator Barry Goldwater's *Conscience of a Conservative* speech.

Yale opened up new worlds to Woodward. During his freshman year, his roommate was dating a black woman, and Woodward opposed the relationship. By his sophomore year, he told Halberstam, he thought that his roommate should marry the woman. His world opened up politically as well, as he progressed from being a conservative Republican to having a greater comfort with socially liberal ideas and thoughts.

At Yale, Woodward majored in English and history, joined the secret society Book and Snake, and was editor of the *Yale Banner* yearbook. His college professors were literary lions Robert Penn Warren, the author of *All the King's Men*, and Cleanth Brooks. "Back then, I saw him as a very complex and creative person," said Kathleen. "The kind of writing he was doing then was very searching and exceedingly introspective and self-reflective and very on the edge. Not necessarily easy to understand. Existential. Very probing and intense. Highly intense. These were qualities I found exceedingly attractive."

It was at Yale that Woodward wrote his first book. "I read his novel," said longtime friend and Yale classmate Scott Armstrong. "I thought it was terrific. I'm sure there must have been something about it that was less than polished. But it was as well written, literary, and complicated as a Russian psychological novel. It had little bitty smidgens that I recognized from his life. I remember that it read well. I didn't have trouble turning pages, but I don't remember action. It was a very cerebral novel."

The novel was submitted to a publisher and rejected. "He was really devastated by that rejection, which was a simple rejection to the effect of, 'I'm sorry, your book is not right for our list.' I actually remember the line," said Kathleen Woodward. "It was very devastating for him because he had envisioned himself as a writer of fiction. I certainly thought he had talent."

After Woodward graduated from Yale in 1965 and then served in the navy for a year, he and Kathleen were married. He was twenty-three. That same year, Carl Bernstein, twenty-two, was joining the *Post* as a reporter. "My fantasy for Bob was that he would become the great American novelist, and I would be a researcher on Wall Street for, say, the photography industry or something and would support him. Isn't that funny?" said Kathleen. "But I didn't go on to grad school in economics. We were stationed in Norfolk first, then San Diego. But I did take courses in English, and here I am a professor of English and that was his major. It still wasn't clear to me that he was not going to be a novelist back then."

By the time of Woodward's Yale graduation, he, like many other young Americans, disagreed with the rationale behind the Vietnam War. He wanted no part of it, but he had made a commitment to the navy. First he served on the USS *Wright*, a communications ship that has since been decommissioned. He hated the navy, finding it boring. He took a correspondence course in romantic poetry just for intellectual stimulation.

In 1967, Woodward received orders to go to Vietnam and felt terrified, but he was smart enough to outsmart the navy. He had no intention of making a career out of the navy, so he feigned an interest in doing so with superior officers. He reasoned correctly that if he presented himself as a navy careerist, the navy would put him on a destroyer, far from the inland fighting. Otherwise his orders would put him in a situation where he was certain that he'd be killed. "I wrote a letter to every senior officer who might be able to help me," Woodward told Halberstam. "I got hold of the Pentagon phone directory and went through it methodically, looking for anyone I might know who might be involved in the decision." The navy put him on a destroyer, the USS *Fox*.

It was on the *Fox* that Woodward played one of the many pranks he would become famous for. This one involved the commanding officer of the *Fox*, when the ship was docked at Long Beach Naval Yard in California. The commander, Captain Robert Welander (who retired as a rear admiral) had his eye on an aircraft carrier tailhook, used to stop landing planes, that was encased in glass. Woodward decided to steal it for Welander. He told Halberstam that one night he got really drunk and hid in a closet, and when it was safe, he came out, smashed the case, stole the tail-hook, and brought it back to the *Fox* to present to Welander.

Back at the Pentagon, Woodward continued to be frustrated with the war. "I didn't like the Vietnam War and I didn't know what to do with that conclusion or emotion," explained Woodward. "I didn't have, quite frankly, the courage or the wherewithal to figure out how to do something about it. So I went along. My most rebellious act was to march in a peace march in my uniform, which was dangerous. I didn't quite realize that. That would have been the year 1969, which was at the height of those demonstrations. I did it in my uniform. At least with my navy jacket on. You know, not for hours, but I made an appearance." No one saw the full lieutenant in the U.S. Navy with Top Secret security clearance marching in a peace parade.

His second rebellious act also occurred at the Pentagon, when he was assigned as a watch officer overseeing TeleType communications for Admiral Thomas H. Moorer, the chief of naval operations. Woodward sent out a memo from the secretary of defense saying that "he'd become aware that there were lots of people who had unnecessary jobs in the Pentagon," Woodward told me. "And that the people who most realized they had unnecessary jobs were the people who held them. And if those people would come forward and identify themselves [Woodward started really laughing as he remembered], they would get their boss's job. They would be promoted [more laughing]. Yes, it was a prank. I gave it some distribution in the Pentagon and there was kind of a minor flurry of who had done this. I thought it was quite funny, and so did others."

By 1970, his years in the navy and varying career paths had taken a toll on his marriage. He and Kathleen decided to split up after four years of marriage. For her, the divorce was a horrible experience. She was teaching in France, and one day went to American Express to pick up her mail. Included was a newspaper clipping with the headline WOODWARD V. WOODWARD, which is how she found out her husband had filed for divorce. "It was news to me," Kathleen said. "Perhaps this is an example of his being demanding, or severe. We didn't really ever talk about it because it was not up for discussion."

When it was time to get out of the navy on July 31, 1970, Woodward wasn't so sure he wanted to go into law. He thought law school was a gutless thing to do for someone who had given five years of his life to the navy. Yet he applied and was accepted to Harvard Law School, though he knew he didn't want to go. But what did he want to do? He wasn't married. He wasn't tied down by loans or family or other obligations.

"I could have gone to law school," said Woodward. "When I was getting out of the navy I was thinking about all kinds of options. I thought about going to grad school, law school. I think Procter and Gamble still has this program where they hire people as a project manager. I interviewed with them. I had a girlfriend at the time who said, 'Oh, so you're going to be Mr. Jiffy Peanut Butter?' They didn't offer me a job. But if they did and that was the first thing that came along, I thought, that will be different. It won't be the navy. It won't be law school. You know, turns in the road."

One thing was certain: he didn't want a navy career. In Woodward's fifth year in the navy, he lived in Washington, D.C., and worked in communications for the Pentagon, though some Woodward critics claim that despite his repeated denials, he was involved in military intelligence.

"I spent my last year in the navy in Washington, D.C., from sixty-nine to seventy and I was working in the Pentagon and saw some of the things going on in Vietnam," said Woodward to a University of Maryland audience in 2002. "And I was reading the *Washington Post* and I realized the *Post* had a better take on what was going on in Vietnam than the generals and admirals in the Pentagon. I realized there was a disparity again between what was really going on and what was being said publicly about Vietnam. The sense the *Post* was a lifeline to what was really happening was very evident to me. That propelled me into the newsroom."

Woodward subscribed to the *Washington Post* and liked the direction its editor, Benjamin Bradlee, was taking the paper. In April 1970, he brashly wrote to the *Post* asking for a job on the major metropolitan newspaper, even though he had zero experience.

"Thank you for your letter of April 23 informing us of your July 31 release from the Navy," the *Post*'s director of personnel wrote, and offered to pass his file on. It wound up on metro editor Harry Rosenfeld's desk. Rosenfeld had become the metro editor in 1970. He agreed to see Woodward.

"I didn't want to just kiss him off," said Rosenfeld. "But normally, I wouldn't see anyone without any newspaper experience."

What made a difference was that Woodward had gone to Yale. This impressed Rosenfeld. So did Woodward's five years in the navy. Rosenfeld knew that sometimes you had to take a chance on people, although he'd once made a mistake by hiring a man with a Ph.D. and a WASPy name with "the third" attached. "He worked as hard as he could," said Rosenfeld. "But he was not a newspaperman."

Yet Rosenfeld knew that this previous unfortunate experience shouldn't warn him off other raw talent. He found Woodward refreshing. "Woodward made a good impression on somebody like me who was used to a lot of hippie reporters, running around with beards and smelling of marijuana. It was a relief to see somebody who looked like an earnest type, a sober citizen."

Rosenfeld decided to give him a two-week tryout and assigned him to his deputy, Andrew Barnes, who had started at the *Post* in 1965. Barnes would leave in 1973, making his way up to become editor of the *St. Petersburg Times* in Florida.

"I'd always been open to atypical candidates," said Barnes. "That's how you get good journalists. God knows, Bob was smart and wanted to do the job. The *Post* newsroom was not the neatest and tidiest, and Bob was so neat and trim. Perfectly shaved. Erect in his bearing. He didn't say, 'Yes, sir,' but he was right on the edge."

No matter what the assignment, Woodward busted his butt. He was always at the paper. Barnes cooked up assignments to cover small-time, unmemorable events, and he was impressed. If another three calls or more trips out of the office were necessary, Woodward made them. The problem was, Woodward didn't know how to write a story or understand the lingua franca of a newsroom. He didn't know what Barnes meant when he used words like *nut graph*, *attribution*, or *lead*.

Barnes was a desk editor. He moved thousands of words of copy a night. He knew who was good and whom he had to worry about on the metro staff. He didn't have time to tutor Woodward, nor was there any system in place for veterans to help green reporters. No matter how hard Woodward tried, Barnes knew it wouldn't work. Woodward never wrote one story that was good enough to go into the paper.

"Bob didn't know how to tell a story," said Barnes. "He had all the facts, but you had trouble tracking the story and it was boring. Bob wanted to succeed, and God knows I wanted him to. But his stories would have taken constant editing, and then I'd worry about a mistake being edited into the story."

At the end of the tryout, Barnes told Rosenfeld that Woodward had some raw talent but needed aging. "I remember saying to Bob, 'I'm with you, but this isn't going to work out,'" said Barnes. "He may have been crushed. But he wouldn't have shown it."

Woodward left the paper in love with reporting and only a little bit discouraged. He knew he had more to learn, but he had found work that he loved. "I left more enthralled than ever," Woodward wrote in *The Secret Man: The Story of Watergate's Deep Throat*. "The sense of immediacy in a newsroom and the newspaper was overwhelming to me."

With recommendations from the *Post*, Woodward got a job at the *Montgomery Sentinel*, a small, respectable Maryland weekly paper where Woodward could learn on the job as countless other gung-ho, inexperienced reporters had done. He did just that. He covered the hell out of whatever he was assigned, and he roamed freely, occasionally doing minor investigative stories.

"One of the stories I wrote was an evaluation of all the high school principals in Montgomery County," Woodward told *Writer's Digest* in 1996. "I'd never written a story that created such a firestorm. Hundreds of people picketed the newspaper. One of the principals sued for libel, unsuccessfully ultimately. Obviously, the quality of education was very important to the people of that community. It was a real eye opener to see the emotions parents felt about saying this principal's good, this principal's not good, this principal's not suited."

Meanwhile, the *Post*'s Rosenfeld, who would soon be Woodward's savior, had heard from his Maryland reporters just how good Woodward was. "I also saw his stories," Rosenfeld said, "and I found that they were most always on enterprising topics, not the normal announcement handouts. But actually they made hard reading. They were good stories, cutting edge for Montgomery County but not terribly easy to decipher. You knew he had a story, but he didn't tell it in the most lucid way."

Nonetheless, once or twice his *Post* competitor Jim Mann had to follow a Woodward story. "He was incredibly inquisitive," said Mann. "It wasn't just what he got in the paper. But I remember interviewing alongside him. He was an incredibly good interviewer. He knew how to establish trust with the people he was interviewing."

That year, when Maryland Governor Marvin Mandel was in a mysterious car accident in the southern part of the state, Woodward impressed Mann with his ingenuity. Mandel had told reporters that he was meeting with Democratic leaders, but no Democratic leaders could confirm that they'd met with him. It turned out that the married Mandel was off with his girlfriend.

"Woodward said, Let's get the gas records and see how much gas was in the car and how far it would have been driven," said Mann. "It didn't turn into a story, but I thought it was pretty clever."

Rosenfeld, too, had been paying attention to Woodward's stories. He had his hands full, however, with a staff of reporters who needed attention. To his mind, many of the reporters were bright, lovely people, but they needed discipline.

Rosenfeld had joined the *Post* in 1966 as the night foreign editor. Three years later, he had been named foreign editor, a job he loved because it involved traveling around the world. He had studied international relations in graduate school at Columbia University and thought that he was well suited to be foreign editor. But executive editor Benjamin Bradlee thought differently. He asked Rosenfeld to take over as metro editor and rebuild the staff of roughly a hundred reporters and editors, by far the largest on the paper.

Woodward was leaving nothing to chance. He sent Rosenfeld his stories and peppered him with phone calls. "He was very much on my mind because he kept himself very much on my mind," said Rosenfeld.

So did Mann, who became Woodward's champion with *Post* editors. In mid-1971, Mann left the Montgomery County beat. When he did, he wrote a memo to Rosenfeld and then city editor Barry Sussman saying that the *Post* ought to hire Woodward. Around the office, some editors teased Mann. "[Woodward] became known as 'my boy,'" said Mann, "as in 'Are we going to hire your boy or not?'"

Woodward wasn't just going after the *Post*. He also applied for a reporting job at the *New York Times*. On May 4, 1971, the *Times* rebuffed him. "I'm afraid we have no staff openings at the present, nor do we anticipate any in the near future," reads Woodward's rejection letter.

During the summer of 1971, Rosenfeld had taken vacation time to paint the basement of his house in preparation for the bat mitzvah of one of his daughters. It was hot, and Rosenfeld hated what he was doing. In the middle of painting, he was interrupted by a frantic phone call from the *Post*. An editorial aide had disappeared, leaving a wife and a young child. The wife was hysterical and Rosenfeld called the police to try to get the young man declared a missing person. Rosenfeld kept going up and down the ladder in his basement, trying to paint and handle an office crisis. For a man with a short fuse, it was not an ideal situation.

In the middle of this, Woodward phoned. Rosenfeld, a hard-charging, nervous man who smoked and was prone to blow-ups, blew up. "I'm busy," he yelled at Woodward. "Call me at the office. Later."

"This guy is calling me every other week," said Rosenfeld, "and I tell him we are going to get to him, but he doesn't leave me alone."

The rest of the story has become legendary. Rosenfeld's wife, Anne, was mystified by her husband's annoyance at Woodward's persistence. "So what are you complaining about?" asked his wife. "This is just the kind of guy you are always saying you want as a reporter."

By August 1971, Woodward was sitting outside Bradlee's office for a final interview. Karlyn Barker was there, too, hoping for a job. "He seemed nervous like me," recalled Barker. "We were both waiting for the thumbs up or thumbs down from Bradlee. Bob was telling me that he'd had a tryout and it didn't work out. I remember thinking, 'Gee, I hope they hire this nice young man.'"

They both got jobs working for Rosenfeld. Before Woodward started on September 15, 1971, he got a letter of acceptance confirming his starting salary of $156 a week, or $8,112 a year, making him one of the lowest—if not *the* lowest—paid reporters at the *Washington Post*.

"Woodward comes on board to do night police," said Rosenfeld. "But Woodward goes to night police not with a chip on his shoulder, like every other reporter I ever sent who hated to cover the pigs. Woodward goes down there, and he brings an extra cup of coffee and a copy of the paper. He establishes himself with the police officers and gets credibility. And he starts to do stories."

Woodward was slogging along doing jobs that most beginners bristle at, only he loved it.

"I was the night police reporter. Working from six thirty p.m. to two thirty a.m. at the *Post*," said Woodward. "And that was my basic job, but I would come in and work during the day because I liked it so much. The world is open to you. The city editor, Barry Sussman, said to me, 'Look, you have an unlimited expense account for all practical purposes.' As I recall, he said, 'You can't take somebody to the Jockey Club every day. But if taking people out to lunch or something helps, do it.' He literally said if you are going to call somebody at the White House or Agriculture Department, check with the beat reporter. The navy was so closed and organized and limited, and all of a sudden the world that had been as narrow as it could be, was open. It was liberating. I was twenty-eight at this point."

The first time Woodward dealt with Ben Bradlee on a story, he was terrified. Shortly after he was hired, a congressional committee was planning to investigate police corruption, a topic Woodward had been writing on. This was just the kind of story Bradlee liked. "It scared the hell out of me," Woodward told David Halberstam. "There was the editor almost leaning over my shoulder. And he was asking these questions: 'Where does it come from? How sure are you?'"

A few weeks later, Bradlee told Halberstam, he took some new reporters out to lunch. "Which one of you is Woodward?" Bradlee bellowed.

Woodward identified himself.

"You are all over the paper," Bradlee said. "Keep it up. Keep it up."

Woodward was assigned to Douglas Feaver, the night city editor. One night Feaver sent him out to cover a triple fatal fire. "He called in his notes and did a spectacular job," said Feaver. "The fire story was on the front page the next two mornings."

Since Woodward worked the overnight slot, Feaver expected that Woodward would go home and get a good night's sleep. "The next morning, on his own time, Woodward went to the building inspectors and found out this building had a record of compliance failures during electrical inspections, and he had another big story. It really impressed me."

Woodward didn't stay on night police for long. He pushed on, turning restaurant health inspection violations into front-page stories. In the early spring, Woodward pursued stories on corruption within the D.C. police department. But he was still green.

Early on at the *Post*, when he was aggressively breaking stories on restaurants being closed down for code violations, a health inspector called. The Mayflower coffee shop got the lowest score ever, he was told. The inspector had never seen anything like it. Woodward dashed over to get the report, returned to the *Post*, and banged out a story.

"One of the things the *Washington Post* still liked was early copy," he told a group of journalists in 2005. "So I turned this story in about lunch time."

He was pretty pleased with himself. This would be a big story because the coffee shop was inside the fancy Mayflower Hotel, where the swells dined and the elite stayed overnight. His editor read the story, thought it good, and then asked, "Did you go over there?"

"No," replied Woodward. "It's all in the record. It's an absolute slam dunk."

"The Mayflower Hotel is four blocks over there," said the editor. "Get your ass out of here and over there."

He did. When he got to the hotel, he asked for the coffee shop and was told that the hotel didn't have one. He looked more closely at the report. Wrong address.

"So I went over to the Statler Hilton Hotel, which was a half block from the *Post*," recalled Woodward. "God knows why they would have a Mayflower coffee shop in the Hilton Hotel, but they did. There it was. I saw it. It said, 'Closed for repairs.'"

He returned and sheepishly asked his editor for the copy without admitting the truth. "I have a few minor changes," Woodward said.

"Fires, shootings, investigations, the gritty and shocking street crimes, and the politics of the police department were all subjects where I could find stories," Woodward wrote in *The Secret Man*. "I loved newspapering so much that I often worked the day shift also." For free. He also told his editors that he didn't think other reporters worked hard enough.

The stories about Woodward the productive workhorse are legend now. When he first started—and nothing changed over time—he worked harder than most other reporters did. In his first months, he had page-one stories on different subjects five days in a row. Stories that other reporters might spend a week on, he'd turn in the next day.

Around this time, Donald Graham, the son of Katharine Graham, who owned and published the *Post*, came by Woodward's desk. The union people were complaining that Woodward was working far more than his prescribed 37.5-hour workweek and wasn't putting in for overtime as the union contract required. That didn't slow Woodward, though. He had discovered his passion and he had all the time in the world to pursue it. No wife. No kids. Nothing but newspapering.

While editors loved Woodward, not every reporter thought so highly of the prolific new guy. "I thought Woodward was a prima donna and an ass-kisser, a navy guy, green lawns of Yale, tennis courts," *Post* colleague Carl Bernstein told Halberstam. "I didn't really think a lot of most of Woodward's stories. I thought they were from the wham-bam school of journalism, making a lot out of very little."

Bernstein, a twenty-eight-year-old *Post* reporter, was the other name that surprised Len Downie as he read about the Watergate break-in from London, where he was temporarily living. Soon he would be returning to the *Post* as an editor. "The story was intriguing on many levels, including the fact that Carl was one of the reporters on it," said Downie. "Because I wasn't sure that Carl would still be working at the *Post* when I got back considering all the trouble he'd gotten into."

If Bob Woodward was strait-laced, clean-shaven, and determined to please his editors, Carl Bernstein was the opposite. Bernstein was an antiestablishment type. He wore his hair long, smoked incessantly, wore military fatigues, and was generally thought of as the office deadbeat. "Carl was a hippie, or a hippie wannabe," said Tim Robinson, a metro reporter who worked with him. "Long hair, very interested in music. I remember some reporter came up to the Virginia desk and said he was going to get an oil change. Bill Curry, Carl's editor, said, 'You ought to take Carl in, too. His hair is getting pretty greasy.' "

Charles Puffenbarger, a former *Washington Star* and *Washington Post* editor, was one of Bernstein's mentors. When Bernstein lived in a house with a couple of guys in Arlington, Virginia, "Carl did none of the work," Puffenbarger told Alan Pakula in 1975. "They were having a party. The guys said, 'You're going to help, Carl. You're going to clean the bathroom.' He said, 'How?' They showed him the brush to clean the toilet. He said, 'Clean the toilet with that? I've been scrubbing my back with it.' "

Unlike many other *Post* reporters, Bernstein was born and raised in Washington and knew well the city's rhythms and history. When he was eleven, his parents, considered leftists, moved the family out to the Maryland suburbs into a predominantly Jewish area. "He lived in a neighborhood that was not only nice but was particularly popular because it had tons of kids," said Gloria Feinberg, who met Bernstein when he was in ninth grade. "He was highly energetic and much more socially aware than other kids in the crowd we traveled in. Carl had a gift which he has now. He sees the big picture. The issues then were civil rights, and there was a big push for white teenagers to understand what the world was beyond their solidly middle-class neighborhood. The schools weren't integrated to any extent. He was far more aware about what was going on than just being concerned about the next school dance. He was thin and wiry. I think he won a Howdy Doody look-alike contest because he had dark brown hair and lots of freckles."

In high school, Bernstein, a phenomenal dancer, was more apt to be playing pool or hanging out with friends or working on B'nai Brith youth activities than studying. He barely graduated from Montgomery Blair High School in Silver Spring, Maryland, in 1961. "My own graduation from Blair is a memory so vivid that I continue to have nightmares about it," said Bernstein, the school's 1976 commencement speaker. "I was never able to send out invitations and those little white cards with your name engraved in script because Mr. Adelman, with good reason, had refused to pass me in chemistry. And I was also flunking gym. The explanation had less to do with my scores on tests or physical dexterity than with the fact that I wasn't in class very often."

He didn't have much success either at the University of Maryland, the only college, he has joked, that would accept him. Parking tickets and poor grades did him in. "Carl was kind of a rough street kid," said former *Post* reporter Stuart Auerbach, who worked with Bernstein. "It's not that he came out of the ghetto. He never finished college, but he worked his way up at the *Washington Star*. But he was more street. He had street smarts."

Street smarts worked for Bernstein. They allowed him to be successful after his father, who knew someone at the *Star*, helped him get a copyboy job at the afternoon newspaper when Carl was only sixteen. By the time he was nineteen, Bernstein said he was earning $86.25 a week. "The best thing I ever did is I got so tired of making those funny little trays in woodworking shop so I finally decided to take typing with the girls," said Bernstein. "The fact that I could type is what got me hired at the *Washington Star* because I could type fast, and I'd taken a journalism course in high school and I could write. It was the one thing I had some skill at, and it was the only reason I was able to graduate from high school."

The first time Bernstein walked into the *Star* newsroom, he was hooked. "I saw that newsroom and it was maybe the most incredible moment of my life," he said. "This clattering of typewriters and people yelling 'Copy.' I never saw anything like it."

Bernstein has often told of his rite of initiation to the *Star* family by an older copyboy, who saw an easy mark. "So it's my first day at work at a newspaper," Bernstein told a *Chicago Sun-Times* reporter in 1974, "and I'm wearing this brand-new cream-colored suit, because I figure that this is the way that you impress people and get a job as a reporter. At 2:30 in the afternoon, one of the older copyboys comes around and he says, 'It's 2:30, and the newest copyboy always has to wash the carbon paper. Unless you wash the carbon paper at 2:30, it's not good for the rest of the day, and we won't be able to get the late editions out.'"

So Bernstein collected all the purple carbon paper he could find in the newsroom, filled a sink in the men's room, and started scrubbing. Purple water flew everywhere, turning his cream-colored suit into a child's art project. He continued scrubbing.

In walked managing editor Newbold Noyes, who said, "What in the name of Christ are you doing?" This would become a classic Bernstein story.

Bernstein later wrote about that formative period of his life in 1981 when the *Washington Star* folded:

> My rites of passage were spent on the dictation bank—an institution in which copyboys and copygirls were lined up along a row of typewriters and made to compete through the grungiest of reportorial hoops. I still have the copy of the dictation I took from Dave Broder in Dallas [in 1963 when President Kennedy was shot]: My hands were shaking so badly that I misspelled Parkland Hospotol in the lead.

At the *Star*, Bernstein became something of a terror to the other copyboys. One of them, Warren Hoge, a contemporary, would go on to become Bernstein's friend and a *New York Times* reporter. Yet in 1964 Bernstein intimidated him. "He seemed an insider," Hoge told Halberstam. "He knew the neighborhood, the underside of Washington life, and he was very 'in' at the *Washington Star*. And he was loud and cocky, the personification of cockiness."

Bernstein was twenty.

He made it clear he was one of the "big boys" and not to be confused with the humble copyboys who ran errands. "He laughed at their jokes," said Hoge, "not at ours."

He paid no attention to copyboys like Hoge. "I almost felt a fear of him," said Hoge. "Then at some point, he realized that I might be a peer and might have something. Very quickly and suddenly, overnight almost, he treated me differently. He offered his friendship. I might have been afraid of asking for it."

Bernstein did become a reporter at the *Star*, but not for long. The *Star* had an unofficial rule that you needed a college degree to write for the paper. Bernstein, who had dropped out of college, had no interest in finishing it. At the *Star*, he was basically a dictationist, a step below reporter, more like a rewrite man. He left the paper in 1965, when he was twenty-one, to follow *Star* assistant city editor Coit Henley to the *Elizabeth Daily Journal* in New Jersey, where Bernstein got his first full-time reporting job.

Henley hired him because he saw a certain attractive quality in Bernstein that would make him a good reporter. "There was something about him, an energy, a passion, something of the street urchin in him," Henley told Halberstam.

In typical Bernstein fashion, though, the budding reporter didn't have enough money to travel from D.C. to his new job. Henley drove down in a rented car to pick up his new charge. "I got there and he was staying at some rooming house, and I had to double-park," said Henley. "While I was waiting, he was having some argument with a woman because he was leaving, and a city bus came by and creamed my leased station wagon."

Bernstein performed well for Henley, however, and made him look good, although some people on the staff referred to Bernstein as "the rotten kid." He quickly won first prizes in the New Jersey press association for a story on teenage drinking and for his first-person coverage of the massive 1965 blackout that cut off electrical power in much of the northeastern United States.

Here is Bernstein, at age twenty-one, writing about hitchhiking in a city that is shut down in darkness:

> He loaded 15 of us into the oversized automobile and started heading uptown. . . . Even at our final stop at 47th Street, the car was still loaded. And what a ride! By now the police had put up huge searchlights at some important intersections and people were walking in the middle of the street and hitchhiking. Grown men in Brooks Brothers suits walking backward on Eighth Avenue with their thumbs out like they were sailors on the Turnpike.
>
> The hotels. Who could ever forget the hotels on the night of the Great Blackout? I walked into the lobby of the Americana,

that grand monument to the nation's conventioneers, and it was a human parking lot. One thousand people, the hotel's PR man said, were sprawled out in the lobby. It looked like two thousand and it was the damnedest thing I have ever seen in my life.

As Leonard Downie wrote in his 1976 book *The New Muckrakers*, Bernstein's long, rambling account of the New York City blackout, written with colorful language, foreshadowed Bernstein's future. "Both reporter and participant, Bernstein wrote about the blackout in Manhattan as a Bernstein Odyssey," wrote Downie. "Bernstein would invariably get mixed up with participants in protest demonstrations, be himself manhandled by the police and spend nights in demonstrators' encampments, sharing their experiences and later offering what amounted to a diary of his adventures as story information for the *Post*."

Yet Bernstein's early prose also shows another side of him, one that any good reporter should have: an unstoppable desire to be at the center of things, a ferocious curiosity that makes it impossible to drive past a group of people where something is happening, whether it's a shooting, a traffic accident, or police officers shoving a teenager. Bernstein always had to be at the center.

"Bernstein thought a lot of himself and his skills, and he lorded it over colleagues," Henley told Halberstam. "He was somebody who knew the editor. He knew he was better than they were, and he let them know it. He was a little bit of a show-off."

Rather than live in working-class Elizabeth, home of noxious chemical factories, Bernstein moved to New York City, into hip Greenwich Village, and quickly accumulated looming debts, a practice that would dog him for much of his life. After he worked for a year at the *Daily Journal*, the *Post* hired him as a reporter for its metro staff. According to Halberstam, before Bernstein moved back to Washington, his father, Alfred, had to drive to Atlantic City and bring several thousand dollars with him to pay off his son's debts.

It was in October 1966 that then city editor Stephen Isaacs hired Bernstein. Isaacs told Halberstam that he had a practice of never reading a job applicant's clips that accompanied the applications. A good rewrite editor could be responsible for polishing the story with stellar prose. Instead, Isaacs listened to how reporters talked, looking for how their minds worked and whether they had an edge. Bernstein certainly did. "The first thing he said when we had the interview was that he wanted my job," Isaacs told Halberstam.

Later, during one of the countless frustrating encounters between Isaacs and Bernstein, Isaacs told his reporter that he would never become city editor.

"Why?" shot back Bernstein, who often seemed oblivious. "I don't trust you enough," Isaacs told him.

Bernstein replied that Isaacs was "full of shit."

"I mean, he was a very combative guy," said Isaacs. Nonetheless, Isaacs liked Bernstein because he was bright, intense, and aggressive and "you could tell he had ink in his blood. Someone said his heart beats at the rate of the press. He is really a newspaper urchin."

On July 4, 1967, Bernstein showed a bit of his early flash in a story about an aviation pioneer:

> Dr. Henri Coanda, who invented a forerunner of today's jet plane in 1910, is still inventing.
>
> He is also still writing, still sculpting, still conducting biological experiments and still collecting art.
>
> However, he doesn't play the cello anymore.
>
> The eighty-one-year-old scientist explained the other day that "when the jet machine crashed, so did my wrist," so he had to give up the cello.
>
> That was in 1910, in Paris.
>
> Now, looking positively spiffy in a blue blazer, black loafers and striped slacks, Coanda recalled that "I never intended to get off the ground; it was an accident."

In the mid- to late 1960s, the *Post* had become one of the most exciting places to work in journalism. Things were changing. In 1965, owner Katharine Graham hired forty-four-year-old, hard-charging, glamorous Benjamin Crowninshield Bradlee, the Washington bureau chief for *Newsweek*, to kick some life into the paper. He would begin as a deputy managing editor, soon to be managing editor. Bradlee, a Boston Brahmin with a rooster tattoo, was ready for the task. By 1968, he was the top editor setting the tone and was determined to undermine the public conception that the *New York Times* was the *only* paper worth reading. He wanted the *Post* to be a national newspaper that pushed the boundaries of lively daily journalism. The premium at the time was on solid, good, creative journalism and not on cost cutting.

Around the same time in the latter part of the sixties, a group of talented and highly competitive male reporters all arrived with Bernstein to populate the metro staff: Peter Osnos, Bob Kaiser, Len Downie, Jim Mann, Sandy Ungar, and Richard Cohen.

"These were bright, lovely people, but they all had the worst habits," recalled Harry M. Rosenfeld, who tried to bring order to the metro staff. "There was anarchy on that side. A lot of factionalism. A lot of reporters playing against each other. All of a sudden there was a strict work ethic. All of a sudden there were standards about what was a story. All of a sudden, it wasn't good enough to pick up a phone instead of getting off your ass and walking six blocks to the bike store that had just been held up."

It was a time when any career path seemed possible. Osnos joined the *Post* in 1966 at age twenty-two, and soon was covering Prince George's County. By 1970, he was heading to Vietnam as a *Post* foreign correspondent. "Carl and Richard Cohen were very close and I was part of that group," said Osnos. "We were all young and hungry." Cohen, who had joined the paper in June 1968 from New York, was assigned to the desk in front of Bernstein. They instantly liked each other, although Cohen thought that Bernstein talked funny. Cohen, Kaiser, Bernstein, and another reporter were sent to cover Resurrection City, also known as the Poor People's Campaign of 1968. Bernstein and the other reporter jumped out of the car for some now-forgotten incident.

Cohen turned to Kaiser and asked, "What kind of accent is that? It's the strangest accent."

"That's a Washington accent," Kaiser replied.

At that time, said Cohen, who still writes a column for the *Post*, there was such a thing as a Washington accent.

"Carl's a very good reporter," said Cohen. "One time there was some kind of event at the Philippine Embassy. Some terrorist thing, a shooting. Everyone went flying over there to the scene. But Carl knew exactly what to do. He got a phone book and started calling people in the building and getting interviews. If you went over to the building, you stood there watching."

Shortly before Cohen joined the paper, Bernstein had married *Post* reporter Carol Honsa on April 20, 1968, just after turning twenty-four. Honsa brought stability to Bernstein's life. The couple lived in a vintage apartment in the Biltmore, and their good friends, Barbara Cohen, a *Washington Star* editor, and her then husband, *Post* reporter Richard Cohen, lived nearby. Honsa was "strikingly beautiful," Barbara told Halberstam. "We used to sit around there, usually on the floor. I remember the first time we were there. Carl was very nice with new people. Everybody was so busy and he was very quiet and made a point of drawing me out. We began to see a lot of them. We were all young and did nothing but talk shop."

The two couples vacationed once on Block Island off Rhode Island's coast, where there were no cars. "There was a restaurant on the other side of the island," recalled Barbara, "and Carol Bernstein refused to hitchhike. So the rest of us went on together and she got very angry. She did stabilize his life and managed it and gave it some structure. But it was not really a very happy marriage."

The union didn't last long. "They were a really odd couple," said a metro reporter who worked alongside Bernstein in the late 1960s. "She seemed very white bread. He was very rye bread. She used to leave him notes with a list of ten things to do, and he'd pass them around, which seemed smarmy to me." Honsa has said that she never discusses the marriage.

Bernstein wasn't ready for marriage. It might not have been a good idea, and at some level, Bernstein knew it. His friend and colleague Robert Kaiser had encouraged the marriage. He thought it was time for Bernstein to settle down. "They started to go out, they got engaged, and Carl asked me to be the best man," said Kaiser. "I was thrilled. I was a completely square and conventional guy, already married at twenty-two. Carl lived a very full and complicated life. A lot of girls. Even with the booze. We all drank too much."

A week before the wedding, Bernstein got cold feet. He and Kaiser went out to lunch, and Bernstein voiced his concerns. "I don't want to do this," he told Kaiser, but Kaiser couldn't hear him. Kaiser had rented a bus for the couple to leave the wedding, which would be held at Bernstein's parents' house in Silver Spring, Maryland.

"Carl, it's time to grow up and settle down," said Kaiser. "Carol is wonderful. She loves you. She'll take care of you. She'll pay your bills."

Bernstein was well known around the office for his chaotic financial life. He had a long list of people to whom he owed money—a list that dated back to when he first joined the *Post* as a reporter at twenty-two. When he wasn't borrowing money, he was bumming cigarettes. And then there were the stories of his womanizing—even after he was married. "There were always calls from creditors," Stephen Isaacs told Halberstam. "There were girlfriends calling, you know, asking for hundreds of dollars that he owed them."

Chuck Conconi, who worked at the *Star* when Bernstein was a copyboy, said that Bernstein enjoyed a reputation as a ladies' man. One day when Conconi was at the *Star*, he was sent to cover a dinner at the Shoreham Hotel, where President Lyndon Johnson was speaking. He ran into Bernstein, and they chatted for five minutes. Three or four days later, Conconi bumped into Bernstein's wife. Honsa said to him, half-joking, "I didn't like it how you kept Carl out that late the other night." Conconi's blank, confused look indicated he had no idea what she was talking about.

"Then I got it, but it was too late," said Conconi. Honsa, realizing that her husband had not been with Conconi, just walked away. After three years of marriage, Bernstein and Honsa separated in 1971 and divorced in 1972, in the early days of his Watergate reporting. (In the Watergate archives is a bill for $175 that Bernstein paid to cover legal expenses for Honsa's attorney in their divorce.)

Marriage may not have been a good fit for Bernstein, but reporting was. He was talented and ambitious, and he loved reporting. He was part of the hard-charging, young metro cohort that was nipping at the heels of the big-name *Post* national reporters such as David Broder, Haynes Johnson, and William Grieder, men who had already earned their stripes. "From 1966 to 1982 was a period of great enterprise and great excitement at the *Washington Post*," said Osnos, who worked there for eighteen years. "The

New York Times was considered stodgy, and the *Post* was innovative and provocative. It helped that the *Washington Star* was taking on the *Post* in an intense competition."

One Saturday afternoon in spring 1969, Osnos and Bernstein, then twenty-five, heard that the *New York Times* was going to have a story in its Sunday paper about some Baltimore indictments that included a congressman. They saw it as a Big Story, and they were going to be scooped. At the time, Osnos was a Maryland state reporter and Bernstein was general assignment working a Saturday afternoon shift.

"We did our best to get the story but didn't succeed," said Osnos. "We had no idea who the congressman was, but we were determined to find out. So we were reduced to finding out what was in the *New York Times*'s first edition."

Osnos asked his mother in New York City to go to Times Square at 6 p.m., buy the first edition, and look for any stories datelined Baltimore. The only Baltimore story was in the travel section. He couldn't expect his mother to hang around Times Square for the second edition.

"It was now about 9 or 10 p.m.," said Osnos, "and Carl got on the phone and called the *New York Times* loading dock on Forty-Third Street and persuaded the foreman to look for a Baltimore dateline and read him the first paragraph. Having been beaten, we found out what they had and then matched it and made the last edition of the *Post*'s Sunday paper. It was a whole hell of a lot of fun. Carl was unbelievably imaginative and zany in his own way. He was a brilliant shoe-leather reporter." Brilliant but never trustworthy. Sanford "Sandy" Ungar, now the president of Goucher College in Maryland, had joined the *Post* in September 1969 as an editorial writer and moved on to the metro staff in 1970 to be a general assignment reporter. In those days, the typewriters were bolted down to heavy gray metal desks on linoleum floors littered with cigarette burns. "Carl's colleagues always regarded him with mixed feelings," said Ungar. "We thought he was gutsy and bold, but not entirely trustworthy. We used to joke that it was a good thing the typewriters were bolted down so he couldn't take them."

By January 1970, Bernstein was working for the new metro editor, Harry Rosenfeld. Bernstein had loved Isaacs, who was more

like a commune leader than the gruff, old-fashioned Rosenfeld—
a real screamer who kept a bottle of Maalox in his desk. Naturally, Bernstein was wary of Rosenfeld.

"One of the first big stories that broke on my watch was the
murder committed by Muffin Mattingly and her biker boyfriend,"
said Rosenfeld. "They killed her daddy by crushing his neck with
a crowbar. I wanted Carl to find out everything that happened to
Muffin from the time she left her mother's breast to incarceration.
The assignment played to his strength. He knew his town. But to
use the word *disciplined* with Carl at that stage would be a con-
tradiction. He was ambitious. He was smart. He was a hustler, but
he wasn't always totally responsible."

But Rosenfeld acknowledges, however, that Bernstein was the
perfect reporter to ask to do that story in a newsroom filled with
young people who'd grown up elsewhere. "Almost unlike every
reporter there," said Rosenfeld, "he was born and raised in Washington and so had the feel of the place, and remembered things
from ten years ago. Most reporters came to Washington to get the
job at the *Post*, including myself, including Barry Sussman. Carl
knew everybody, and that was his kind of story." The Muffin Mattingly story ran on January 13, 1970, under the headline MUFFIN
"TOUGH AS NAILS, BIKER TOUGH":

> Two weeks ago, fourteen-year-old Debra Mattingly (nicknamed
> Muffin) phoned her former counselor at Washington's Runaway
> House and announced that she had married a Hell's Angel.
>
> "I didn't know whether to believe her or not," the counse-
> lor, Judy Swannell, 26, said yesterday. "With Muffin you could
> never tell where fantasy left off and reality began. She told me
> they (Muffin and her husband) were sitting around fondling their
> knives."
>
> The man Muffin identified as her bridegroom, Eugene Louis
> Comeau, 19, was the latest of a string of boyfriends who shared
> what Miss Swannell called "Muffin's motorcycle fetish."

Rosenfeld was pleasantly surprised by Bernstein's work on the
story, especially after the *Washington Star* beat the *Post* for the
first two days. But Bernstein made up for it with the kind of compelling human-interest story that, somewhat unusual at the time,
is common in today's journalism.

Rosenfeld's first exposure to Bernstein soured him. Before taking over the metro staff, Rosenfeld was on the foreign desk. He didn't know Bernstein, but he knew of him by reputation. He also knew Bernstein's parents. "They were always asking in a very concerned way how their son was doing," noted Rosenfeld. Rosenfeld had heard the office talk about how this kid Bernstein was always striving to get off the local section. "He would volunteer himself to every national editor to do every bit of scut work," said Rosenfeld. "Just so he could get away from metro."

Rosenfeld first worked with Bernstein on a story that was popular in the late 1960s about young men who had escaped to Canada to avoid the draft during the Vietnam War.

"Somebody gave Carl the assignment to go to Canada to interview draft dodgers, so the story fell to me," said Rosenfeld. "He went away and came back from Canada and no stories were produced. 'Carl, where's the story?' I asked. Finally, I said to him, 'I've got to have the story.' He eventually produces this mountain of copy. It was terrible and I didn't use it at all. I came to find out that when I had given Bernstein the ultimatum, his editor sat down with him and batted it out. It was a piece of crap. The draft dodger story never got in the paper. He had a hard time doing it because he didn't do it right away. If he's not focused, nothing happens." This experience would be a harbinger of things to come.

But Bernstein also made a lot happen. He wrote about communes, protests, sleazy housing projects, and quaint neighborhoods. He usually did it in a style that pleased his editors when he finally got the story in. That was the problem: he couldn't make deadlines. He drove his editors crazy pushing a story until the last minute.

In fact, that is why Bernstein happened to be in the office on Saturday, June 17, 1972. He did not like to work weekends. But his editor, Tom Wilkinson, on the Virginia desk where Bernstein was assigned, was unhappy with Bernstein. Bernstein had been working on a story about shoddy construction practices at a Virginia high-rise project and should have turned in his story on Friday for Sunday's paper. "I knew pretty early in the week he wasn't going to make it," said Wilkinson. "I pressed and started hearing that litany of reasons why he couldn't get it done in time."

Wilkinson ran out of patience and ordered Bernstein to work on the story that Saturday. Bernstein resisted. People weren't returning his phone calls. No one would be around on Saturday. He didn't have all the records. He was having internal structural story problems. "I told him he had to come in," said Wilkinson. "He wasn't happy. But he came in."

There were other reasons Bernstein's editors were wary of him. He was sporadic as a reporter. When he liked a story, he would be all over it and do a bang-up job. When he was less than enthused, it showed. Sometimes he would disappear from the office. He was tossed off the city hall beat when an editor paid a surprise visit to the city hall press room and found him asleep on a couch at noon, even though Bernstein said he was sleeping off a migraine.

"Stories he didn't particularly like, he waltzed around a lot, procrastinated, dawdled, found small crevices that somehow became big problems," said Wilkinson. "All the kinds of roadblocks, real and otherwise, that creative reporters can dream up." In 1972, though not officially, Bernstein was on probation, in danger of losing a job he wasn't sure he wanted. He thought after six years he should be on the national staff, but editors thought otherwise. He'd already asked unsuccessfully five times to be sent to Vietnam as a correspondent.

Just a few weeks before Watergate, Bernstein heard that Hunter S. Thompson was leaving *Rolling Stone* magazine, and he applied for a job. Bernstein was restless. He felt underutilized and underappreciated at the *Post*. Writing about Virginia, where he didn't even live, was not his idea of where he should be after six years. He should be on the national desk. Or, as someone equally passionate about rock and roll and classical music, he should be writing about music. Or covering the Vietnam War. But those things weren't going to happen. Bradlee was closer to firing Bernstein than to offering him the prestigious job of war correspondent.

So it was not surprising that in London on that morning when Len Downie read the first Watergate story, he was amazed to see his old friend Bernstein still working at the *Post*. What he did not know as he read the June 18, 1972, story was that soon the three of them—Woodward, Bernstein, and Downie—would be working together on the most spectacular story in American journalism and that his relationship with Woodward would grow more difficult and strained over the years as each man grew more powerful at the *Post*.

2

Trust

Their careers have played out very much the way they were as young reporters. Bob is prodigious and productive and formidable, and Carl is brilliant in spurts. The combination at the early stages of their careers created something historic.

—Peter Osnos, a former *Washington Post* reporter

On Sunday morning, June 18, 1972, only Woodward and Bernstein showed up in the *Post* newsroom to work on the strange story of the Watergate break-in. Neither reporter was particularly glad to see the other. Although they shared an individual fascination with the story, the only other thing they shared was mutual distrust.

To Bernstein, Woodward was a suck-up, plain and simple. He'd been at the paper for only nine months and had moved up the editorial food chain uncommonly fast. Few reporters do as well as quickly as Woodward did. The editors loved him. Bernstein thought that Woodward's rapid rise had little to do with his hard work or all his front-page stories on failed restaurant inspections and police corruption. Bernstein thought of him as the "rat turd" reporter and believed that Woodward's success had everything to do with his establishment credentials: WASP, Yale graduate, navy lieutenant. He was too straight to be a down-and-dirty investigative reporter. He was just the type that Ben Bradlee liked. Bradlee, dashingly handsome with a Boston pedigree, had been executive editor of the *Post* since 1968. He'd gone to Harvard, served in the navy during World War II, and been press attaché in

Paris at the U.S. embassy. Bradlee had even been friends with President John F. Kennedy and his wife. Woodward and Bradlee were cut from the same cloth, as far as Bernstein, a college dropout and the son of left-wing Jews, was concerned.

To Woodward, Bernstein was a quasi-counterculture journalist, a long-haired freak who rode a bicycle and didn't even own a car. And he smoked cigarettes endlessly. He was the type who would be out protesting the war if he weren't a journalist and didn't know better. And even though he knew better, Bernstein still managed to get caught up in peace demonstration scrapes. An early tidbit from an editor sealed Woodward's impression. "One of the first things I learned about Carl was a complaint from the managing editor [Howard Simons] at the *Post*," Woodward told an interviewer in 1974, "that Carl had rented a car and had forgotten about it and the *Post* had to shell out $500." He knew the rap on Bernstein. In every way, the two were opposites. Woodward was a registered Republican who had voted for Nixon in 1968, and he was sure that Bernstein had not. He was right.

What they shared, though, was an intense drive and an equally strong suspicion of and respect for all things powerful, although not for the same reasons. They also, particularly Woodward, recognized that things are rarely what they seem.

On that Sunday, they learned that they'd been badly scooped by the Associated Press. While Woodward had nailed down that burglar James W. McCord Jr. had retired from the CIA, Woodward hadn't gotten the full picture. Over the wires on Sunday came a story that indicated that McCord was *also* the security coordinator for the Committee for the Re-Election of the President, known as CRP and pronounced "creep" by journalists.

"We got beat the first day of the story," Bernstein said on CNBC in July 2005. "And I remember walking to the back of the newsroom where the wires were and thinking, 'Jeez, how did this happen that we didn't get this?'"

For Monday's paper, June 19, 1972, Woodward and Bernstein wrote a story on McCord's real identity that ran above the fold on the front page.

One of the five men arrested early Saturday in the attempt to bug the Democratic National Committee headquarters is the salaried security coordinator for President Nixon's reelection committee. The suspect, former CIA employee James W. McCord Jr., 53, also holds a separate contract to provide security services to the Republican National Committee, GOP national chairman Bob Dole said yesterday.

"It was a big story, saying, 'Look, the guy who led the burglary team into the Democratic headquarters happened to be the security chief for the opposition,'" said Woodward on CNBC in July 2005.

Woodward got a break late that Sunday night from a fellow reporter, Eugene Bachinski, who covered overnight cops. Had Bachinski been more ambitious, he might have parlayed his knowledge into a more important role during Watergate. Bachinski, however, essentially handed Woodward a great story that Sunday night, day two of the embryonic Watergate story.

Bachinski had been covering night cops for nearly three years and knew about a hundred people inside the D.C. headquarters, where he had a desk. His regular shift began at 6:30 p.m. and went to 2:30 a.m. An editor asked him to work that night to see what he could scare up on the Watergate story from police sources. Bachinski hadn't even read the story, but he was willing to work on it.

Bachinski operated like any good beat reporter. If he could do something nice for the people he covered, and it didn't compromise him, he would do it. Each night at 10:30, when a truck dropped off twenty copies of the *Post*, he walked around the station handing out free copies. A few weeks earlier, he'd helped a sergeant get a mention in a *Post* column about a police fund-raiser.

"My guy couldn't have been happier," said Bachinski. "So that night I asked him what he knew about the Watergate. He says, 'I know everything. Why don't we have a drink later?' Later I went out to his house and had a couple of drinks. He had spread out all the property seized from the burglars on his kitchen table."

Among the items were two personal address books. Inside one were the initials H.H. and a White House phone number: WH 202-456-2282, as well as Howard Hunt's home phone number. There was also a never-mailed envelope with Hunt's check for $6.36 to pay a bill at a local country club.

On June 20, 1972, a Woodward and Bachinski story appeared (Bernstein had the day off) on the front page of the *Post*: WHITE HOUSE CONSULTANT TIED TO BUGGING FIGURE.

> A consultant to White House special counsel Charles W. Colson is listed in the address books of two of the five men arrested in an attempt to bug the Democratic National headquarters here early Saturday.
>
> Federal sources close to the investigation said the address books contain the name and home telephone number of Howard E. Hunt with the notations, "W. House" and "W.H."

Not long after that, however, the story dried up. Bernstein was taken off it after one week, and soon Woodward was sent back to other assignments. Bernstein did a smart thing, though. He wrote a five-page memo titled the "Chotiner Theory," suggesting that Nixon's old friend Murray Chotiner might be involved in the Watergate bugging attempt. Back when Nixon ran for Congress in California, Chotiner was in charge of something loosely called "ballot security," which consisted of tactics the Republicans employed to prevent Democrats from stealing the election. Bernstein sent the memo to Woodward and his editors.

"I do remember the Chotiner Theory," said Harry Rosenfeld, thirty-three years later. "An editor has to do two functions. Goad people sometimes into doing something, which I didn't have to do with Woodward and Bernstein at all. And then there comes a time where the editor has to become the screamer: 'Wait a second. How do you know this? Are you going too far?' Murray Chotiner is a good example. Carl was positive it was Chotiner. He was the sleazy kind of guy who would do something like this. Of course, it wasn't true. His was the one name that never appeared in Watergate."

Yet Bernstein's memo showed ambition and made a mark, although Bernstein didn't know it. He went back to writing about flooding from Tropical Storm Agnes and the closing of the *Washington Daily News*. He was sick of the *Post*, but the paper still owed him almost four months of vacation time, and he was trying to get it together to use it for a cross-country bike trip.

Two weeks later, Bernstein would forget about the cycling trip. His fortunes changed dramatically, and the Chotiner memo helped to make the difference. So did the *New York Times*.

By then, Woodward and Bernstein had begun to reassess each other. Although Woodward had considered Bernstein a lazy reporter who was screwing over the *Post*, his opinion changed almost immediately. He saw that Bernstein could be imaginative and creative in figuring out who to call and how to handle them. When Bernstein was captivated, he could be a far more serious reporter than Woodward had imagined. Conversely, it took Bernstein longer to "get" Woodward and to come around. He was fascinated and impressed by Woodward's endless energy and his commitment to a story, but he still thought that Woodward was an ass-kisser.

On July 25, 1972, everything changed for Woodward and Bernstein. They had no idea how deeply a single story in another paper would affect the rest of their lives. On that day, the *New York Times* ran a hot front-page story. Previously, the *Times* had pursued the White House–espoused theory that four restive Cubans were behind the Watergate break-in. On this day, however, reporter Walter Rugaber had a story saying that phone records showed that burglar Bernard Barker, the ringleader, had placed at least fifteen calls to Nixon's campaign headquarters. Rugaber wrote, "Records of the calls, made available by sources involved in the investigation of the break-in, suggest more direct and extensive links between the incident and the Committee for the Re-election of the President than previously reported."

That story and a second one by Rugaber on July 31, 1972, made *Post* managing editor Howard Simons furious. The second story, datelined Mexico City, indicated that the fifty-three $100 bills found on the Watergate burglars were part of $89,000 discovered in Barker's Miami bank account and that a well-known Mexican lawyer had deposited the money into Barker's account. The story had nothing to do with a Cuban connection and only escalated Simons's suspicions that there was much more to the break-in.

"I decided that we weren't doing anything," Simons told Woodward and Bernstein when they interviewed him in 1973. "I went storming across the room. And I went out and grabbed Barry [Sussman] and said, 'Godammit, we've gotta do more on Watergate. It's a great story and we've got to go after it. I want an investigative team full time and I don't care who you put on it. Just full time and nothing else.'"

At the time, Sussman, who had joined the *Post* in 1965, jumping from the *Bristol, Virginia-Tennessee Herald Courier*, was the city editor. He was in charge of city news and supervised a staff of six editors and more than thirty reporters. From the first moment that Sussman heard about the break-in on a Saturday morning and assigned Woodward to it, Sussman loved this story. He inhaled every small detail, filed it in his memory, and became the glue that the *Post* relied on to piece the puzzle together. He had just the kind of mind that recalled every fact, as well as an intense fascination that led him to become the central editor on Watergate. On July 5, 1972, Sussman was assigned to the story full time.

"Sussman became a walking compendium of Watergate knowledge, a reference source to be summoned when even the library failed," Woodward and Bernstein wrote about their immediate boss in *All the President's Men*. "On deadline, he would pump these facts into a story in a constant infusion, working up a body of significant information to support what otherwise seemed like the weakest of revelations."

For Sussman, adding Woodward to the Watergate investigative team was a no-brainer. Ever since Woodward had joined the paper, he'd been gung-ho. Ben Bradlee often held Woodward up to other reporters as a guy who knew how to "crack the code" and get stories into the paper with good play. "You'd give him a real shit detail," Bradlee told David Halberstam. "The next day he'd have it on Page One. I was using him before Watergate as an example of someone who could always get in the paper."

Woodward possessed a trait that was antithetical to Bernstein. Woodward wanted to please his editors. He did what they asked. Not only was he enormously hardworking and committed, he found genuine satisfaction in his job.

"He seemed in fact," Rosenfeld told Halberstam, "almost a generation older in his sense of the work ethic. He's not looking for glory outside other than his work. He finds a genuine fulfillment in his job. He doesn't really need the extra accoutrements of title and whatever. He was already somebody we thought of as special—a comer. A hot reporter."

Bernstein was more problematic. He bridled against authority. Sussman wanted him, though. Bernstein was good at poking around. He was sensational at working the phones, and he knew how to work people to get information. Sussman realized, however, that Bernstein would be low on Simons's list of probable candidates.

"I never had the problem with Carl that others did," Sussman told Halberstam. "He did have a tendency to exaggerate the importance of his story and his information and you had to be careful because you did not want to take too powerful a description of a Bernstein story into a news conference. But he was bright and he was hungry."

At the time, Simons was terribly irritated with Bernstein over his expense accounts, and everyone in the office knew it. His expenses were huge (about $6,000, Bradlee told Halberstam), and his paperwork was always late. Plus, the now-legendary rental car story had turned out to be true. Bernstein had rented a car while covering the Virginia legislature, had left it in a garage, and had forgotten about it.

"The paperwork comes by, and it's horrendous," said Rosenfeld, who worked under Simons but over Sussman. "It's so typical Carl. So typical. I got called into Ben Bradlee and Simons's presences, and they said, 'Get rid of that sonofabitch. Who does stupid things like that? Get rid of him now.' I said, 'For the first time in his benighted life he's really working, he's really producing for the paper. This is no time to get rid of him.'"

Simons wasn't so sure. He considered Bernstein irresponsible, lazy, and unreliable—traits that would instantly sink most journalists' careers.

"You were always sort of the enfant terrible at the *Post* in your behavior, your conduct," Simons told Bernstein in the 1973 interview. "You were very erratic. You did brilliant work and then you did lousy work and every once in a while you had to be spanked. And when you were spanked, you did well for a little while and then you'd fall back into your slovenly habits. There was some worry about what you were doing. Accuracy. Trust. I think you were your own worst enemy."

As far as Bernstein was concerned, Simons misread him. The young reporter was just overzealous. "I'd try to sell everything to

Page One," Bernstein told Halberstam. "I was quite ambitious. I was always trying to make up my own assignments. They wanted me to do little nickel and dime things."

What Bernstein thought, however, didn't matter. What did matter was that Sussman was willing to take a chance on him. He called Bernstein at home on his day off, asking him to follow the *New York Times* story. Bernstein's reaction was hardly one of undying gratitude. He was angry. He was sick of being put on the story, taken off, then put back on. He knew that the *Post* editors were keen on keeping Woodward on Watergate but were not so sure about him. He absolutely did not want to be the inexperienced Woodward's sidekick. "I think I'm better than he is," he yelled at Sussman. This was the last time, he said, that he would come in on a random basis.

Bernstein, make no mistake, wanted in on the story, but he wanted to work on it as Woodward's equal, not to be yanked around at the editors' whims. Sussman agreed. Once the tantrum had passed, Bernstein began making phone calls, trying to follow the *New York Times*'s story. He called his contact at the phone company (he always made a point of knowing people who worked inside the phone company) and began working the phones as few others could. It led him to sources in Miami. Soon Sussman was sending Bernstein to Florida without telling his bosses.

"Barry came into my office that afternoon and said, 'Now, sit in your chair and don't go up through the roof. Please relax. I've assigned Carl Bernstein to the team, and I've sent him down to Florida,'" said Simons. "And I went right up through the roof."

Bernstein did not disappoint. He and Woodward broke a story for the next day's paper on August 1, 1972, that was a major turning point in the saga. The *New York Times* had written about four Mexican checks. Bernstein found a fifth cashier's check for $25,000 made out to a Kenneth H. Dahlberg that had been deposited into burglar Barker's Miami account. He called Woodward, who quickly tracked down Dahlberg at home in a Minneapolis suburb. Dahlberg told Woodward that he did fund-raising for Nixon, and he had collected $25,000 in cash. "So I recall making a cash deposit while I was in Florida and getting a cashier's check made out to myself," Dahlberg told the *Post*. "I didn't want to carry all that cash into Washington."

Scrawled on a yellow legal pad found in the Watergate archives are two pages of Woodward's notes for that day. "I gave it to Stans," wrote Woodward. Dahlberg had given the $25,000 check to Maurice Stans, the finance chairman of Nixon's reelection committee.

"Well, obviously I'm caught in the middle of something," Dahlberg told Woodward.

The story ran on the front page of the *Post* on August 1, 1972, under the headline BUG SUSPECT GOT CAMPAIGN FUNDS:

> A $25,000 cashier's check, apparently earmarked for President Nixon's re-election campaign, was deposited in April in a bank account of one of the five men arrested in the break-in at Democratic National Headquarters here June 17.
>
> The check was made out by a Florida bank to Kenneth H. Dahlberg, the President's campaign finance chairman for the Midwest. Dahlberg said last night that in early April he turned the check over to "the treasurer of the Committee (for the Re-Election of the President) or to Maurice Stans himself."

Simons loved the story. He was almost ready to forgive Bernstein his transgressions. Almost. He knew it was a good story and later confessed that "money laundering," which was what the Nixon reelection campaign was doing, was a new term to him. Simons had to have the two reporters explain laundering to him.

The Dahlberg check story put the *Post* back on the map. First, the *Post* had a really detailed story about the break-in; then Woodward connected the story, ever so tenuously, to the White House, through Barker's address books; and now a campaign check for $25,000 had been found in a burglar's bank account. "The check was the third stepping stone to really beginning to widen the story way beyond just a normal burglary," said Simons in 1973. "Way beyond it." It was only August 1972.

That night, when Woodward was on the phone to Bernstein in Miami, Simons asked to speak to Bernstein. "Watch your expenses!" he bellowed into the phone. "And ride a fucking bicycle." (This was code for "Don't rent a car.")

Simons later told Bernstein that it was a reference to "both the fact that I was mad about the expense accounts, but I was delighted you were down there covering the story."

The deal was sealed. Woodward and Bernstein were forever a team, soon to be known around the newsroom as "Woodstein" or "the kids" or "the Bobbsey Twins." Woodward was twenty-nine; Bernstein, twenty-eight.

By this point, Woodward had been working at the *Post* for only one year. He had two years of reporting experience under his belt. Bernstein, in comparison, was a veteran.

"When we started working together, besides being young I had precisely one year and nine months' experience in the newspaper business," said Woodward. "He had twelve years. Carl taught me an immense amount. He knew the ropes. He taught me an immense amount about keeping notes and going back."

"It was mutual. We learned from each other," said Bernstein. "He might have had less experience, but I also learned from him. I learned restraint. In some ways I might push to get something into print a little faster than he. Sometimes he was more willing to compromise with management or editors than I. Those skills, when transferred to me or accepted by me, often serve me well. Not always. But the great thing is, there's no question, the synthesis of the two, the sum of the two produced something extraordinary."

Their next break came in late September when they were able to tie John N. Mitchell, a close Nixon friend, a former U.S. attorney general, and the former head of the Nixon reelection effort, to a secret unregulated slush fund that was used to finance the break-in and other activities.

"The Watergate team was essentially sequestered on the other side of the newsroom, and whatever was going on was largely kept under wraps," said Douglas Feaver, a cityside editor during Watergate. "Stories would show up later that were not on the news budget. The story about the Dahlberg cash didn't get in until the second edition. I never saw any story at the *Post*, save for the Pentagon Papers, handled with such secrecy."

By this point, Woodward and Bernstein had established that there was a secret slush fund and that it had financed the break-in and other espionage activities. Former CRP treasurer Hugh W. Sloan Jr. had told them that John Mitchell was one of the five people who controlled the fund. Woodward and Bernstein were about to write a story saying that the former attorney general was a criminal. It was published on September 29, 1972, under the headline MITCHELL CONTROLLED SECRET GOP FUND:

John N. Mitchell, while serving as U.S. Attorney General, personally controlled a secret Republican fund that was used to gather information about the Democrats, according to sources involved in the Watergate investigation.

Beginning in the spring of 1971, almost a year before he left the Justice Department to become President Nixon's campaign manager on March 1, Mitchell personally approved withdrawals from the fund, several reliable sources have told the *Washington Post*.

Those sources have provided almost identical, detailed accounts of Mitchell's role as comptroller of the secret intelligence fund and its fluctuating $350,000–$700,000 balance.

The Mitchell story prompted one of the most memorable quotes from Watergate, as Mitchell screamed into Bernstein's phone that "Katie Graham's gonna get her tit caught in a big fat wringer if that's published."

In Simons's 1973 interview with Woodward and Bernstein, Simons conceded that some of "the kids' " stories both scared and worried him and Bradlee—but they never publicly admitted that to anyone.

"We had sort of a pact," said Simons. "And the pact went like this: that he and I would worry. Are they right? Are we right? Are we doing right? My God. But the pact was that we'd never let anyone on the staff know, ever, that he and I had any doubts at all."

They questioned each other behind closed doors and then came out to the newsroom with a united, confident front. "But we had our private doubts," said Simons. "What the hell if we were wrong? And the least of it was Ben and I would have to resign."

The stories scared Woodward and Bernstein, too.

"I just remember the basic reporting of it," said Richard Cohen, who reported alongside them on the metro staff and remains friends with both. "We would talk a lot. I remember they were scared. Carl was scared. It was scary because the story was so immense. You didn't know what to expect. At the time, no one knew what was going on. If they were wrong, they were wrong on a scale that nobody had ever been wrong on before."

The next story that certainly made the editors sweat was the Segretti story. To Woodward and Bernstein, it was the seminal story that changed everything. Here's how Woodward spoke about it when he began giving speeches eleven months later:

"On October 10, we published probably the largest and most significant story—the one saying that the FBI had, during the course of the Watergate investigation, uncovered an elaborate espionage and sabotage campaign directed from the White House against the Democrats.

"It identified a White House aide who was a former reporter at the *Washington Post* as saying he wrote the so-called 'Canuck letter' during the New Hampshire primary—in which Senator [Edmund] Muskie, the Democratic frontrunner, allegedly condoned a racial slur on French Canadians as 'Canucks.' The letter, in part, contributed to Muskie's famous—and politically damaging—crying speech in front of the office of an anti-Muskie newspaper.

"The White House declined to comment on the story, and the President's reelection committee said, 'The *Post* story is not only fiction but a collection of absurdities.' They refused to discuss the specifics.

"That story also told of a young California attorney named Donald H. Segretti who traveled the country, crisscrossing it at least ten times during the second half of 1971, to conduct political sabotage and recruit undercover agents.

"Five days later we identified the president's appointments secretary, Dwight L. Chapin, as the contact for Segretti's spying activities. Segretti's other contact was Watergate defendant [Howard] Hunt. He was paid $35,000 by the president's personal attorney, Herbert W. Kalmbach."

The Segretti story proved that the Watergate break-in was not an isolated event. It was but one of many illegal and corrupt schemes the Nixon administration had masterminded. The Segretti story really angered Ken Clawson, a former *Post* reporter. He'd gone to work at the White House as deputy director of communications in February 1972. Clawson hated the stories that his former employer was publishing.

One day that fall in 1972, Simons was having lunch at Cantina D'Italia with William Safire, a Nixon speechwriter. Safire was fuming about "the kids'" October 10 story.

"How could the *Washington Post* attack and just destroy a sweet guy like Dwight Chapin, who was just a nice, innocent boy?" Safire scolded. "How could you do that to Ken Clawson, who is suffering from diabetes? What kind of a newspaper are you?" (Chapin subsequently served eight months in jail, and Segretti spent four and a half months behind bars.)

In reality, though, the *Post*'s Segretti story didn't get picked up much outside of Washington. Many more newspapers ran stories the next day that led with the administration's denial of the *Post* story. After that, according to Simons, Clawson began a whisper campaign against Woodward and Bernstein. First he went to Bradlee and Simons, questioning how they could let "two young punks" cover a national story. "Clawson was hissing in everybody's ear—too young, a jerk like Bernstein and everybody knows he's a jerk and a snotnose like Woodward and everybody knows he's a snotnose," recalled Simons. "You know, you can't trust them."

The *Post* wasn't completely out on a limb, though. Shortly after its Segretti story, the *New York Times* broke its own Segretti story about phone calls he'd made to "sweet" Chapin, who sat near the president's Oval Office. Bernstein had gotten Segretti's credit card records; the *Times* got his phone records. "Thank God," Bernstein recalled saying when the *Times* ran a Segretti story. It added legitimacy.

The *Times*'s October 18, 1972, story, written by Steven V. Roberts, reported—albeit on page 30—that phone records showed that Segretti had made at least twenty-eight calls to the White House, to Chapin's home, and to E. Howard Hunt's home and office.

Just two days before that, Nixon campaign director Clark MacGregor had lashed out: "The *Post* has maliciously sought to give the appearance of a direct connection between the WH and the Watergate—a charge the *Post* knows, and a half dozen investigations have found, to be false."

Two weeks later, Clawson, MacGregor, and the White House felt vindicated. Woodward and Bernstein had made a mistake.

3

The Best Obtainable Version of the Truth

One story, Watergate, will be the story of the year and maybe the story of the decade. It is also rare that one newspaper and one pair of reporters are so clearly identifiable and so clearly ahead of the rest of us covering the story. The pair of reporters, of course, are Carl Bernstein and Bob Woodward of the Washington Post.

—William Small, CBS News, *Quill* magazine, June 1973

The national press corps, such as it was in the early 1970s, was an elite bunch of middle-aged white men who had worked their way up to a spot covering the White House. They moved in the world of Washington dinner parties, amid the powerful and the glamorous—a world foreign to Woodward and Bernstein. The White House press room was more clubby than competitive, as it later became. Then, White House correspondents reported on what was happening at the White House. Nobody was breaking blockbusters.

They were making good money, though. White House reporters earned "perhaps $20,000 a year to upwards of $60,000 or more," said the *Columbia Journalism Review* in the summer of 1973. (Woodward and Bernstein together earned less than $30,000.) "If there is a journalistic law to which they and the organizations they represent universally subscribe it would be: What the President of the United States or the White House says is news."

In the early 1970s, White House correspondents tended to have a more deferential and respectful attitude toward the presidency, one that wouldn't be recognizable today or, for that matter, evident in the White House press room after Watergate. Back then, they tended to write what the White House told them. Woodward and Bernstein, however, were not White House reporters. They weren't worried about making the White House angry and losing access. They just went after the story.

"Woodward and Bernstein did something other reporters didn't do at that time," said CBS lifer Bob Schieffer, who came to Washington in 1969 as a Pentagon reporter. "That is, they went to people's houses after work and knocked on doors. Reporters didn't do that then. Washington was a place where everybody played by the rules. You dealt with people in the office. You picked up the phone. If they returned your call, fine. If they didn't, fine. I don't want to say it was more gentlemanly, but it was. There were rules. You didn't make a pest of yourself. Watergate was when the stake-outs first started."

At the time of the break-in, it was customary for sixty to seventy White House reporters to attend an 11 a.m. briefing and turn handouts into news stories. Little was known then about how the White House worked or who the people behind the president were, unlike today. Reporters knew Ronald Ziegler, a nonjournalist, as the public face of the White House. If Ziegler said something was or wasn't true, reporters printed that. And he was skilled at handing out a press release close to the reporters' deadlines.

"The White House press corps is more stenographic than entrepreneurial in its approach to news gathering," criticized Bill Moyers, who had been President Lyndon Johnson's press secretary. "Too many of them are sheep."

Reporters countered that try as they might to penetrate the White House, it was impossible. Nixon and his top aides had set up a so-called Berlin Wall.

When Woodward and Bernstein wanted to learn more about H. R. Haldeman, they went to the *Washington Post* library to see what the *Post* had written about him. (Haldeman, Nixon's chief of staff, would later serve eighteen months in jail.) "We went to our library and elsewhere and found virtually no clips of substance on him," they wrote in a December 1972 speech given at the National Press Club. "We couldn't even find a recent picture, and the wire services were of little help (luckily, Haldeman has the same crew cut he wore three years ago). Haldeman was, in effect, a mystery man. There is no reason to have mystery men running this Republic. Right from the start of the new administration here is something that the press and TV can do better. Take away the mystery."

The release of the Pentagon Papers on the Vietnam War in 1971, which Nixon unsuccessfully tried to keep the *Post* and the *New York Times* from printing, played a role in shifting reporters' attitudes toward government. The Pentagon Papers became symbolic of the government trying to hide something. Yet even so, White House reporters felt hamstrung. They were up against a White House public relations machine that understood how to successfully manipulate the news media far better than the news media understood the White House. Nixon and his vice president, Spiro Agnew, had successfully run a campaign convincing the public that the Nixon presidency was a victim of a hostile, vindictive press. The campaign was so effective that it made White House reporters gun-shy, especially as the *Post* and the *Los Angeles Times* broke more serious Watergate stories around the November presidential election.

"For several months after the initial burglary, the *Washington Post* was almost alone in disclosing the wider implication of the Watergate break-in," said the *Post*'s Howard Simons, giving a commencement address in June 1973. "And it was a lonely time. Normally, there is a herd instinct in journalism. A good story by one newspaper or magazine or television station brings the rest of the media to it like bees to a spilled honeypot. Not so this time. Only a few other media organizations reported the story. With magnificent hindsight it is not difficult to understand why most editors outside of Washington ignored the story. Here was the *Washington Post*, a newspaper not especially notable for empathizing with the up-trodden, publishing stories on page one implicating the White House and basing its reporting on anonymous sources. And the White House, in turn, vigorously denying all."

During Watergate, two untenable trends had come together to threaten democracy. The White House press corps had become both complacent and jaded, and the White House itself had become corrupt.

Woodward and Bernstein had the energy, the ambition, and the outsider status to pursue the story, but they had more than that. They had the full might of a major newspaper behind them, pushing them to get the story.

The *Post* gave them a reporter's favorite gifts: time and flexibility. Publisher Katharine Graham and the top editors encouraged them to doggedly pursue lead after lead, meet secretly at night with sources, and hound officials by day on the telephone, always in pursuit of "the story."

"The important thing you must know about this story is that we really didn't know what we were going after," *Post* editor Barry Sussman told David Halberstam. "But we knew in some way that it was big. In the early days, each day, each week, we kept adding on."

In the beginning, Woodward and Bernstein knew they had a good story, and there was a mystery to solve. They had no idea where it would lead, although by the fall they had a good idea that the break-in was not an isolated incident and that the Nixon administration was clearly involved.

For Woodward, in the initial months of Watergate, it was just another good story. He'd already enjoyed a great run of front-page stories. The super-energy he devoted to Watergate was the same fanatical energy he gave all his stories. Woodward never shut down. He was a man in a hurry. He felt that he'd wasted five years of his life in the navy and had to catch up. "I didn't have any great perspective on Watergate in those days," he told Halberstam. "A story was a story. I was trying to get on other big stories. There was no sense yet that this was the super story."

Bernstein and Sussman were certain sooner than Woodward was that this story led to the Oval Office. Bernstein realized that Nixon was tied to the break-in when the *Post* was about to publish a story that John Mitchell, the former attorney general and the former head of the reelection effort, was one of five people who controlled a rich slush fund used for the break-in. In essence, they were saying that Mitchell was a criminal. As Woodward and Bernstein discussed the story in a vending room off the newsroom, Bernstein said that he got a chill.

"Oh my God," he said to Woodward. "The president is going to be impeached."

Woodward was not nearly as convinced but told Bernstein never to say that publicly. That's how it often was in reporting on Watergate. Woodward was the hard-working reporter; Bernstein, the conceptual guy. The Tortoise and the Hare.

One simple line of thinking kept Sussman stubbornly on the story. He was sure that if there had been a scandal like the Watergate break-in at the *Post*, executive editor Ben Bradlee would have known. Sussman knew enough about how Nixon operated to realize that Nixon delegated little and was keenly aware of what went on inside his White House.

Woodward and Bernstein trusted Sussman. He was a reporter's editor. They knew he was their ally, always pushing their stories and advocating for bigger and better play. They had other allies. Metro editor Harry Rosenfeld loved it that his "boys" were out front on a local story with national implications. Howard Simons, the managing editor, supported them because he smelled an important story. His boss, Ben Bradlee, came late to the Watergate story, not putting his full energies behind it until the fall. Bradlee's desire to turn the *Washington Post* into a force to threaten the *New York Times* fueled the atmosphere for the story to thrive. On top of that, publisher Graham, a smart newswoman, believed strongly in Bradlee.

"Ben Bradlee has been with me since 1965 and he's never let me down," Graham told the *Columbia Journalism Review* in 1973. "I had no reason not to have confidence in him. I was surrounded by about 10 editors who wouldn't back off. If I had said we're not going ahead, our newsroom would have been a helluva lonesome place—some of them there would have walked out."

It can't be overstated how important this structure and level of trust were to Woodward and Bernstein's ability to plow ahead. The story was coming perilously close to implicating the president of the United States. Nixon was mean-spirited and Kay Graham knew this. As publisher, and being fairly new in her role, she feared that the Watergate reporting might hurt the *Post* financially. "The thing I remember most about Mrs. Graham is that she seemed so shy to me," said James McCartney, whose piece on the *Post*'s Watergate coverage for the *Columbia Journalism Review* appeared in 1973 before the *Post* was vindicated. "I remember sitting in her office, and she was wearing a conservative blue suit. The thing she was most concerned about and talked about was the implied threat against the *Post*'s television stations in Florida, and she was worried about the effect on the *Post*'s stock."

Graham was right to be concerned. It was one thing to report on the break-in, but quite another to incrementally report that the president of the United States might be involved in a political scandal of major proportions. Nixon, true to form, was spiteful. "The main thing is the *Post* is going to have damnable—*damnable*—problems out of this one," the Nixon tapes reveal him saying on September 15, 1972. "They have television stations, and they're going to have to get them renewed. . . . Well, the game has to be played awfully rough." Nixon said this on the same day the Watergate grand jury indicted the Watergate burglars.

By the beginning of 1973, the *Post*'s stock had fallen from $38 a share to $21, after the Nixon team had orchestrated four challenges to two *Post* Florida TV station licenses that were up for renewal. During four previous years, only eleven challenges had been lodged against any of the 701 commercial TV stations in the whole country. None were made against the other 34 Florida TV stations up for renewal in 1972.

And yet the *Post* and its editors still backed their young reporters.

Other newspapers and television stations weren't as fortunate, which is one explanation for why the other members of the Washington press failed to put the same energy into covering Watergate. Most editors were suspicious of the story. They believed Ziegler's statement that it was nothing more than a "third-rate burglary."

It was inconceivable to the well-entrenched media elite in 1972 that a president could be a criminal. "It was beyond the imagination of the powers that be—people like [*New York Times* Washington bureau chief] Max Frankel—that the president of the

United States could be involved in something like this," said Richard Reeves, a former *Times* reporter who wrote a book on Nixon.

So there was a tendency to dismiss the *Post*'s early Watergate stories because the White House dismissed them, and also because Woodward and Bernstein were young metro reporters. If the *Washington Post* thought this was an important story, surely it would put its heavyweight, big-name national reporters on it.

"All of us who had been around for a while were inclined to dismiss the story because it was controlled by these two young reporters, neither of whom we knew, and it was embarrassing to be beaten every day by two young punks," said Jack Germond, then a White House reporter for Gannett News Service. "A lot of the competitive reporters were originally pooh poohing the story, but it kept getting bigger and bigger. After a while, we realized this was a big story."

It's just as well that *Post* editors didn't turn the story over to the national staff. Not only was national editor Richard Harwood skeptical about the story, his reporters might also have shrugged at the Nixon campaign high jinks. William Greider, a *Post* star national writer, complimented Woodward and Bernstein after the *Post* ran the so-called Donald Segretti story on October 10, 1972, which made it clear that the break-in was not an isolated event.

"I said Segretti was good. But that goes on in every campaign," Greider told Halberstam. "They just looked at me. I was saying that I would not have gone after that with the same set of facts. They were very polite. Then they said, 'Just don't tell us that because it happens all the time, it isn't wrong.' They were right. I was wrong. Woodward and Bernstein are modern-day, clear-eyed prophets saying the money changers are in the temple."

In 1972, few Washington bureaus had reporters working full time on the Watergate story. That was both a comfort and a terror. It gave the young reporters freedom to explore the story without competitive publications breathing down their necks. Yet the lack of other news outlets jumping on the *Post*'s "hot" story did make Woodward and Bernstein's editors occasionally question their own judgment. If this is such a great story, *Post* top editors asked, where is the *New York Times*, where are the wire services, the newsmagazines, the networks?

"I was the Watergate correspondent for ABC," said longtime ABC veteran Sam Donaldson. "But like most news organizations, ABC just followed along with the *Washington Post*. We were all just impressed with their stories and what Woodward and Bernstein were doing."

Even without the intense pressures of today's twenty-four-hour news cycle, TV networks did an abysmal job of covering Watergate. TV correspondents jumped on the police story about a break-in but let it go later because the story lacked any visuals. The story gave CBS veteran Lesley Stahl her first break. "I went and covered Watergate, which they gave me as the new kid because they didn't think it was a big deal," she told CNN's Larry King.

Then the story got complicated, however, and TV doesn't do complicated well. It was difficult to follow a Woodward-Bernstein story because the reporters often relied on anonymous sources, and there were few documents to show viewers and few people to interview on camera—with the exception of White House officials willing to go on camera to disparage press reports. In fact, when CBS ran a two-part special on Watergate in October 1972, with anchor Walter Cronkite adding gravitas to the story, the network pleaded with the *Washington Post* to share its documents to provide visuals.

"For the first time in a long time in major American journalism there were no documents," said *Post* managing editor Howard Simons. "This was just gumshoeing, classic journalism. CBS wanted to photograph the documents for its stories. But there were none. What we decided was, we wouldn't tell CBS we didn't have documents. We'd let them think we had documents."

CBS's October 27 and 31 specials were a turning point for the Watergate story. The first story ran for nearly fifteen minutes in a twenty-two-minute broadcast—the unprecedented equivalent of a newspaper turning two-thirds of its front page over to one story. The second story was truncated to nine minutes after the Nixon White House pressured CBS brass. CBS brought the story to a national audience, many of whom had never heard of Watergate because the mainstream press coverage was so spotty. A Gallup poll in October 1972 showed that 48 percent of the country did not recognize the word *Watergate*.

Most of the country was in the dark because influential newspapers like the *New York Times* and others never quite got the hang of the story. A January/February 1973 *Columbia Journalism Review* article explained that the dearth of coverage had to do with fall 1972 being the height of the presidential election season, and the majority of newspapers in America had endorsed Nixon for reelection. "There was abundant evidence that the 'Watergate Affair' was an extraordinary and ominous story of major proportions," said the article. The story "exuded the odor of official corruption that sets conventional investigative and page one juices flowing." And yet the coverage was scanty. Reporters preferred the soft political handout stories to scratching beneath the surface. Out of some two thousand reporters in Washington, only about fourteen actually covered Watergate with any gusto.

This is not to say that only Woodward and Bernstein broke stories that kept the spotlight on the Nixon administration's connection to the break-in.

"Except for the *Post*, the *New York Times*, *Time* and *Newsweek*, American media reported mostly about things happening out there in broad daylight—George McGovern picking the wrong man for vice president or making campaign blunders, Richard Nixon acting out the role of the president, well above sordid politics," wrote the *Christian Century*, a respected biweekly in Protestant and Catholic circles, in a congratulatory editorial two years after the break-in.

Why the *New York Times* reported sporadically on Watergate had more to do with internal machinations than to lack of hunger for a good story. The *Times* started out of the gate almost as quickly as the *Post* did. For the first three days, it had equally strong stories, and, like the *Post*, it petered off. One reporter whom the *Times* assigned to the story was Tad Szulc, who had broken the *Times*'s scoop uncovering plans for the Bay of Pigs invasion before it occurred. Szulc was a natural because the Nixon administration was leaking information to reporters about a Cuban connection to the break-in. The leaks perpetuated the theory that the break-in had been organized by a right-wing Cuban exile group because four of the five burglars were Cuban.

Internally, however, the *Times* was going through changes. In summer 1972, its longtime Washington bureau chief, Max

Frankel, was made Sunday editor, which meant that he was in transition. In September 1972, national editor Gene Roberts, who would have been involved in the story, left to become editor of the *Philadelphia Inquirer*. Washington correspondent Bob Smith, who had been pursuing the story through Justice Department sources, got fed up with the *Times* and went to law school that fall. He left behind a memo. Sources had told Smith to follow up on a guy named Donald Segretti. But no one ever did. Segretti would become a key figure in helping Woodward and Bernstein break their seminal story.

"I remember it was hard to get people interested in the story at the *Times*," said Roberts. "We had a couple of reporters assigned to it early on. Smith was finding out that once you got out on the story and started banging on doors, you might not get information, but the sense of fear was palpable." It was that same sense of fear that Woodward and Bernstein picked up on and conveyed to their editors, which is why they could stick with the story.

Even though Frankel would spend six more months in Washington, he initially distanced himself from the story. The *Times* didn't cover local crime. Former *Times* managing editor Arthur Gelb said that the Washington bureau didn't even have the local police number. Frankel also found the idea preposterous that the break-in could be linked to the White House.

"The real secret to Watergate was that it wasn't done by reporters who called [Nixon's national security adviser Henry Kissinger] 'Henry,'" said James McCartney, who spent decades in Washington for Knight Ridder. "The real news in Washington doesn't come from the top. It comes from the bowels of bureaucracy. Unfortunately, the media tended to venerate the official statement when often it wasn't the truth."

The *Times*'s Washington bureau initially took Kissinger's assurances that the break-in and the *Post*'s stories were much ado about nothing, wrote former *Times*man Seymour Hersh in the *New Yorker* in 2005.

"Our Washington bureau had no ties to the capital police or courts," Frankel wrote in his book *The Times of My Life and My Life with the Times*. "We were too sluggish even after the White

House was implicated. Not even my most cynical view of Nixon had allowed for his stupid behavior. . . . I was so envious of the *Post*'s lead that I allowed myself to be skeptical of some of its revelations."

By the fall, the *Times* sent down Clifton Daniel to take over as bureau chief. In December 1972—six months after the break-in—Daniel put Hersh, a rabidly dogged investigative reporter if there ever was one, on Watergate. First, however, Daniel bought him a box of Brooks Brothers shirts and sweaters to spruce up the sartorially challenged Hersh. It didn't take him long to advance the story. Hersh is credited with revealing on January 14, 1973, that Watergate involved a cover-up and hush money to keep the burglars quiet, a story that Woodward and Bernstein were slow to report. "The word *cover-up* did not appear in our paper until after January 1973," Sussman told David Halberstam. "We kept looking for things on the burglary and the break-in, when it was in fact the cover-up that brought him down."

The *Los Angeles Times*'s Washington bureau put three reporters on Watergate, although not initially. "We treated the first story as politics as usual," said Ronald Ostrow, who worked full time on the story in the fall of 1972. "We were frustrated. We knew it was a good story, but we didn't get the kind of support that Woodward and Bernstein did. We did a story based on a source inside the Committee to Re-elect the President [CRP] about covert funds that said that's what people there were really worried about coming out. It was played on page ten and cut by two-thirds. But that didn't stop us. We kept trying to out report Woodward and Bernstein."

While the *L.A. Times*'s national editor, Ed Guthman, liked the story, others at the *Times* did not. To them, it seemed like typical political hanky-panky. The other problem that Ostrow and investigative reporters Robert Jackson and Jack Nelson faced was that even when they had a good story, it appeared in a newspaper three thousand miles across the country. This was long before the days when the Internet made time and distance meaningless. The *L.A. Times* did share a wire service with the *Washington Post*, but that relationship, said Ostrow, hampered competition. The joint wire service meant that either paper could see what the other was doing before stories were published. "It got so they were so distrustful of us, and we of them, that we'd keep stories off the wires until nine-thirty p.m. or ten p.m.," said Ostrow. "But it got to a point where it hurt us. On many stories they'd always find a way to do our story. They'd put something in the bottom of the story that said elements of this story were first reported in the *Los Angeles Times*. It was frustrating. But we never could prove that they got the story only from us."

On October 5, 1972, Nelson and Ostrow badly scooped Woodward and Bernstein on a story. It was the first hard-hitting story to document by name one of the burglary participants' experiences. Much of Woodward and Bernstein's reporting was attributed to unnamed sources. The power of the *Times*'s story was that it ran a verbatim taped account by Alfred C. Baldwin III. From a Howard Johnson motel room across the street, Baldwin had monitored the eavesdropping devices the burglars planted at the Watergate. A former FBI agent, Baldwin traded his testimony for immunity and was considered a major government witness. He told the *L.A. Times* that the wiretap information was gathered for and sent to the Nixon reelection committee.

The Baldwin interview was tough to get. Baldwin and his lawyers wanted to tell his side of the story, but only for money. Since reputable news organizations never pay for information, no news outlets wanted to do business with Baldwin. That, however, didn't stop *L.A. Times* reporter Jack Nelson, another intrepid investigative reporter. Nelson wasn't going to pay Baldwin, but he also refused to take no for an answer. Long after other reporters gave up on Baldwin, Nelson persisted. "I kept pestering the lawyers, saying this guy [Baldwin] needs to get his story out," said Nelson. "That way, you'll get the other reporters off your back. It won't have any credibility if you sell your story."

Nelson was right, and the lawyers knew it. A story sold for money is just that. If Baldwin wanted to get his whole, uninterrupted story out before he testified against the other burglars, he needed to tell a reputable news organization. At last, the lawyers relented. "Jack spent almost a week in Connecticut trying to make his point," said Ostrow. "It was a sales pitch really. Jack's a great salesman."

Suddenly, Ostrow got a call from his boss. "Drop what you are doing. Get to Connecticut. Jack needs you." Ostrow left so fast, he had to buy a shirt and later figure out how to get it covered on his expense account.

Nelson interviewed Baldwin. After the interview, Nelson stayed up all night transcribing the tape so that the *L.A. Times* could run a straight first-person account—the only way that Baldwin had agreed to talk. Ostrow wrote the news story. The entire time, both men were terrified that Baldwin or his lawyers would change their minds. Yet it was the *L.A. Times*'s lawyers who objected to running the story because the Watergate judge in the burglar case, John J. Sirica, had issued a gag order. The prosecutors were threatening to pull Baldwin's immunity if the interview came out. "I ran the first-person story by Baldwin, and he and his lawyers approved it," said Nelson (although Baldwin did object to Nelson referring to him as chunky and insisted they take that out). "I argued that we should run it, and we did. Nothing ever happened."

The *Washington Post*, however, did not run the Baldwin story offered on its wire service. When the competing afternoon paper, the *Washington Star*, saw that, they wanted it, but Bradlee vetoed this. The next day, the *Post* ran the Baldwin story with a piece by Woodward and Bernstein. "The Baldwin story was a big deal," said Nelson. "It created a hell of a story because you had an eyewitness talking. It was a big explosion at the time. It was not an 'informed source or official.' It put a face on the Watergate story."

Even so, Nelson admits that in October 1972, he didn't believe the story was connected to Nixon. "To me, a hard-bitten cynical reporter, it boggled the mind to think that a president could be involved in a crime like that. Most of the reporters felt the same way." Ostrow added, "The story just kept mounting. But I never thought Nixon would be dumb enough to be at the bottom of it."

While Nelson, Ostrow, and Jackson did stellar work, they did not have what Woodward and Bernstein did: youth and freedom. All three men are about a decade older than Woodward and Bernstein. They were married. They had kids. With young families, they couldn't work the long hours that the story demanded.

"Woodward and Bernstein were indefatigable," said Ostrow. "Bob Jackson had three daughters. One was hearing impaired. Jack and I had kids. We couldn't spend all our time on the story. I know it sounds like sour grapes. But that's the reality."

Other news organizations worked on the story, including *Time* magazine, whose Sandy Smith did exceptional reporting. "Sandy Smith of *Time* is very good, like a cop, not secretive at all, very easy, very friendly," Woodward told Halberstam. "He really has a lock on the FBI." Yet it was the *Washington Post* that the White House chose to single out with searing criticism. Its orchestrated attack had the intended effect. A slew of other newspapers either ignored the Watergate stories or wrote about the White House denials.

"The hostility and pettiness of other newspapers, not only helped to suppress the Watergate story, but also had the effect of isolating the *Post*—which was precisely what the administration wanted," wrote Timothy Crouse in his landmark 1972 book *The Boys on the Bus*. "The White House strategy was to make the issue out to be the *Washington Post* rather than the Watergate affair and they succeeded."

The *Washington Post*, with 201 staff-written stories, was the most prolific in the critical first six months, from June 17, 1972, to December 31, 1972. Yet there was more reporting going on by other news organizations than is generally acknowledged. In that same time period, the *New York Times* ran 99 staff-written stories, and the *Los Angeles Times* published 45 staff-written stories, according to Louis Liebovich's book *Richard Nixon, Watergate, and the Press*.

"I don't resent the fact that Woodward and Bernstein get all the credit," said Nelson. "They did a lot of hard work. But so did others."

Others, however, did not write a best-selling book or have Hollywood turn their tale into a box-office success.

About a year before Carl Bernstein ever associated "Watergate" with anything other than a ritzy Washington address, a book agent named David Obst, age twenty-six, had approached him. Obst had already made investigative reporter Seymour Hersh a star. He wanted to talk to Bernstein about turning his July 1971

Post series on crooked career schools into a book. In those days, there were few, if any, literary agents in Washington. Obst and Bernstein, about the same age and both antiauthority, hit it off. Yet instead of becoming a lifelong friend, Obst would join a short list of people who were instrumental in helping Woodward and Bernstein publish their best seller, *All the President's Men*, but who today are not on friendly terms with either Woodward or Bernstein.

No one knew where Watergate was going when Obst began discussions with Bernstein about writing a book called *The Hope Business*. It would be based on career schools Bernstein had discovered that advertised through third-class mail. They promised extensive training in areas like disc jockeying, creative writing, broadcasting, dentistry, and medicine after students plunked down expensive tuitions. Bernstein's stories reminded him that things are rarely what they seem, which would help him in covering Watergate. Instead of launching students into lucrative careers, the schools left students poorly trained and with few job prospects. That book, however, was never written. Obst took an editing job, and the idea fell by the wayside. In September 1972, Obst, a tall blond with a bushy beard, got a phone call from Bernstein asking whether Obst thought this "Watergate stuff" could be turned into a book.

Ten days later, Woodward and Obst met at Bernstein's apartment to talk about how to put together a proposal for an interpretative history book on Watergate. "The guys were still ahead of the story, but there hadn't been a whole lot of revelations yet," said Obst. "It was still a hands-off story. The story doesn't really break open until June '73 when Nixon's counsel John Dean goes public and after the FBI director jumps ship. Then it all started to fall apart."

Yet nobody knew that in the fall of 1972.

When Woodward and Bernstein first talked with Obst, they wanted to write a book on what they'd uncovered about Watergate. It would be a traditional nonfiction book. Never was there talk early on of a book about them. Bernstein said that the original book was going to begin with gadfly Martha Mitchell, the wife of Nixon's attorney general, John Mitchell: "She wakes up in a motel, turns and her husband isn't there. 'John, John. Where are you?' was one beginning. He wasn't there. He was on the phone to the Western White House. There was trouble."

"That was the tone," said Obst, who took the proposal to New York for an auction. "I received zero bids."

No book publisher wanted to touch Watergate. The story was too new. Political books at that time didn't enjoy good track records, and people rightfully were afraid of the Nixon White House, especially since it seemed certain that Nixon was about to be overwhelmingly reelected.

Even so, Obst thought he had a winner. He had already sold his client Daniel Ellsberg's book to Simon & Schuster. For that reason, Obst wanted to offer the Watergate book to another publishing house because he worried that Simon & Schuster would have too much power over his authors. "But when everybody turned it down, I called the then [Simon & Schuster] publisher Dick Snyder," said Obst, "and set up a meeting in Washington with him the next morning."

Snyder was interested enough to come to Washington in September 1972 to meet with Woodward, Bernstein, and Obst. "Carl and Bob left the Hay-Adams, and Dick Snyder said he was going to pass on the book," said Obst. "I burst into tears. I did something I never did before. Piteously weeping, I implored him to buy this book, and he did. I knew he just had to buy it. I had kind of a mentor relationship with him at this point. He'd hired me as a scout for Simon when I was working at *Ramparts* magazine. He had seen something in me at a very young age and taken me under his wing. I really did become emotional. So Snyder said, 'Okay, if it means that much to you, I'll buy it.'"

A Simon & Schuster editor who worked for Snyder in 1972 recalled Snyder talking about the Watergate book at the regular Thursday lunchtime meetings. "It was going to be a short, quick book about Watergate," said the editor. "We talked about it but not for very long. Nobody was terribly interested. But Dick was very interested."

Snyder was smart—smarter than Obst, or maybe just in a more powerful position. He agreed to buy the book, but he wanted *all* rights. When the deal was done, Snyder walked away with the subsidiary rights, too—for a paperback edition, a movie, and foreign language books—which would turn out to be far more lucrative than anyone could have imagined at the time.

Snyder, Obst, and the Watergate sleuths met again in late October. Woodward and Bernstein had stayed up until dawn working on the book outline. The noon lunch on October 25, 1972, at the Hay-Adams Hotel was a disaster. Woodward and Bernstein had a major story in the paper that day saying that Nixon's chief of staff, H. R. Haldeman, "was one of five high-ranking presidential associates authorized to approve payments from a secret Nixon campaign cash fund." Earlier they had named Mitchell; now they were taking Watergate to the door of the Oval Office. Haldeman was so close to Nixon that Nixon referred to him as the assistant president. Rather than enjoying the glow of a great exposé, Woodward and Bernstein were mortified. They had made a small mistake, but it felt like a career-ending blunder.

The morning before the story ran, Sussman came in to find Woodward at his desk. He gave Sussman the thumbs-up. "We've got Haldeman," Woodward told him.

"I was impressed by what he said, and later at Bradlee's office, Bradlee gave him a very tough interrogation, very tough, very adversarial," Sussman told David Halberstam. "The question was whether we should go with it. Howard seemed almost dubious, and I got a little nervous because we really weren't quite finished."

Simons had been uncomfortable with the story all along, he later said. Yet the *Post* editors had what they thought was a fail-safe system. There were three rules for a Watergate story to be published: the story had to be read and approved by at least one top editor, another publication's Watergate story had to be independently corroborated before they'd run it, and any set of facts had to have at least two independent sources.

With the Haldeman story, Bradlee, Rosenfeld, and Sussman were comfortable with three sources. Simons wanted one more. When the story went into the paper headlined TESTIMONY TIES TOP NIXON AIDE TO SECRET FUND, it had four sources, although Simons characterized one source about as reliable as "reading eyebrows." One of the sources was Sloan, the reelection committee's treasurer who had resigned shortly after the break-in rather than participate in a cover-up.

"The lowest moment came over our story about a $350,000 slush fund controlled by White House Chief of Staff H. R. Haldeman from the White House," Bradlee wrote in the *Post* on the thirtieth anniversary of the break-in. "We watched the news a lot in those days to see how TV was playing our stories, and we were all horrified one morning to see Dan Schorr of CBS shove a microphone into Sloan's face and to hear Sloan deny he had said any such thing to the grand jury. We went to general quarters and told Woodward and Bernstein to find out what had gone wrong."

The mistake Woodward and Bernstein had made was one of attribution. The source did say that Haldeman controlled the money. He just had not told the grand jury. Woodward and Bernstein felt beyond awful. Woodward wanted to turn back the clock, hold the story a day, and get it right this time. He kept beating himself up. Such a stupid little mistake, and it was going to hurt the paper while giving the White House a public relations boost. Woodward had a feeling that some people in the newsroom were trying to stifle smiles. The "boys" had screwed up.

"We were careless, in hearing what we wanted to hear," Bernstein told Halberstam later. "We didn't ask the right questions. We made an assumption of logic that what Sloan told us, he told the grand jury, and we were wrong."

White House press secretary Ron Ziegler leaped at the chance to discredit the *Post*. "I personally feel that this is shabby journalism by the *Washington Post*," Ziegler thundered at a press conference where he spent thirty minutes trashing the *Post*. "I think this effort on the part of the *Post* is getting to the point, really, of absurdity."

The mistake, even while minor, damaged the paper. "We took a giant step backward in our credibility at that time," Bradlee told Halberstam. "It was a very tough thing on us. It kind of underlined the whole thing and the fragility of where we were. It was hard to win and so easy to lose."

It was the worst day emotionally during the twenty-six months that Woodward and Bernstein covered Watergate. They considered resigning. During their lunch with Snyder, they could barely concentrate. They had gotten their first story wrong, and Bradlee was pissed. While many people would later accuse them of being fame-hungry glory-hounds, with a major book deal within their grasp, their main concern was always the quality of their reporting.

The *Post* could not afford any more mistakes. Editors were terrified that the White House might do something to set up the *Post* as its young reporters began to penetrate the Oval Office. Bernstein did have something controversial in his parents' background, and he talked to his bosses about it, but they were willing to take the risk. The *Post* was not going to give up Bernstein now.

The Haldeman error did not set them back with Simon & Schuster, though. The pair signed a contract and was given a $55,000 advance. It was impressive for two unknown journalists with zero national recognition—especially two journalists whom the president of the United States had called liars. They had just unwittingly taken their first tangible step toward becoming international celebrities, though nothing could have been further from their minds.

The unexpected book windfall was welcomed, but they were working so ferociously that they did not have time to enjoy it or even start the book. They were suffering under the so-called Haldeman Slump. They were desperate to advance the story to get them out of this dry period, but no story was panning out. Woodward and Bernstein and the *Post* were admittedly gun-shy after the Haldeman story, especially since Nixon beat McGovern in a landslide. By then, Bernstein and Woodward had written fifty-one stories on Watergate. "What happened to us was that we were beginning to feel the pressure of those persons who were saying, in effect, 'Aha! You see. It's true. They were working for McGovern,'" Simons told Woodward and Bernstein in 1973. "I knew and Ben [Bradlee] knew in our hearts that everybody dried up. Nobody was going to talk. Who was about to talk with Nixon taking 49 states out of 50? So we were anxious."

Bradlee and Simons kept coming by their desks, pressing, "What have you got? Come on, you've got to get something. Anything you can develop?"

Sources really had evaporated, though. People weren't talking because they feared the retributive Nixon White House and because the burglars' trial was coming up in January. The pressure to produce was behind one of Woodward and Bernstein's more foolish moves, even by their own admission. Hoping for a scoop, they contacted Watergate jurors at their homes during the first weekend in December. None responded, but the jurors told Judge Sirica, and he hauled all the reporters covering Watergate into court on December 19, 1972, threatening jail if it ever happened again. Sirica never mentioned Woodward or Bernstein by name. "We thought we were going to be named and unmasked and probably sent to jail," Woodward told ABC's Ann Compton in 1974. "We went down there quite scared."

After the hearing ended, Woodward and Bernstein ran for the elevators to avoid being asked questions by colleagues. "We went out in the hall and engaged in our own cover-up," said Woodward.

ABC reporter Sam Donaldson was at the Sirica tongue-lashing. "We were all abuzz. Who was Sirica talking about?" recalled Donaldson. "The session ended. I got on the elevator with Carl and Bob and Daniel Schorr from CBS. Either Schorr or I said, 'I'll bet it was you who were trying to contact the jurors.' I remember Bob particularly. His response was, 'Why would you accuse us of that? How could you ask that question?' The door opened and they left. They didn't deny it. On the other hand, they didn't admit it."

"A number of times we were confronted with ethical questions just like the people at the White House," Bernstein told Compton in 1974, adding that they would never visit jurors again. "Perhaps we started to do what some of the people we wrote about did. Justify our actions, thinking that any means may be reasonable."

It wasn't until the end of December, almost two months after the election, that the *Post* had a major exposé. Bernstein began going through a three-inch folder labeled "To Be Checked" that the pair kept. He discovered a special White House telephone that bypassed the switchboard. Oddly, the phone was listed in the name of a White House secretary, and bills were sent to her house. Bernstein got an on-the-record interview with the former secretary. She explained who the White House "plumbers" were and that their mission was to investigate leaks to the news media. The story, on December 22, 1972, put Woodward and Bernstein back in business.

The pair kept meaning to get back to their book, tentatively titled *A Point in Time*, but daily reporting interfered. Typically, they worked sixteen-hour days. It got to the point where Woodward complained to Sussman—not about working, but that he had no time to buy soap. He was showering with shampoo. That was an easy problem for Sussman to solve. He sent a copyboy to the store with fifty cents to buy Woodward three bars of soap.

"You couldn't even pay your bills," Bernstein told a reporter later. "At least, I couldn't. Everything got out of hand."

By January 1973, for the first time the Watergate reporters were feuding with their editors. They were especially angry at metro editor Harry Rosenfeld. They desperately wanted and felt entitled to cover the January Watergate burglar trial, but Rosenfeld assigned the *Post*'s court reporter to do it. He wanted Woodward and Bernstein to continue investigating around the edges. He felt that it would be a waste for them to sit in court day after day for a trial that would last nearly a month.

If they couldn't do that, then the pair wanted to at least write a pretrial news analysis exploring all of Watergate's unanswered questions. They wrote the story, expecting it to run the day before the trial, but it got held. Woodward and Bernstein were furious. They thought it had to do with the editors not trusting them anymore.

According to their Watergate archives, Simons didn't want to run their story because he thought it looked like the *Post* was editorializing or telling the prosecutors how to do their job. He also wasn't comfortable with Woodward and Bernstein writing a news analysis. Their story finally ran, much to their dismay, after former Nixon aides G. Gordon Liddy and James W. McCord Jr. were convicted of conspiracy, burglary, and wiretapping in the Watergate incident in late January. The other five—E. Howard Hunt, Bernard L. Barker, Frank A. Sturgis, Virgilio R. Gonzalez, and Eugenio Rolando Martinez—pleaded guilty to avoid a trial.

Always looming in the background was Simon & Schuster's book, technically due at the end of 1973. The publisher was expecting a short, quick book about Watergate. It would be edited by one of Simon & Schuster's new editors, Alice Mayhew, who had been lured away from Random House. "But they weren't working on it," said a former Simon & Schuster editor. "Dick told me to take Alice and go down and have dinner with these guys and find out what's going on. We all met at the Jockey Club at six-thirty p.m. and stayed until they closed the restaurant. This was the first time they met Alice."

It wasn't that they didn't want to write the book, but in January there was the Watergate burglars' trial. In late February, there was FBI acting director L. Patrick Gray's confirmation hearing, where he testified that during the FBI's Watergate investigation, he provided files to the White House. Gray's testimony was the first crack in the White House wall of silence. The next month, on March 23, burglar McCord dropped a real bombshell. Threatened with a long jail sentence and angry that the higher-ups had left him to take the fall, McCord wrote a letter to Judge Sirica. McCord said that perjury had occurred at the trial, that he was under political pressure to plead guilty, and that others were involved. He added that several family members feared for his life.

Even with stories breaking, Woodward and Bernstein did manage to eke out two different approaches for their Watergate book, neither of which was about them. An outline for an early draft submitted in 1973 began:

> Chapter one. Taking either November 1960 when Nixon defeated or November 1963 when Kennedy assassinated,—select a specific day and describe the life and action of the 17 major conspirators. The American way.
> - Political Saboteur Donald H. Segretti was in USC managing Dwight Chapin's campaign for the Sigma Chi presidency.
> - Up the coast in LA, Bob Haldeman was reviewing copy at J. Walter Thompson for Black Flag insect spray.
> - In Seattle, John Ehrlichman was winning a zoning case, bringing a gas station to what had formerly been a park.
> - Howard Hunt was an undercover CIA agent (involved in) the Bay of Pigs.
> - In Washington, a young attorney, Charles W. Colson, was handling constituency mail for his boss Sen. [Leverett Saltonstall, elected last in 1960].

- John Dean was in college, dating the prettiest girls and hoping to get into law school.
- Henry Kissinger was at Harvard lecturing on morality and international relations.
- In Connecticut, L. Patrick Gray was drawing his Navy retirement pay and drawing up wills for friends—part of his "beloved" law practice.
- In New York, an obscure financier, Robert L. Vesco, was making small deals to get money.
- FBI agent G. Gordon Liddy was planning a bag job on the [Ku] Klux Klan.
- Daniel Ellsberg was working at the Rand Corporation.
- Richard Helms is plugging away in the CIA bureaucracy.
- In the Midwest, Maurice Stans is. . . .
- On the West Coast, Herbert W. Kalmbach has built a law practice.
- In New York, John N. Mitchell is selling bonds.
- And Richard M. Nixon is _____

A little later, according to their Watergate archives, they tried a different approach. This time the book would begin with the four Cuban burglars arriving from Miami and getting off an airplane at Washington National Airport, where they rented a black 1972 Chrysler and drove to the Watergate Hotel.

Woodward and Bernstein wrote in a first draft: "They registered at the desk under the same assumed names listed on their plane tickets and in their rooms, prepared for dinner. In the candlelit Watergate Terrace Restaurant that evening, three of them, joined by another man, dined on shish-kabob, lobster tail, filet mignon and New York strip steak. The tab ran $44.45, plus tip."

"I wrote a chapter on E. Howard Hunt," Woodward told the *Houston Chronicle* in 1974, as he explained how the book was initially to be written, "and Carl did a chapter on the origins of Watergate. We had a lot of information that we didn't want to put in the paper. Carl wrote about the 1968 elections, how the White House used violence as an issue and about Colson's dirty tricks. It was sort of 'this is the secret side of the White House.' I did a chapter on campaign financing and Carl did another on Haldeman."

Woodward, in fact, wrote thirty-eight pages on Hunt that read like a novel but never made it into the book. This is just one excerpt:

> It was 12 days before Christmas of 1972 and an eight-car funeral procession pulled slowly into River Road that leads out of Washington DC to the Maryland suburbs. . . . A handful of mourners gather for a brief graveside service and funeral held for Dorothy Hunt. It was Dec. 13, 1972. Howard Hunt, 55, stood by the grave, the wind blowing relentlessly. He was a ruined man. His life had collapsed. His wife had been killed in a United Airlines plane crash the week before in Chicago. Her purse, found among the wreckage, contained $10,000 in $100 bills, money that he said was purportedly being carried to Chicago for a business investment. But that much money—like much of what Howard Hunt touched—remains a mystery to this day.

By the spring, the public had become increasingly interested in Watergate as more came out in the press and in public government proceedings. What had begun as a third-rate break-in on June 17, 1972, had blossomed into the makings of a first-rate scandal. By mid-1973, the rest of the press pack was all over the Watergate story. Court testimony—with pictures and people testifying—was something tangible the media could cover. Television and other news outlets, once wary of *Post* stories with unnamed sources, could now attribute information found in court or on Capitol Hill. Other news outlets began breaking big stories that the *Post* missed.

"Then the whole thing broke and became a shark frenzy and everybody was after it," said Howard Simons in 1973 in an interview with Woodward and Bernstein. "We really were reacting more than we were acting. That was the toughest period. We were a little hurting. You were hurting. We were hurting. We knew it. But at the same time I don't think we panicked. We decided that we'd just take the lumps and do our own good works."

All the while, Simon & Schuster editors were awaiting the book. "There were actually rumblings of, well, maybe this isn't such a good idea," said Obst. "Maybe we should talk about them returning the advance. Then it all went crazy."

On April 30, 1973, Nixon's two top aides, Bob Haldeman and John Ehrlichman, as well as Attorney General Richard G. Kleindienst, resigned. The president fired White House counsel John Dean, who would later publicly turn against Nixon. The news was stunning. Watergate had to be more than a third-rate burglary if Nixon's most trusted aides were being forced to resign. (Three days earlier, as revealed on the Nixon tapes, Nixon told aide David Gergen to tell Bob Woodward, "They better watch their damned cotton-picking faces.")

The *Post* was secretly thrilled but refused to gloat.

"There was a mistrust of our reporting for a long time, because Spiro Agnew had done his job well. He'd laid the seeds of doubt in the minds of many people and distrust of the Eastern Establishment media was high," Bernstein told *Time* magazine in April 1973. "As for ourselves, we don't feel any kind of glee. This affair does great damage to a fragile, delicate system of government. There was a time, right after the burglary was discovered, when this situation could have been dealt with more easily, without the tragic dimension for so many people that it's now shaping up to be. Even now, there's no candor from the White House."

As luck would have it, reporter James McCartney was in the *Washington Post* newsroom at 11:55 a.m. on April 30, 1973, when the resignation news broke. He was writing a story for the *Columbia Journalism Review* about the still relatively unknown Watergate pup reporters.

"They knew right then for the first time that they were bringing down the government," said McCartney, who is a generation older than Woodward and Bernstein. "I was just lucky to be sitting there when that happened. To me, they were young kids. I remember them that way because of their mannerisms, particularly Carl. He wore his hair long. They lounged around with their feet on the furniture. They were both very informal but intense. Carl looked like a hippie with a relaxed mien to him. Woodward had this sort of intensity and seriousness when I was interviewing him. He'd talk in very measured tones as Bernstein was making jokes. They were certainly not celebrities."

They were celebrated the next day, though. Much to the surprise of news outlets, White House spokesman Ron Ziegler, who had viciously attacked the *Post* more than a dozen times, was cowed, one might say humiliated, by the resignations. On May 1,

1973, Ziegler stood before the White House press corps, now more raucous and angry as they realized that Ziegler had lied to them countless times. He apologized to the *Post*. "When we're wrong, we're wrong," said Ziegler.

United Press International wrote this story:

> White House press secretary Ronald Ziegler publicly apologized today to the *Washington Post* and two of its reporters for his earlier criticism of their investigative reporting of the Watergate conspiracy.
>
> At the White House briefing, a reporter asked Ziegler if the White House didn't owe the *Post* an apology.
>
> "In thinking of it all at this point in time, yes," Ziegler said. "I would apologize to the *Post*, and I would apologize to Mr. Woodward and Mr. Bernstein. . . . We would all have to say that mistakes were made in terms of comments. I was over-enthusiastic in my comments about the *Post*, particularly if you look at them in the context of developments that have taken place."

The *Post* had been correct. The White House press corps would never be the same. This was a turning point in the relationship between the White House and the press. Never again would White House reporters be so trusting or respectful of a press secretary pushing the administration's agenda. This occurred because reporters who did not daily enter the hallowed halls of the White House—Jack Nelson, Ron Ostrow, and Bob Jackson of the *Los Angeles Times*; Sandy Smith of *Time*; Seymour Hersh of the *New York Times*; and Woodward and Bernstein and a few others—had stayed on the story, challenging the White House at every turn, even when it appeared that the press was wrong and the White House right. They were not worried about the White House punishing them by denying access for stories it didn't like.

"Woodward and Bernstein came at this as outsiders," said Alex Jones, the director of the Joan Shorenstein Center on the Press, Politics and Public Policy at Harvard. "They didn't have access to protect."

After Ziegler apologized, the *Detroit Free Press* wrote an editorial praising Woodward and Bernstein for succeeding in making Watergate a household name. A few days later, on May 7, 1973, *Post* executive editor Ben Bradlee called the staff into the newsroom and stood up on a desk to make an announcement. The Pulitzer Prize board had given the *Washington Post* the Gold Medal for Distinguished Meritorious Public Service for its Watergate coverage. The journalism industry was bestowing its ultimate accolade.

Yet it almost hadn't. When the Pulitzer jurors first gathered to wade through the pile of submissions for public service, they ignored the Watergate stories. Five other newspapers were selected as finalists. Bradlee was astonished. There was about a month between the time that jurors submitted three finalists in each category to the full Pulitzer board and the board met to select the winners. During that interval, Haldeman and Ehrlichman resigned. The full Pulitzer board quickly regrouped, deciding to award the public service prize to the *Post*.

> "The *Washington Post* from the outset refused to dismiss the Watergate incident as a bad political joke, a mere caper," announced the Pulitzer board. "It mobilized its total resources for a major investigation, spearheaded by two first-rate investigative reporters, Carl Bernstein and Robert Woodward. As their disclosures developed the Watergate case into a major political scandal of national proportions, the *Post* backed them up with strong editorials, many of them written by Roger Wilkins and editorial cartoons drawn by the two-time Pulitzer winner Herbert A. Block (Herblock). Other public-spirited newspapers took up the case but the *Post*'s lead in the investigation helped it to continue to produce disclosures that deeply involved various figures in the Committee to Re-elect the President as well as the White House."

The *Post* paid a price. There had to be a trade-off. Two *Post* entries slated for Pulitzers would not get them. Yet winning the top prize was the perfect antidote to six months of rough and professionally dangerous reporting in 1972.

Telegrams and letters poured in from around the country and the world:

> Congratulations from the only place on earth where nobody has heard of Watergate.
> > Best, [*Post* Moscow correspondent Bob] Kaiser
>
> Congratulations. Splendid work. Dig on.
> > —from 27 *New York Daily News* staffers

Warmest congratulations for winning the 57th annual Pulitzer prize for Distinguished Public Service in investigative reporting for your coverage of the Watergate scandal. Never have so few done so much for so many.

—WBRC Television, Birmingham, Alabama

You gave the tree a mighty shake and the big ones tumbled out. Many congratulations.

—telegram from *Post* correspondent
Don Oberdorfer in Japan

Kudos arrived not only to the newsroom, but to Bernstein's parents as well. Letters congratulating the Bernsteins on their son came from Los Angeles, Chicago, Wichita, Switzerland, and Spain. "Boy—are we kvelling!" wrote Eleanor Belser in a postcard to Sylvia and Al Bernstein after the Pulitzer.

Dear Mrs. B—You must be very pleased that your son achieved such a distinction. I have been following the accounts written by Carl that are carried in the *Sun Times* regarding the Watergate incident. You can imagine my pleased surprise to see his byline all the way in Chicago.

—from a friend of Carl's sister, Laura

Congratulations were sent to the two reporters as well:

Dear Mr. Bernstein: The main reason for this letter . . . is to try to express a very heartfelt appreciation to you and Mr. Woodward for the absolutely inestimable service which your excellent and very professional craftsmanship has rendered the entire nation.

—Bill Pharr, Little Rock, Arkansas

While the public congratulated Woodward and Bernstein, it was the newspaper—*not* Woodward and Bernstein—that won the 1973 Pulitzer Prize. This fact made them angry. They had wanted their work submitted in the investigative reporting category, which, if they won, would convey all credit to them. The duo was so incensed that they planned to quit when they learned that the *Post* had submitted Watergate as a package with reporting, editorials, and cartoons. Roger Wilkins, a *Post* editorial writer who had concentrated on Watergate, was equally annoyed. "The boys were not simply upset," said Wilkins. "Bob and Carl came pounding into my office yelling, 'We gotta quit. Can you imagine they would do this to us? We got screwed!'" Later, over drinks, Wilkins managed to calm them down, telling them they'd be crazy to resign. If they did, they'd forever be known in journalistic lore as the guys who quit the biggest political story of the century.

That didn't stop them from busting into Bradlee's office, however, claiming that the paper was screwing them. "I was almost more upset than Carl," Woodward later told David Halberstam. "There was a sense that something was slipping away from us." Yet Bernstein was mad, too. They figured that a reporter gets only one, maybe two, shots at a Pulitzer in a journalistic career, and they felt that they were being robbed of theirs.

Bradlee was prepared for them. In Bradlee-esque form, he reminded them that the paper had risked and staked its reputation on their stories. "The paper had its cock on the chopping block," he told them, stressing the importance of loyalty. The paper had been faithful to them. Didn't they owe something to the paper? He also said something that would become prophetically true: "No one will ever forget *who* wrote those stories." He was right. Decades later, news stories about the pair repeatedly and mistakenly say that Woodward and Bernstein—omitting the *Post*—won a Pulitzer. By May 1973, they'd already won a passel of impressive journalistic awards—George M. Polk, Heywood Broun, Worth Bingham, and a Sigma Delta Chi—and garnered almost $10,000 in prize money. The public may not have been aware of the team's Watergate digging, but the journalistic community had finally taken notice.

It would not be long, though, before the American public became well versed in Watergate. In February 1973, the Senate formed a select committee to look into Watergate. On May 17, 1973, TV began airing the Senate Watergate hearings. Each day, as Watergate figures testified, more information spilled out about the criminality, the chicanery, and the cover-up. The hearings captivated the public in a way that has rarely ever happened again. Between May 17 and August 7, some thirty-two Watergate witnesses told their stories, filling 237 hours of television, according to Liebovich's book *Richard Nixon, Watergate, and the Press*. They watched on public television after the three commercial networks decided not to provide full coverage. Only the nonprofit PBS aired the entire procedure. The average U.S. home watched thirty hours of the hearings.

This no longer was a story people knew nothing about. Mesmerized viewers quickly became saturated in Watergate minutiae. As the White House conspiracy began to crumble, Woodward, Bernstein, and their Simon & Schuster editors began to rethink how much the public would want a rehash of Watergate.

4

In Demand

Dear Sirs:

I am doing a class project on Watergate and would appreciate it if you would answer some questions that I have. Did your life change in any way or were you treated any differently after uncovering Watergate?

—Kenan Siegel, Miami, Florida, April 22, 1975

Contrary to what one might imagine, it was Woodward who first brought up the idea to Bernstein of writing a first-person book. But the idea did not just come up out of the blue. It was actually inspired by Robert Redford, a popular actor at the time, who was starring in one hit movie after another. Between shooting scenes and promoting movies, Redford read about Watergate and became captivated with making a movie about these two punk reporters. He was never interested in a political story; Redford was instead fascinated by the unlikely pairing of two opposites and their youthful, fearless determination to take on the Nixon White House. Before Woodward and Bernstein had written a word of their book, Redford approached them asking for permission to turn their story into a movie. They blew him off, but Redford had planted a seed. Instead of writing a story about Hunt, Liddy, and Mitchell—one idea they had tossed around—Woodward and Bernstein decided, thanks to Redford, to write a book that only they could write: the story of the road they traveled reporting Watergate. Rather than writing a whodunit, because that was already well known, they would write a howdunit about the whodunit.

Bernstein initially hated the idea. A first-person book would be self-aggrandizing, as if they were on some big ego trip. Besides, how would they be able to separate what Woodward did from what Bernstein said? "Bob sat down and wrote what was very loosely the first part of the first chapter, and I read it and thought it would never work because it was 'we,'" said Bernstein. "We did this. We did that. It was too awkward."

Bernstein had an idea of how it might work, though. He had been bowled over after reading Norman Mailer's 1968 Pulitzer Prize–winning book *The Armies of the Night: History as a Novel, the Novel as History*, where Mailer writes about himself in the third person, giving his firsthand account of the 1967 anti–Vietnam War march on the Pentagon. Coincidentally, Bernstein had covered the event for the *Post*. In the book, Mailer places himself at the center and writes about the experience with brutal honesty.

So Bernstein took what Woodward had written, rewrote that, and finished the first chapter by writing about himself and Woodward in the third person. "Woodward left his one-bedroom apartment in downtown Washington and walked the six blocks to the *Post*. . . . That morning, Bernstein had Xeroxed copies of notes from reporters at the scene and informed the city editor that he would make some more checks."

The style, though jarring at first, was in the nascent stages of becoming a popular writing technique, especially by journalists, although it is still rare even today for reporters (the exception might be war correspondents) to write books where they make themselves protagonists.

While the twosome acquiesced to the unusual writing style, they insisted on being self-critical and fiercely blunt in telling their story. They would include errors as well as triumphs. They also wanted to make sure that credit was evenly distributed. While initially wanting to grab the glory, they came to realize that Bradlee was correct; they could not have done the reporting or written the book without the courageous support of the *Post* hierarchy, its resources, and its reputation. "If it wasn't for the *Post*, these revelations would've been just stuff we wrote in letters to our mothers," Woodward told the *Boston Globe* in 1974. After all, the newspaper had risked its financial stability and reputation in confronting a powerful president.

The book could illustrate the hard work involved in shoe-leather reporting and could tell how Woodward and Bernstein had unearthed facts from relentless digging; how they culled sources, conducted countless interviews, and knocked on doors of timid sources late at night. Little was handed to the two reporters. They fought for every scrap. It was neither romantic nor glamorous. They hit dead ends. They barely slept. They ate poorly. They had no social life. They made scores of phone calls each day, each week, each month. They fought with each other, with their editors, and with the White House. "They were often upset with each other," their direct editor Barry Sussman told Halberstam. "Woodward more often with Bernstein. Woodward doesn't really leave anything to judgment. He is very, very careful. Carl has a little bit of an instinct to generalize. There were a lot of times when Woodward would come to me and complain about Bernstein." They would put it all in. The mistakes they made, including the Haldeman error and the story where they erroneously named three White House officials as recipients of wiretap memos (a mistake made in a competitive moment that damaged the reputations of the men named). The palpable paranoia they felt when they traveled at night to the homes of people working inside Nixon's reelection effort. The ethical slips made when they broke the law by contacting grand jurors at home and when Bernstein wheedled private phone records from a telephone company source. They would give credit to other news organizations that made a difference: the *New York Times*, the *Los Angeles Times*, the *Washington Star*, CBS, *Time*, and *Newsweek*.

Yet the book would be more than their story. It would be a kind of textbook on investigative reporting. By offering the step-by-step process that they had negotiated inside the newsroom and out, Woodward and Bernstein wanted to give a glimpse behind the curtain and show the public how a newspaper works. Most Americans have no idea how decisions are made inside a newsroom. In this book, however, readers would get a firsthand view. It would achieve Woodward's foremost journalistic maxim—take away the mystery—for the subject of journalism itself.

They'd write about how *Post* editors determined whether a story was newsworthy, when an incomplete story was tossed back, and how hard editors rode them. They'd tell about the three rules the *Post* had established to allow any story to be published. The most important one, which would set a precedent for other newspapers on investigative stories, demanded that any set of facts must come from at least two independent sources.

The book would explain their detectivelike approach to reporting. "It's a question of building up your information," Woodward said in a July 1974 interview with *Mass-Comm Arts*, which is included in their Watergate archives. "In the initial Watergate story, five burglars were arrested. What do you do? Do you go over and have lunch at the San Souci Restaurant with some FBI official to find out what's going on? No. You study the five burglars and find out where they're from, where they live, where they work, who they talk to, who they socialize with, what their background is, how old they are, what their children do, where they go to church, where they bank, who their neighbors are. It's exactly what TV's Columbo does."

It's a messy world inside a newsroom, but their book would show the public something it needed to see: that journalists work phenomenally hard, possess integrity, struggle to be fair, and agonize over whether to run certain stories. For everyone at the *Post*, the reporting was never about getting Nixon; it was about getting to the truth. All a newspaper has is its credibility; if journalists lied, if they were sloppy or unfair, the paper would be hurt. In the end, it would be a book about journalism and what it was like to pursue the greatest political story of the twentieth century. The book would also do something else, though that was never the original intent: it would trace Woodward and Bernstein's growing friendship and the grudging respect they felt for one another. To anyone who knew them, the biggest surprise, then and now, is that the two men developed a lifelong, though complicated, friendship.

Yet before they could focus on the book, there was another blockbuster development, a twist that ensured, although it was uncertain at the time, that Nixon could not remain in office. In May 1973, when the Senate Select Watergate Committee published a list of people it intended to interrogate, Alexander Butterfield, Nixon's deputy chief of staff, was not on it. "I was sort of surprised but relieved since I had nothing to do with Watergate," said Butterfield.

Then Butterfield got a phone call in July 1973. The Senate Select Watergate Committee wanted to talk with him behind closed doors on Friday, July 13, 1973, to see what he knew. Butterfield had an explosive secret. He knew that in February 1971 Nixon had had a taping system installed. Only a handful of men knew. He was one of them because he had ordered the installation. He wondered whether he'd be asked about the taping system. He talked to his wife. "I didn't want to lie," recalled Butterfield. "I never entertained the thought of lying. But I knew what a big secret this was to Nixon." This is what he decided: "If the investigators asked me an indirect or fuzzy question, I was justified in giving an indirect, fuzzy answer."

After a few hours, he thought he was okay. Then the question came. It was direct. "Were there ever any recording devices in the Oval Office other than the Dictaphone system you mentioned?" asked Senate investigator Scott Armstrong, who had gotten the job after Woodward recommended his old friend.

Butterfield hesitated, took a deep breath, and answered, "Yes." The room fell silent. The excitement was palpable. "I felt ten times older than any of them," said Butterfield. "They were young. They were ecstatic. I said, 'Wait a minute. Let's be serious. I know this information I gave you is monumental. Let's think this through.'"

It was too late, though. The Watergate investigation had turned a major corner that Friday the 13th. Nixon had tape-recorded his conversations. Woodward quickly found out about it the next day, but not from Armstrong, who intentionally kept a distance from his buddy. Another staffer told him. Woodward called Bradlee. He didn't think it was much of a story. "See what more you can find out," he instructed Woodward, "but I wouldn't bust one on it."

The *Post* had missed a big scoop. On Monday, July 16, 1973, in front of the Senate Select Watergate Committee and with the nation watching on television, Butterfield revealed that Nixon had installed a taping system in 1971.

While news of the tapes was shocking, it would be months before any became public as Nixon ferociously fought the courts and Congress to keep the tapes private. In the meantime, the pair got back to working on their book. They would need a research assistant. Robert Fink was hired after he won the competition for the job. "Woodward loved to play games," said Fink, who worked on the book for seven months. "He said a lot of people wanted this job. We had to pick a character from Watergate, anyone we wanted, and go out and find as much as we could, then write it up. I won that handily." (Fink wrote about Nixon campaign finance chairman Maurice Stans.) They already had hired *Post* library researcher Elisabeth Donovan to keep their clip files in order.

"Bernstein asked me to be a full-time researcher maybe three months after the break-in when they got the book contract," recalled Donovan. "I had just come back from a leave and didn't want to quit again. Bernstein convinced me and said the *Post* would pay me overtime to do it. When I started, I was about three months behind. Bernstein handed me three folders and clippings he had borrowed from a private organization. He was really good about taking files and never returning them. About a year later, they got really upset and wanted their files back."

In their Watergate archives is an acknowledgment that Woodward and Bernstein paid Donovan forty dollars. "That must have been Bernstein paying me back money he'd borrowed," said Donovan. "It was always ten dollars here, ten dollars there. He would just hang around. 'Could you give me a few cigarettes?' He never had any. 'Can I borrow ten dollars?' People would do it. I've never met anybody who was so good at making you do what he wanted you to do. He wouldn't stop until you agreed to do it."

Woodward took a week off that summer and wrote 110 pages on how the two sleuths got started. The story began, as most mysteries do, with the crime. After Bernstein read what Woodward had written, they agreed that the unusual style might work. They knew they had some leverage with Bradlee (they still felt that he had screwed them a bit with the Pulitzer). They asked for and got a six-week leave of absence. It wasn't the first leave given to a reporter, but it was still much less common than it is today at the *Post*. They collected their files, notes, memos, news stories, and clippings, and went to Naples, Florida, where Woodward's mother kept a winter home. They batted out the first draft—seven hundred pages double-spaced, Woodward told the *Book of the Month Club News* in 1974. If there was a period that Bernstein knew more about, Woodward left it blank. Then Bernstein—acknowledged by Woodward to be the better writer—rewrote Woodward's draft, banging away on an old-fashioned portable typewriter on a table by the swimming pool. Woodward worked inside on an electric typewriter.

According to "an early draft," in their Watergate archives, they struggled with how to write about the man they both respected and feared: *New York Times* reporter Sy Hersh. Five times, they tried to write a paragraph paying tribute to Hersh, thirty-six, who was the first person to reveal the White House cover-up.

> Among the few Washington reporters who had consistently penetrated the White House veil of secrecy, none had more of an impact on the Nixon administration. . . . [stops there]
>
> If there was a single Washington reporter who would never fall victim to that sad axiom, Bernstein and Woodward were sure, it was Seymour Hersh of the [stops there]
>
> WHAT THEY WROTE: If there was one Washington reporter unlikely to be taken in by White House manipulations, Bernstein and Woodward thought it was Seymour Hersh of the *New York Times*. . . . He was unlike any reporter they had ever met. He did not hesitate to call Henry Kissinger a war criminal in public and was openly attracted and repelled by the power of the *New York Times*.

Hersh was a close friend of David Obst's, Woodward and Bernstein's agent. At one point, Obst introduced the three intrepid reporters.

"We finally had this very funny clandestine meeting out in Virginia at a Chinese restaurant," said Obst. "It was Nixon's worst nightmare. It was like watching the World Series of poker; it was really fascinating. Carl kept saying things, and Woodward gave him these withering looks, like shut up.

"The upshot of the whole thing that's a funny coda of the piece," continued Obst, "is we went back after dinner to Larry Stern's house, who was a wonderful reporter for the *Post*. We were hanging out at Larry's and having some drinks. Sy is the most antisocial guy imaginable, and I wondered why he was there. Woodward comes back from calling the desk, and he's white. Sy had broken this big story that was going in the *Times* the next morning about Watergate, and the *Post* needed to match it and couldn't find Woodward and Bernstein because Sy had taken them out that night. Woodward was pissed. They just stormed out of there." (The story was that burglar James McCord had secretly testified that the cash payoffs to the burglars came from the president's campaign fund.)

By December 1973, a strong first draft was ready for their editor, Alice Mayhew, who was relatively new at Simon & Schuster. Around that time, Mayhew's boss, Dick Snyder, decided to have a companywide contest to name Woodward and Bernstein's book. *Reporting Watergate* was too mundane. Daniel Green, then the marketing director for Simon & Schuster, came up with the title— and all he got was a bottle of champagne. "We all joined Dick in his office and started throwing out names," said Green. "I came up with *All the President's Men* because it was appropriate. This was a case in which the whole White House was involved in covering up a crime." Coincidentally, at Yale, one of Woodward's favorite professors had been Robert Penn Warren, who wrote the 1947 Pulitzer Prize–winning book *All the King's Men*, one of the most famous and widely read works in American literature.

They may have had a title, but changes still needed to be made on the manuscript, according to a typed memo in their Watergate archives. One of the men (the comments are unsigned) thought a description was needed on how they handled the October 25 botched Haldeman story: "That was the difference between Woodward and Bernstein. When things went wrong, Woodward made himself an Ovaltine milkshake; Bernstein called a girl." Then there were holes that required work: "Need more internal Woodward to balance internal Bernstein, mention amount of sleep, or lack of it, state of Bernstein's desk, Segretti needs tightening, need something of Barry Sussman; his personality not defined."

Although Sussman's personality and background were eventually defined in the book, there is something the pair omitted. Pre-Watergate Sussman and Woodward had enjoyed a close rela-

tionship. What editor wouldn't love a pliable young reporter willing to work day and night and, to boot, work harder than the rest
of the staff? Woodward had the energy of a gazelle. Sussman
helped Woodward work on his writing at a time when colleagues
joked that for Woodward, English was a second language. Sussman showed Woodward how to take his hard-earned facts and
massage them into readable stories. Woodward did not always
know what a story was or whether he even had a story, something
not unusual for a reporter with only a year's newspaper experience. Woodward and Sussman became genuine friends. Woodward
went to Sussman's home on the weekends, brought girlfriends,
and played touch football. It was an atypical newsroom relationship between an editor and a young reporter; Sussman was almost
a decade older than Woodward. Bernstein thought it was unusual
because Woodward did not have a lot of friends in the newsroom.
He wasn't a collegial, let's-get-a-beer type, largely because he
wanted to work 24/7.

Initially, there was talk of Sussman writing the book with
them. He wanted to do it, he told David Halberstam, especially
when the plan was to write about the tale behind the break-in.
Then, however, Woodward and Bernstein decided that they
wanted to work alone. They didn't want to hurt Sussman's feelings, keenly aware of all he had done for them and how he had
often improved their stories. They thought he was a brilliant editor, but they didn't need an editor now. They would get that from
Simon & Schuster. What really bothered Bernstein was that he
didn't think Sussman could write. He thought Sussman would be
more of a liability than an asset. "If you have three people on
a book and two of them are not writers, then you have a lot of
problems," Bernstein told Halberstam. Eventually, they cut Sussman out. By the time *All the President's Men* appeared in May
1974, Sussman had stopped talking to them. "I've never read the
book," he told me. Sussman wrote his own Watergate book in
1974, *The Great Cover-Up*, a dispassionate overview that received
wide acclaim but never took off as the Woodward-Bernstein
book did.

"Barry Sussman was a great editor for us and an immense
help," said Woodward. "I feel sorry. You know, it was a reporter's

story to tell. Not an editor's. His role is fully laid out in the book *All the President's Men*."

When I called Sussman three decades later, he was curt. "I don't have anything good to say about either one of them."

By June 1973, a year after the break-in, Woodward and Bernstein's lives barely resembled what they had been a year earlier. Fellow *Washington Post* reporter Ivan Goldman wrote the following on June 9, 1974, in a review of *All the President's Men*: "Once I was driving along a downtown street with a companion in the early hours of the morning after a scrumptious feast at Trader Vic's, which just happens to be President Nixon's favorite Washington restaurant. Down the street I saw Carl Bernstein exiting from a greasy diner, walking along a dreary 15th Street. He was a solitary figure in the neon, predawn darkness. . . . He was heading back toward the *Post* building only a block away, returning to more work in the huge, nearly empty newsroom."

They worked hard, but it was paying off. Nixon's press secretary, Ron Ziegler, had publicly groveled in apology to them, and the *Post* had won a slew of awards. A year earlier, a mention of either name in public would have drawn blank stares. Now, suddenly, Bernstein and Woodward were sought after as public speakers. They weren't quite celebrities; that would come later. Yet they were well known for what they cared most about—the quality of their investigative reporting.

They signed up as speakers with the American Program Bureau, based in Boston and run by Robert Walker, who then had cornered the college lecture market. "They were in great, great demand at colleges and universities," said Walker. "And in 1973, who knew how the story would break? No one knew their names. They were just two reporters, but as the story got bigger, everybody wanted to hear from them. People wanted to know what was going on. It was just weird. They had more dates than they could even handle. And this was before the movie." Their fees varied between $1,200 and $2,000 for each college stop. Walker said that as their fame grew, they sometimes got $7,500 for each lecture. (Roughly three decades later, Woodward's minimum fee is $10,000, and it rises to $50,000, depending on how far he has to travel. Bernstein gets between $10,000 and $15,000, speaking fifteen times a year about what he sees as the sorry state of the media.)

In the fall of 1973, as the embattled White House fought to keep the Nixon tapes private, Woodward and Bernstein were running around the country speaking about Watergate and attacking the media for doing a lousy job. Over and over, they told audiences that their job was to get the "best obtainable version of the truth." As journalists, they were required to keep searching for bits of truth until the full picture emerged. It fit with influential journalist Walter Lippmann's theory about how a free press works. Lippmann, who died in December 1974, used to say that if the press is allowed to report without constraints, the truth will eventually emerge, but rarely does it spill out in one perfect account.

On October 8, 1973, the Watergate duo spoke at a Boston forum before eleven hundred people. Police reported that three hundred more were turned away.

While telling the story of how they reported Watergate before crowds of college kids, Woodward often lashed out at the media. His and Bernstein's success came not just from what they did, but what the rest of the press did not do. "There has been an obscene affection in Washington for the official version of a story," said Woodward, then age thirty, in the *Boston Globe*. "Big-name reporters were merely stenographers. Watergate has proved that that is not enough."

In the early 1970s, the lecture circuit afforded each man an opportunity to attack his critics and colleagues. Years later, Bernstein developed this nascent press criticism into a stock speech given more than three decades after Watergate, but Woodward eventually dropped the press attacks. Yet in Woodward's notes from 1973, he calls reporters "captive prisoners, who have an 'obscene affection for the official version,'" a "superficial toughness" but are "not doing a good job sorting through information." Reporters who didn't dig were no more than "sophisticated stenographers transcribing what the administration says," Woodward told University of Manitoba students. Bernstein was no less critical in taking on soft press coverage of Watergate.

Bernstein was twenty-nine; Woodward, thirty. The colleagues they were criticizing were typically a decade or two older. It wasn't that Woodward thought what he did was so special or difficult to replicate. He didn't claim to have a unique skill. It was simply that the rest of the press corps had forgotten how to report beyond the official version.

As the two journalists traveled, one or the other, but rarely both, often flew into a college town, met with local and student press, gave a lecture, and then stuck around for questions. "It's a racket," Bernstein cracked to a Minnesota college reporter in June 1973. "Woodward and I could do just this and we'd be rich."

When Woodward spoke at Brandon University in Canada in the fall of 1973, a pink program was passed out. It introduced Woodward in this way: "This could be THE most explosive story in the political history of the United States. Even though the investigation is still going on, we are quite fortunate to have someone who was there from the start. Here is one of the men responsible for the awakening of America to the fact that corruption may exist in today's political system."

Woodward and Bernstein liked speaking, and they didn't like it. Neither one was really comfortable being interviewed, and it took them away from reporting. "I'm not used to doing this," Bernstein said in the *Cleveland Plain Dealer* in May 1973. "I want to get back to work. I just took a day off to come here but I've been in touch all day with the *Post*. I don't want to be a public figure. I just want to do my job right."

In Cleveland, Bernstein, twenty-nine, wore a brown suit and was described as chain-smoking Kool cigarettes before speaking to two hundred students at Cleveland State University for $1,000. He said that the pair received seventy letters a day, most of them complimentary, and that they were besieged by offers to speak and appear on TV. They did go on NBC's *Today Show* and *Dick Cavett*. "We could do a lot more [appearances]," he said. "We even signed a book deal last October. But we're dropping everything until Watergate is over."

In October 1973, Woodward gave eleven speeches, and in November, he logged twelve more, including three in Canada. Their Watergate archives indicate that Woodward spoke at small colleges such as Louisburg in North Carolina, Ottumwa Heights in Iowa, Quincy in Illinois, Park in Missouri, St. Gregory's in Oklahoma, and Golden West in California. By November 1973, the *New York Times* reported that Bernstein and Woodward "are booked solid. They are perhaps the hottest speakers on the circuit at this time. Jack Anderson, the columnist, and his former associate, Brit Hume, are also in great demand."

Here's part of Woodward's typed speech attacking his colleagues:

> The press did not respond well to the Watergate—initially the reaction was that it was too stupid to be related to the White House. Listing the characters involved in the case, the respected *National Observer* said: "It is an unlikely grouping that might turn up as characters in a novel by Snoopy or guests at a party on *Laugh-in*."
>
> For a long time, it was called the Watergate caper. Can you imagine someone saying the My Lai caper? [a U.S.-led massacre broken by Seymour Hersh where American GIs killed at least 350 Vietnamese civilians in the village of My Lai.]
>
> But the press was confronted by a public relations mechanism at the Nixon committee and White House that is unparalleled.
>
> First, a series of leaks were floated out—traceable to the White House—that because four of the five arrested in the Watergate were Cuban, it was some type of Caribbean adventure. The *New York Times* bought this for several weeks. The afternoon paper in Washington—the *Evening Star*—responded favorably to that thesis for at least one day.
>
> Another measure of the effectiveness of the White House press machinery is that the biggest file in our many file cabinets on the Watergate affair, is the one labeled, "Responses and statements by Ziegler, Dole, MacGregor and CRE-EP."

During this period in late 1973 and early 1974, Woodward and Bernstein were frantically trying to balance their time between reporting the story and speaking about it. If one of them was traveling, he was on the phone to the other. Meanwhile, Simon & Schuster executives were getting ready to roll out *All the President's Men* and make history in book marketing. The book company was moving on a crash schedule that cut the production and printing time to less than half of normal. For the first run, Simon & Schuster planned to print 35,000 hardback copies and sell the book for $8.95.

"At this point, we decided in terms of marketing that we would do something relatively new and strange," said marketing director Green. They had assigned the book a healthy $75,000 budget to drum up publicity, but media coverage, it turned out, would not be difficult. Simon & Schuster decided to embargo the book, a practice rarely used at the time in publishing. Publishers typically distribute galleys, or advance reader copies, weeks before the publication date to give book reviewers time to read them and write copy. For *All the President's Men*, however, reviewers would get the book the same day as the public. The strategy wasn't completely new. In 1968, Little, Brown delayed sending out review copies of Gore Vidal's novel *Myra Breckinridge*. Something similar was done for William Manchester's *The Death of a President*.

But things rarely work according to plan. *Women's Wear Daily* got a pirated copy of *All the President's Men* and broke the embargo by writing a story. The hoped-for effect was accomplished. That created more buzz than any prepublication galley could. "This, for nonfiction, was still totally new," said Green. "In this case we were saying nobody could look until the actual publication date. The reason for that was there was going to be much news in the book. I had to deal with reviewers and explain that they would have, in effect, no time for reviewing."

That was not a problem, though. Bernstein and Woodward's book quickly became a hot property. No one knew that better than Mildred Marmur, Simon & Schuster's director of subsidiary rights. Her job was to get deals for the paperback, the book club, and foreign rights. Another agent handled movie rights. Marmur said, "I went to Dick Snyder in January 1974 and said I was going to spend the next three months focusing on *All the President's Men*, and he said, 'Absolutely.' Dick had fallen in love with the book, and we all worked like crazy to create this industry buzz. We all loved the boys. It was so exciting and so much fun."

Marmur did quite well for "the boys," as they were known. They had no idea just how quickly their book would turn their lives inside out and fatten their bank accounts. In early February 1974, Marmur was negotiating a contract with Book of the Month

Club for $105,000. The House of Representatives made her work easier when it voted to authorize the House Judiciary Committee to look into grounds for Nixon's impeachment. Impeachment hearings would only help the book, said Marmur. It's useful to remember that no one yet knew how Watergate would turn out. Marmur got the Book of the Month Club to make *All the President's Men* its July selection, *Playboy* Book Club got August, and *Fortune* magazine got September.

A key part of Simon & Schuster's strategy was finding the right publication to excerpt the book before it appeared in print. Marmur held an auction. Participants had to sign a nondisclosure statement. *Playboy* won, paying $30,000 for excerpts in its May and June issues, which then sold for $1 on newsstands.

By April, things were crazy. Simon & Schuster had already upped its print run from 35,000 to 75,000. In April, they bumped it up to 100,000 copies. Three weeks before the book's official publication date, June 18, 1974, Simon & Schuster had printed 210,000 books.

Marmur wrote in an April 10, 1974, in-house memo:

> Our publicity department is being inundated with requests by mail and phone for personal appearances by the authors. As far as we can assess, every national magazine is preparing a major story (in many cases covers) on the book or on the authors.

- Flash! Newsweek Condensed Books has just acquired condensation rights for its volume.
- Dan Rather will review *All the President's Men* in *Rolling Stone*.
- *Cosmopolitan* magazine just asked the authors to be Bachelors of the Month.

Bernstein and Woodward were clearly in the money. Marmur held an auction for the paperback rights on April 15. Before it even opened, she had a guaranteed bid for $750,000. Much to industry amazement, Warner Paperback Library paid a record $1 million for the paperback rights. "The book was really important to us because we were a small fringe company then," said Howard Kaminsky, Warner Books's agent. "Dick Snyder pushed it really hard. But we didn't really make money until the movie came out in 1976. Then we redistributed the book with the movie stars on the cover. I published like ten thousand books in my career, but I would put that book in the top hundred."

The $1 million was split—half to the hardcover publisher and half to Bernstein and Woodward. Each man got $250,000, less an agent fee. The sale "is a record setter, in financial terms, for a book that has not yet appeared in hardcover," crowed an April 17, 1974, *New York Times* article. "Other books have garnered $1-million for paperback rights, but they were already run-away bestsellers when the deals were struck. The Bernstein-Woodward hardcover will not appear until June 18."

What would the *Post*, which made it all possible, get from the 349-page book? What the newspaper would *not* get was serial rights, which it wanted for September. Simon & Schuster, worried (unnecessarily) about sales, refused to let the *Post* excerpt the book.

"Today I received a call from Henry Robbins of S&S who said that after due consideration it was decided 'not to run the risk of hurting book sales' by scheduling a newspaper series at this time," wrote a *Post* employee to editor Bradlee on July 11, 1974. The *Post* was invited to ask again in six weeks.

Of greater concern to the *Post* were royalties. As the book captured everyone's imagination, sales skyrocketed, and it became clear that Woodward and Bernstein were going to make a significant amount of money on royalties and rights. It was agreed, by contract on September 5, 1974, that the duo would pay the *Post* 5 percent of their net royalties for the hardcover version and 5 percent of their net share of books sold to book clubs. In return, their employer would waive claim to any other rights.

By the year's end, Woodward, only thirty-one, and Bernstein, only thirty, had earned a minimum of $567,000 in royalties and rights from their popular book, according to their Watergate archives. On top of that there was the money earned from speeches. Woodward, ever the more productive one, earned $14,874 from speeches in 1974; Bernstein got $7,894. In 1974, had they stuck with just their reporting jobs and not hit the big time, Woodward would have earned $15,130.32 and Bernstein $18,527.24.

The money was one thing, and it was a good thing, but the publication of *All the President's Men* turned Bernstein and Woodward into the most celebrated journalists of the day. Woodward told one interviewer that he didn't think that they'd become celebrities. "But if we have become celebrities, we know that fame is a fleeting thing," he said in 1974. This would turn out not to be true for either man.

The first news of the book broke with *Playboy*'s May issue, which came out in mid-April. While *Playboy* of the 1970s was considered a more serious magazine than it is today, it still catered to an audience consumed by sex. "Bernstein and Woodward Reveal How They Exposed Watergate—America's Worst Scandal" was the cover promo, where the centerpiece featured a woman in a see-through light purple bra, her nipples exposed. The promo for another story: "A Ten-Page Pictorial on the Occult."

"Playboy sales for last month up 10 percent—a phenomenal increase in sales," penned *Post* colleague Richard Cohen in a note. The magazine received a stack of letters, not all flattering. Nixon was still in the White House, and he retained loyalists. Woodward and Bernstein were called irresponsible and egotistical. Referring to a *Playboy* note to readers about the issue, C. Budar of San Rafael, California, wrote on May 23, 1974, "You said it best. We are especially proud of this issue's fiction."

In spring 1974, Nixon was still battling the courts to prevent turning over the tapes. Impeachment hearings in the House began on May 9, drawing unprecedented media attention. In this environment, Simon & Schuster delivered the hardback version of the book with a picture of Nixon, the presidential seal, Haldeman, Dean, and Ehrlichman on the cover. The hardback jacket promo trumpeted *All the President's Men* this way: "All America knows about Watergate. Here, for the first time, is the story of how we know."

The byline listed the authors alphabetically as Bernstein and Woodward, a name order that would not stick as the decades passed. Instead, as they grew ever more famous, their names became forever entwined in the public consciousness as "Woodward and Bernstein." Just like Lewis and Clark, Lerner and Loewe,

Tracy and Hepburn, Laurel and Hardy, and Rodgers and Hammerstein, "Woodward and Bernstein" stuck.

Strong reviews followed the book's debut in English and in every language imaginable—German, French, Japanese, Arabic, Spanish, and Hebrew. Ninety-eight percent of them were glowing. In publishing, it didn't get much better.

"Why now read *All the President's Men* since most of the 'facts' have been endlessly detailed in the media?" asked reviewer Ruth Kaltenborn in the *Palm Beach Post*. "Politics aside, it is still a fascinating read even though we know the ending. The book shows how enterprising reporters can take a thin thread and work it into a spool, ending up with a rope strong enough to become a noose."

"Sure, we are in the midst of a Watergate deluge—hardback, paperback, television, radio, magazines, newspapers," wrote Ivan Goldman in a June 9, 1974, review. "And so, even if you feel you couldn't stand another Watergate tract, even if you have plodded through edited tape transcripts until your eyeballs begged for mercy and your stomach threatened to turn, I urge you to read this book. It's different from all the others."

"This astonishing account of how the hideous mess behind the Watergate burglary attempt was first uncovered by two young reporters on the *Washington Post* makes a book which is absolutely not to be passed up," said a June 1974 appraisal in *Los Angeles* magazine.

"Bernstein and Woodward were in a sense the Wright Brothers of Watergate," said the Norfolk, Virginia, *Virginian Pilot* review on June 23, 1974. "Everything that came afterwards was dependent upon their pioneering work."

People magazine dubbed them Batman and Robin, although it didn't say who was who. *New York* magazine had Superman dashing into a phone booth and emerging as the newly powerful, mild-mannered, newfangled "Investigative Reporter." Journalistic legend Jimmy Breslin called them "the two that saved the country." Before Watergate, reporters had not warranted a whole lot of attention, but Bernstein and Woodward had glamorized an old role, making popular the concept of Investigative Reporter. It was a title that Bernstein didn't particularly care for. To him, good reporting was good reporting. You didn't have to dress it up with a fancy title. "I feel all this talk about investigative reporting is a myth," Bernstein told UCLA's student newspaper in 1973. "It's always been done. I've done it for years. Truman Capote did it in *In Cold Blood*." Ironically, when he said this, people hadn't yet realized that Truman Capote wasn't the most reliable of investigators.

Criticism of *All the President's Men* covered two areas. Some reviewers, including CBS Watergate colleague Dan Rather, wanted more than the book delivered. "There are personal flashes, but overall the authors don't tell enough about themselves," complained Rather in *Rolling Stone* on June 20, 1974. Had Rather and readers gotten an early draft, before Simon & Schuster editor Alice Mayhew laid hands on it, they might have learned much more about the authors' personal lives. Woodward had written an early draft of 700 pages. Bernstein worked on it, adding 300 more pages. Mayhew cut out 40 percent, mostly the autobiographical details, because it slowed down the story. It was a tale that used the story arc of Watergate to illustrate the vagaries and the complexities of reporting Watergate. In retrospect, this makes even more sense now than it did then. Nothing interests Woodward more than pulling back the curtain on secretive organizations. He doesn't just want to reveal secrets; he wants to make secret processes transparent, from the White House to the Supreme Court to the *Washington Post*. If investigative reporting was now an important cultural phenomenon, then it made sense that Bob Woodward and his lifelong book editor would want to pull the curtain back on that, too.

To the extent that the book *was* personal, it traced Bernstein and Woodward's begrudging respect and eventual friendship, and their realization that their synergistic partnership allowed them to do something neither could have done alone. "Neither of us is an advocate of the New Journalism in general, but there's one aspect of it that is good," Woodward told Walter Goodman in a July 1974 interview for the Book of the Month Club. "Writing about your own personal experiences, getting close to your own feelings and reactions. That's what we tried to do in our book."

The book was also criticized for not being analytical and for failing to give enough credit to the role that the grand jury, Congress, and the court system played in unraveling Nixon's undoing. The first criticism would dog Woodward's future books, but it was never the duo's intent to analyze what went wrong; they were writing a book about journalism. "There is no message in our book," Woodward told college students in 1974 who were putting out a magazine on "success." "It is about two reporters who worked on this story—their methods and legwork. It is also about how newspapers work, who makes the decisions, and what the power structure is like." Bernstein added, "The book is about human frailties, including our own. We tried to tell the story as honestly as possible."

But that didn't stop such criticism.

Leonard Orr, in a review in *Ms.* magazine, took the book to task for its self-congratulatory tone and for perpetuating a myth that Woodward and Bernstein took down the president. "But after the Nixon mandate eroded," wrote Orr, "journalists looked for their own heroes, found Bernstein and Woodward and invested that very competent pair with magical powers. It is entirely understandable that *All the President's Men*, which had to be written quickly from Bernstein and Woodward's huge Watergate file, would tend to exaggerate their role in the affair."

Orr called the book "unimaginatively written, sloppily structured with dull details." The *Arizona Republic*'s book review took the reporters to task for employing some of the same methods to get information that the Nixon administration used. Yet the majority of reviewers praised the structure, called the writing dramatic, and congratulated the authors.

As the prodigious amount of fan mail shows, reaching Bernstein and Woodward became more difficult and demand for them even greater. Everybody wanted something from them: a speaking engagement, an autograph, a favor, advice, an interview, a job, or a donation. Mostly, however, people gushed. Others wanted them to be saviors. Letters arrived begging them to investigate fluoride, haunted houses, pollution, tax evasion, medical conspiracy in the armed forces, religious cults, and even "Mrs. Kronick's husband's predicament." Someone else wanted them to look into the Kennedy assassination.

> "Your book was THE best I've ever read. I feel you can be trusted."
>
> —Mrs. Eileen Perry, Forest Hills, New York

"Dear Mr. Woodward: I hope you take an interest in this letter. I can give you one of the biggest stories since your Watergate story!"

> —Frances S. Siekmann of Los Angeles,
> tempting them but offering no details

"I'm half-way through your book and it's just great!"

> —Donald F. Sullivan, who hoped that Bernstein would take a look at his son's writing to assess his journalistic talent

"Dear Mr. Bernstein: I need some information for one of my classes. What is the name of the man who found the tape on the Watergate door? And if possible I would have to have his address."

> —Deane Reilly, of Plantation, Florida,
> one day after Nixon resigned

"At what age did you start writing for the *Washington Post*?"

> —Robert Calhoun, age nine, Valley Stream, New York

"Dear Carl,
Just three things. 1. Don't jump to conclusions. 2. You must some day try to understand that not everyone realizes that you are as famous (?) as you (and some others) obviously think you are. 3. I love you."

> —Rhona Kane, Toronto, 1974, typed on onionskin paper

But, really, most of the hundreds of letters about their book might best be called love letters. Scores thanked Woodward and Bernstein for explaining Watergate in a way the public could easily understand. Their early *Post* stories had dribbled out as news broke, but they did not necessarily convey the import of Watergate. The book put the story in context. They received letters such as:

"Dear Mr. Bernstein,
I just don't know what to say. I have never read a book as fascinating as yours. I can't believe it. It's becoming my bible. I think I'll just read it over and over until I'm dead."

> —Liz Clarke, Oxon Hill, Maryland

"Mr. Bernstein & Mr. Woodward,
I'd like to thank you for sticking to your investigation of Watergate. You did me a great service. I was 17 at the time and believed in God & the Government. To me, all reporters were flunkies for Big Business. I've changed my thinking since then."

> —Annette Lessman, Concord, California

"P.S. Have you ever thought of becoming detectives?"

"Dear Mr. Bernstein and Mr. Woodward,
Consider this a fan letter—or better yet, a note of overwhelming gratitude. I think you two come as close to achieving heroic proportion as any figures in our lifetimes. The source of my trust in our system of government is that two men such as yourselves could have helped precipitate the historical events which we've just witnessed. Anyway, someday I'll tell my two daughters about what giants strode the earth—even in Washington once."
—Mrs. Barbara Bengels, Garden City, New York

The public onslaught forced them to hire newsroom clerk Laura Quirk as their personal assistant to handle the flood of calls and letters. They certainly did not have time; they were about to start a nationwide book tour.

Before they left, Simon & Schuster threw a lavish book party for seven hundred people, with hot hors d'oeuvres and ice sculptures on the terraced garden behind the Textile Museum in Washington. Lady Bird Johnson's former social secretary was hired to ensure that the party was a smash. Two casualties of the Nixon administration were on hand: former attorney general Elliot Richardson and his deputy, William D. Ruckelshaus, who both quit before Nixon could fire them. In their Watergate archives are eighteen legal-size sheets of names of the people Woodward and Bernstein wanted to invite.

"The guests, who came after invitations that promised 'unrecorded conversations,' included scores of non-working members of the press, plus a sprinkling of the cast of public characters of the Watergate drama," wrote Jean M. White, who covered the party for the *Post*. "Sen. Lowell P. Weicker (R-Conn), who became an afternoon television star as a member of the Senate Select Watergate Committee, was at the party, along with Sam Dash and Fred Thompson, the committee counsels."

On June 17, two years to the day after an editor roused Woodward on a Saturday to work on a suspicious break-in and Bernstein joined the story, the Watergate partners began a harried two-week, five-city book tour, starting in New York City. On the first day, they told their story in five interviews. On the second, they began with the *Today Show* at 6:30 a.m. and ended with a party at Rockefeller Center for four hundred people that evening.

After three days and at least thirteen scheduled interviews in New York, they flew to Chicago (ten interviews in two days) to appear on the *Phil Donahue Show* and have their day chronicled by *Chicago Sun Times* writer Bob Greene.

"For the talk shows, Woodward and Bernstein have their routine down smoothly," wrote Greene. "They have set answers to every conceivable question. . . . When their answers begin to ramble, they have unobtrusive signals that they flick at one another to make sure that they keep it short, and do not tax the attention spans of their viewing audience. They are purposely and consistently reluctant to criticize the president, feeling that talk show partisanship would hurt their credibility as reporters."

Jon Van of the *Chicago Tribune* caught up with the pair and noticed that they had spent so much time together, they finished each other's thoughts. Instead of Watergate, they told Van that what they really wanted to be working on was the Patty Hearst story. Hearst, the granddaughter of newspaper legend William Randolph Hearst, had been kidnapped on February 4, 1974. The Symbionese Liberation Army, an urban terrorist group, was still holding her prisoner in California.

> "I know right now, if we weren't working on this," says Bernstein, "I'd love to be working on Patty Hearst. I mean that's—"
>
> "I'd drop everything in three minutes and get out there," breaks in Woodward.
>
> "Not just to write about the S.L.A.," Bernstein resumes, "but to write about the cops and what they did in that shootout; find out about the family. It's a great human story."
>
> "And it's all there," Woodward continues. "The role of the media, the race movements, the radical movements. We don't need to say it."
>
> "Modern, nomadic California," Bernstein says with growing enthusiasm. And the pair is lost in a reverie of stories still unwritten, headlines not yet set in type.

Then to Detroit for an evening TV appearance, to L.A. for twelve interviews in two and half days, and up to San Francisco for eleven more in two days, then home. They were asked the same questions, and they told the Watergate story over and over until it seemed that they had tired of it. Bernstein talked about

Woodward's never-ending stories about rat droppings in fancy Washington restaurants. Woodward told about Bernstein forgetting to return a rental car. Mostly, they teased each other, clearly not comfortable on the other side of the notebook. Reporters scrambled for any new scrap. Interviewers probed for tension, trying to explore how overnight wealth might have changed the two rookie reporters.

Charles T. Powers in the *Los Angeles Times* tried this approach to capture their new lives:

> Then, of course, came the big movie sale. Woodward bought a new car.
>
> "I went over to him when I heard that," Bernstein said, "and told him I could see it starting. He'd better watch out. It wasn't a fancy car, or anything but I just figured."
>
> "It's nothing special," Woodward said, looking at his plate. He didn't want to tell. Finally he said, "It's a BMW."
>
> Bernstein bought an apartment.
>
> "A huge apartment," Woodward said. "It's got about 19 rooms."
>
> "I call it Xanadu of El Barrio," Bernstein said.
>
> Bernstein doesn't own a car. He did buy a new bicycle.
>
> "I gotta tell you this story about Carl," Woodward said, and proceeds to tell the rental car story for the umpteenth time.

The two men could barely breathe they were so busy. "It's extremely difficult to get work done now because of all our appointments," Woodward told one interviewer.

"A reporter covets his anonymity," half-complained Bernstein in the same interview, "and we've lost that. On the other hand, there are special compensations for fame. For instance, it is easier to get people to call you back."

As the airwaves sizzled with talk of *All the President's Men*, and as their bank balances shot skyward, there was still one thing that bothered thirty-one-year-old Bob Woodward. He owed a lot to one particular invaluable source who had helped them uncover the corruption that rocked Nixon's White House. In the book, they called the source Deep Throat. From the earliest days of their Watergate reporting, Woodward had reached out to this man and relied on his guidance. They often met late at night in an eerie,

empty parking garage in Arlington, Virginia, just across the Potomac River from D.C. Sometimes Woodward took two taxis, traveling a circuitous route to reach his friend, a man old enough to
be his father. Woodward was bursting with curiosity.

What, he wondered, did his friend think of the book? Had he
read it? Was he surprised, even shocked to learn that around the
Post newsroom he was known by the nickname Deep Throat?
Was he angry at Woodward for quoting him in the book, even
though his name was never used?

Everyone in Washington and the rest of the country was talking about Deep Throat. Each interviewer grilled Woodward and
Bernstein every which way. Who is he? Who is he? Who is he?
Bernstein knew the uber source's identity, but he was the only one.
Woodward's bosses didn't even know. Yet in those early summer
months, as Deep Throat's name began to be as well-known as they
were, Bernstein and Woodward reaffirmed a vow they had made
in 1972 to never reveal his name until he died or released them.
It was a secret they would keep for thirty-three years.

5

The Source to End All Sources

Consider this a fan letter—or better yet, a note of overwhelming gratitude. . . . I'd send "Deep Throat" a thank you letter too—if I knew where to address it!

—Mrs. Barbara Bengels, Hofstra University,
Garden City, New York, May 26, 1976

The legendary Deep Throat made his first-ever public appearance in *Playboy* magazine, which ran two excerpts of *All the President's Men* in its May and June 1974 issues. He was one of many sources that Woodward and Bernstein used, but he got the lion's share of attention because he had a sexy moniker. Woodward and Bernstein's reporting had put anonymous sources at the center of political reporting. Over time, though, it would become clear that there was never a more spectacular anonymous source than the man they called Deep Throat. When the excerpt first appeared, there was tremendous curiosity about just who this mysterious uber source was.

But Woodward had a tremendous curiosity of his own. He was dying to know what his source thought about *All the President's Men*, now topping the best-seller lists. The man would have had to be living in the depths of the Amazon rain forest to have missed the clamor. When the news media began singing the book's praises, Woodward, now thirty-one, decided he had to call Deep Throat, whom he first met sometime between late 1969 and early 1970 when he was twenty-six or had just turned twenty-seven and was a full lieutenant in the navy. The two met by chance in the basement of the West Wing of the White House. Woodward was there delivering Pentagon documents. "After waiting some time that evening, a tall man with perfectly combed gray hair came in and sat down to wait," Woodward wrote in *The Secret Man*. "He was probably twenty-five to thirty years older than I. He too carried a file case or a briefcase. He was distinguished-looking and had a studied air of confidence, even what might be called a command presence, the posture and calm of someone used to giving orders and having them obeyed instantly and without question." Unbeknownst to either, the two men were about to embark on the most famous reporter-source relationship in journalism history.

Now it was more than three years later and Woodward, who had once phoned the man freely, was afraid to call. It's hard to imagine a Pulitzer Prize–winning investigative reporter like Woodward being timid about calling anyone, let alone one of the single most important sources of his career, but Woodward had experienced one blistering encounter already with Deep Throat and was reluctant to face the man's wrath again. While writing *All the President's Men*, Bernstein and Woodward had approached several anonymous sources they had used during their newspaper reporting to ask whether they could use their real names in the book. The former treasurer of Nixon's reelection campaign, Hugh Sloan, a key anonymous source, was willing to go public. Maybe Deep Throat would, too. He had left his government job in June 1973. Many Americans might consider him a hero for the role he played in exposing unprecedented presidential corruption. Woodward was dreaming, though. His source had been forced to resign from his executive branch job because he was suspected of leaking a story about illegal wiretaps to the *New York Times*.

Woodward "very gingerly" asked if he could use Deep Throat's name.

"He exploded. Absolutely not," Woodward wrote in *The Secret Man*. "Was I mad even to make such a request? He went further, suggesting at one point that he didn't know what I was talking about, as if he might be taping the call to create deniability. It was about as emphatic a no as anyone could receive. Angry and unhappy, he told me, Don't call here again."

Now Woodward was aching to call him to see what he thought about the book. He dialed the number and waited.

Woodward had not forewarned his source that he would appear in the book under such a titillating, embarrassing name, but since he wouldn't let the two reporters use his real name, they created a literary character instead, calling him Deep Throat. The name, the book, the movie, and the mystery all conspired to leave the impression on the wider world that Woodward and Bernstein had only one source. The truth is that they depended on scores of sources, both high and low level, and many of them Republicans. With a name like Deep Throat, though (Woodward referred to him around the office as "my friend"), it lent the source a cachet that would last a lifetime. They got the name Deep Throat from *Post* managing editor Howard Simons, who playfully borrowed it from the popular 1972 pornographic movie of the same name. Deep Throat is mentioned 24 times in 349 pages. Over time, Deep Throat would become a mythic figure in the public's mind, often given too much credit for his role in Watergate. No one ever imagined that the secret would last thirty-three years.

It did, however, because Woodward had made a promise. He'd guaranteed his source anonymity. In their book, this is how they wrote of Deep Throat:

> Woodward had a source in the executive branch who had access to information at CRP as well as at the White House. His identity was unknown to anyone else. He could be contacted only on very important occasions. Woodward had promised he would never identify him or his position to anyone. Further, he had agreed never to quote the man, even as an anonymous source. Their discussions would be only to confirm information that had been obtained elsewhere and to add some perspective.

Woodward initially never told his editors the man's name. He confided only in Bernstein. All that Woodward told his bosses was that the source was a high-up official in the Justice Department. "Everything he told us was true, and in that sense that was all I needed," Ben Bradlee later said.

In fact, Bradlee and managing editor Howard Simons didn't want to know the source's name. "Ben and I made a decision that on some of them [sources] we wouldn't ask it," Simons told

Woodward and Bernstein in a 1973 interview. "For instance, Deep Throat. You know, we've never wanted to know."

A surprised Woodward asked, "Why didn't you want to know that?"

"Because you really didn't want to tell us," Simons said. "Sure. At one point we could have said to you, 'Okay. We must know.'"

They didn't, though. Woodward eventually revealed Deep Throat's name to Bradlee on a park bench near the *Washington Post* offices in 1976. Simons died before it ever became public. No one else was told for years. (Woodward later told his wife and *Post* editor Len Downie before *Vanity Fair* broke the story in 2005.)

The trust that Bradlee and other *Post* editors placed in Bernstein and Woodward is crucial to a successful editor-reporter relationship inside a newsroom. It is the kind of trust that is not built up over time but must exist immediately, from the moment a reporter is hired and writes the first story. An editor cannot go out and do the reporting, nor does an editor in any medium have time to double-check a reporter's facts or read back quotes to named sources. The editor has no choice but to trust that the reporter is playing by mainstream journalism's well-established rules. Reporters don't lie to get a story. They don't make up facts or quotes. They do their best to objectively report a story, telling it with fairness and accuracy as their two-pronged goals. Editors know this. Reporters know this. In a delicate and imperfect relationship, they must rely on one another to do the right thing when the other isn't looking.

Decades later, in a plethora of high-profile scandals inside big-city and small-town newsrooms, a batch of reporters would violate that sacred editor-reporter relationship, destroying their careers and hurting journalism's credibility along the way. Since an editor has to be able to trust a reporter to behave honestly and ethically, once the trust is broken, the relationship almost always is irreparably damaged. Unlike in politics, business, or art, a journalist who lies and gets caught will never work in journalism again.

In 1972, when Deep Throat first appeared as one of many unnamed sources in the *Washington Post* (he was never identified in a newspaper story as Deep Throat), it was because *Post* editors completely trusted Woodward and Bernstein. Equally important,

Woodward and Bernstein relied on their editors to guide and support them when the pair came under attack.

Bradlee even supported the two reporters when they made their biggest mistake concerning the Haldeman story in October 1972. When news organizations barraged Bradlee with phone calls, he backed his boys. "We stand by our story," Bradlee wrote in a statement. However imperfect the editor-reporter relationship, it's all that Woodward had when it came to protecting Deep Throat's anonymity. He knew the *Post* would never force him to reveal Deep Throat's name in the newspaper and break the confidential relationship he had forged with his source. He knew, too, that his editors understood and respected this sacred relationship.

Deep Throat was strictly Woodward's source. Bernstein never met him during Watergate. In *All the President's Men*, the reporting team chronicled Woodward's odd, late-night meetings with Deep Throat. The source set strict rules. Woodward could contact him only on important stories. He would not be a routine source. Woodward could never use his name. Woodward could never identify him by his job. Deep Throat would only confirm information that the reporters got from somewhere else. He would provide guidance. In fact, his insistence that if Woodward kept digging, he'd always find more became the foundation of Woodward's later reporting. Other journalists might give up, thinking they'd reached as far as the story went, but Woodward always kept going. Deep Throat may not have given him a lot, but he encouraged the two reporters to keep asking questions, and this was his most valuable advice.

In the history of journalism, there have certainly been other important unnamed sources that provided news outlets with vital information that others wanted hidden. There is little dispute, however, that Deep Throat is the most famous and most well-known anonymous source throughout history. Over the years, journalists have come to say "off the record" or "not for attribution" to convince reluctant sources to talk. In return, reporters promise not to quote the person by name. Whether the inducement is "deep background" or "off the record," the result is the same: information is given to a reporter and used in a story, or a reporter quotes someone and attributes it to an unnamed source, often a "senior administration official" or a "former staffer." Either way, the public has no way of knowing where that information came from or what motive is behind an unnamed source's decision to open up to a journalist. Therein lies the biggest problem with anonymous sources: they are never accountable. The other problem: they sometimes, under the guise of anonymity, use reporters to settle political scores, attack rivals, or push agendas.

"I think there are a few major historical developments that happened in journalism—the Pentagon Papers, maybe Watergate—where anonymous sources had a more positive influence than a negative impact," said Allen H. Neuharth, the founder of *USA Today*. "But on balance, the negative impact is so great that we can't overcome the lack of trust until or unless we ban them." *USA Today*, the largest daily newspaper in the country, all but forbids the use of anonymous sources.

Some journalists say that important stories would be missed if there were a prohibition on anonymous sources. Whistleblowers would be reluctant to come forward, as would people whose safety or jobs might be jeopardized by their speaking publicly to a reporter. Defenders of confidential sources, chief among them Woodward and Bernstein, say that these sources bring to light important stories that otherwise would never surface. If used carefully, unnamed sources are a valuable tool.

"The job of a journalist, particularly someone who's spent time dealing in sensitive areas, is to find out what really happened," Woodward told me. "When you are reporting on something inside the White House, the Supreme Court, the CIA, or the Pentagon, you tell me how you're going to get stuff on the record. Look at the good reporting out of any of those institutions—it's not on the record."

The good stuff, Woodward has said time and again, is never said by named sources.

Woodward and Bernstein, throughout their careers, have never wavered in their support of anonymous sources as an indispensable tool in a journalist's arsenal. "Look at all the stuff that's been from anonymous sources over the years, and very little of it has been wrong," Woodward told me in 1994. "In fact, I would argue it's often more correct because the reporter knows his or her rear end is on the line."

And, he added, government officials are also capable of lying on the record. "You can go up as a White House correspondent and quote the president of the United States in a televised press conference. If it turns out he's lying, as it often has turned out, no one comes back and says to the reporter: 'Why did you print what the president said on the record in public?' The standard has to be: What's the quality of information?"

Deep Throat's information was first-rate, but why was he sharing so much insider knowledge with Woodward? Even Woodward didn't know. "Did Deep Throat want to get caught so he would be free to speak publicly?" he and Bernstein wrote in *All the President's Men*. "Was there a love-hate dialectic about his government service? Woodward started to ask, then faltered. It was enough to know that Deep Throat would never deal with him falsely. Someday it would be explained."

Since no one knew who Deep Throat was, no outsider could judge whether he was motivated to help the *Post* because he was offended by the criminality of the Nixon White House or whether he had a vendetta because he'd been mistreated by Nixon or his own boss. Decades later, when his identity finally became public, Deep Throat, who had spent a lifetime denying this identity, was not mentally competent to provide the answer.

In 1972, though, Woodward was less concerned about Deep Throat's motivation than about the accuracy of his information, and Deep Throat had never let him down. "The man's position in the executive branch was extremely sensitive," Woodward and Bernstein wrote in *All the President's Men*. "He had never told Woodward anything that was incorrect."

Although, at the time, Woodward was following typical journalistic procedures by keeping Deep Throat's given name quiet, it was a decision that would influence the rest of his career. By honoring the verbal contract with Deep Throat, Woodward and Bernstein hit gold that they could spend the rest of their lives. Future confidential sources knew that if they spilled secrets to either man, the secrets would be kept.

"This is an absolute contract," Woodward said at a December 2005 forum at Harvard. "This really is an unbreakable contract unless somebody is dishonest with you. If somebody lies to you, you go back and say, 'You broke the bargain.'"

Even more important to journalists is the notion that every source deserves a reporter's protection, regardless of whether that person is a hero or a heel. As long as the source tells the truth and sticks to the bargain that's implicit in a confidential relationship, the journalist will go to jail rather than reveal the name. "During Watergate, our sources for the most part were not necessarily all the good guys," Bernstein said at the Harvard forum.

Woodward, however, was never put in a position with Deep Throat where he was legally forced to reveal the man's name or go to jail. Not even after the president and a top aide correctly guessed who the source was a few months after the break-in. The Nixon tapes later revealed that Nixon and H. R. Haldeman knew who Woodward's source was but feared that if they fired him, confronted him, or retaliated, the source would cause major damage by going public on network television.

When the first Watergate story broke, Woodward called his secret source for help on June 19, 1972. What did he know, Woodward asked, about White House consultant E. Howard Hunt, whose name was listed in a Watergate burglar's address book? Deep Throat confirmed that Hunt was a prime suspect in the break-in, although Hunt hadn't yet been named as a burglar. Over the next months, Deep Throat would confirm stories and provide invaluable guidance. Woodward and Bernstein used dozens of sources as they pieced the story together, some of whom were disgusted Republicans working for the president. "Deep Throat was nice to have around, but that's about it. His role as a key Watergate source for the *Post* is a myth, created by a movie and sustained by hype for almost 30 years," wrote Barry Sussman, the *Post* editor directly over Woodward and Bernstein from the story's inception. "It wouldn't be correct to say we never got any help from him . . . [but] an investigator in Miami who helped us one time was a lot more important than Deep Throat."

Woodward went further. "He was one of many sources," he told an interviewer on C-SPAN in 2005. "He provided a context and explained that Watergate was much larger and much more abusive. Others hinted at that but didn't quite have the concept of the scope and magnitude."

Nixon's former White House lawyer, Leonard Garment, wrote in his 1997 book *Crazy Rhythm* that Deep Throat most accurately understood the corrupt atmosphere inside the Nixon White House. "He provided the *Post* with eye-popping stories, preceding disclosures by law enforcement people, that built momentum and drew in the rest of the press at a time when Watergate might otherwise have faded from public view," said Garment. "I'd say he accelerated the pace of Watergate by somewhere from six months to a year. If Nixon had had this added time, Watergate would have continued past the 1974 congressional elections. There might have been a changed political atmosphere, a changed makeup and mood in Congress, and a different outcome to the impeachment proceedings. Woodward and Bernstein and the *Washington Post* didn't do it all, but they did a lot."

With Deep Throat, Woodward and Bernstein had invented a literary device that provided an enduring mystery. Everyone knew what happened to Nixon. Less than two months after *All the President's Men*'s official debut on June 18, 1974, Nixon resigned. Yet no one knew Deep Throat's identity. Woodward and Bernstein's book left just enough clues to start a national guessing game that would last three decades. Rarely, if ever, when Woodward or Bernstein spoke in public, were they not asked, Who is Deep Throat?

The *Wall Street Journal* kicked off the game with a front-page middle-column story, prime real estate for one of the country's largest newspapers. The June 25, 1974, headline read: IF YOU DRINK SCOTCH, SMOKE & READ, MAYBE YOU'RE "DEEP THROAT." The subhead read: "Almost Anyone Can Qualify as Capital Tries to Guess Watergate Story Source." In the book, Deep Throat is described as a man who smoked, drank, and "knew too much literature too well."

As Bernstein and Woodward traveled the country in 1974, interviewers pestered them with, "Who is Deep Throat?" Both men quickly formed a stock reply. People could guess all they wanted. Woodward and Bernstein would never reveal their source until he died or released them. That didn't matter, however; the questions never stopped (not even thirty years later). From 1974 onward, they received letters from book readers asking for confirmation of this or that educated guess. Americans wrote as if each letter writer might be the person with whom Woodward would share his secret. On August 16, 1974, after Nixon resigned, a woman named Nancy Klock wrote to thank Woodward and

Bernstein, adding that her curiosity about Deep Throat was "almost uncontrollable, especially after the events of the past two weeks! P.S. The book is almost impossible to find in the bookstores."

Official Washington had a new parlor game. Everyone was trying to figure out who this mystery man was. The man himself straight-out lied in the *Wall Street Journal* piece. Newspapers ran columns speculating on the source's name. Pundits offered candidates. Even Nixon's henchmen proffered their guesses. In May 1975, former Nixon lawyer John Dean, who spent four months in prison for his role in the Watergate cover-up, wrote a piece in the *Washington Post* fingering Earl Silbert, a U.S. attorney who prosecuted many of Nixon's men. In their 1991 book *Silent Coup*, Len Colodny and Robert Gettlin are certain that Deep Throat was former Nixon chief of staff Alexander Haig. Colodny and Gettlin allege that White House counsel Dean was behind the burglary and orchestrated the cover-up. In 1992, CBS News ran a ninety-four-minute special concluding that Deep Throat was L. Patrick Gray, the head of the FBI under Nixon. Leonard Garment wrote a book in 2000, *In Search of Deep Throat: The Greatest Political Mystery of Our Time*, pinning Deep Throat as Republican strategist John Sears. In October 1993, journalist Michael Kelly concluded in the *New York Times* magazine that the man behind Deep Throat had to be Nixon White House operative David Gergen. Later, Dean, who turned Watergate into a side career, published an online book on the thirtieth anniversary of the Watergate break-in. In his 2002 electronic book *Unmasking Deep Throat: History's Most Elusive News Source*, Dean could make no conclusion. This time he offered a "short list" of candidates. He was sure that Deep Throat could not have been in the FBI. He was wrong.

People trying to "out" Deep Throat scoured every page of *All the President's Men*, searching for definitive evidence. In 1989, when Woodward offered a hint in a *Playboy* interview that Deep Throat was not in the intelligence community, Throat-seekers pounced, although Woodward never elaborated on what he meant by "intelligence community." Arguably, no one did a more thorough job than University of Illinois journalism professor William Gaines. On April 22, 2003, his investigative journalism class announced with complete confidence that Dean's assistant White House counsel Fred Fielding had to be Deep Throat, although

Fielding vehemently denied it. The class presented its conclusions at the infamous Watergate hotel in Washington. Several classes had spent four years sifting through clues and doing computer research. Gaines, a two-time Pulitzer Prize–winning investigative reporter, had worked for the *Chicago Tribune* before teaching. Although Gaines was criticized for trying to disclose a confidential source, especially by Bernstein, he and the sixty-plus students who worked on the project weren't deterred. After they made the pronouncement, Gaines appeared on more than a dozen broadcast outlets, and their findings were picked up by more than thirty newspapers around the world.

"Everything that we have, we show there's a document," Gaines intoned. "It's not interpretation, it's not guesswork."

But it was wrong.

Over the years, as no prime candidate emerged, a theory began to take shape that Deep Throat was a composite or even a hoax. Some believed that there was no such actual person, but that the character Deep Throat represented a compilation of several important sources. Those who doubted Deep Throat's existence believed that he had been created to spice up *All the President's Men*. Woodward and Bernstein's first literary agent, David Obst, published a book in 1998 titled *Too Good to Be Forgotten*. Obst claimed that since Woodward and Bernstein had never mentioned Deep Throat when he negotiated their contract for *All the President's Men*, the man must not exist. It was faulty logic because the first manuscript was not about them. By the time Obst's book came out, Woodward and Bernstein had long since severed their relationship with him, and the two men expressed contempt for Obst. "He has no evidence of it," Woodward said in a 1998 Associated Press interview. "He had nothing to do with writing the book. He helped sell our book, and now it's obvious he's trying to market his own book."

Although the man who was Deep Throat never made a dime until it was too late for him to enjoy it, Deep Throat's existence spawned a cottage industry where others profited. Deep Throat was not only a mystery; he was also a tightly held secret, and one doesn't have to have a Ph.D. in psychology to understand the deep pull in human nature to aggressively try to find out what someone else doesn't want you to know.

"The question everyone is asking is 'Who is Deep Throat?'" wrote Ida Lewis in the now-defunct *Encore* magazine in August 1974. "One cannot help being tantalized by this mysterious informant, Deep Throat."

Deep Throat was not just a quixotic mystery. His debut in 1974 changed journalism, because he lent credibility to the notion of using anonymous sources. Through their rigorous reporting, which relied so heavily on confidential sources, Woodward and Bernstein succeeded in popularizing the use of anonymous sources. "To be absolutely clear, there is no way our reporting on Watergate could have been done without the use of anonymous sources," Bernstein wrote in an October 2005 *Vanity Fair* piece. "In fact, in our first 100 stories, there is not a single named source who revealed anything of substance about the undercover activities of the Nixon White House."

After Watergate, the use of anonymous sources flourished, with many reporters considering it sexier to have an unnamed source than a named one. ABC chief Washington correspondent John Cochran covered the Pentagon and the White House from 1972 to 1977. At a March 2005 conference in D.C. on anonymous sources, Cochran concluded that the explosion of anonymous sources could be traced back directly to the *Post*'s inseparable reporting team. "Woodward and Bernstein have a lot to answer for," said Cochran. "When I was here, I think as a young broadcast reporter, because Woodward and Bernstein were doing it, it was cool to talk about senior administration officials or officials or to have anonymous sources. I honestly can remember doing stories where I'd say, late in the afternoon, 'I think we can get somebody to say this on camera. It won't be somebody in the administration,' and somebody would say, 'It sounds better if we just say sources.' It was cool during that period, I really do believe that. I honestly think you could go on the air or get in the paper easier if you had an anonymous source. I think it's less so now. I don't think it's nearly as cool. I think it's an admission of failure when we have an anonymous source."

The legacy of Watergate, helped out by Deep Throat becoming a journalistic legend, is that reporters feel comfortable using confidential sources. Few people disagree that they are an invaluable and effective reporting tool, but often, because of competitive pressure, many print and electronic reporters are too quick to grant anonymity, sometimes even before it's requested. The over-use of anonymous sources hurts journalism's most valuable asset, its credibility. "Out of Watergate came the legitimization of anony-mous sources," said Geneva Overholser, a chaired professor at the University of Missouri's journalism school. "They certainly existed before, but they were glorified by Watergate. Anyone who is an absolutist on anonymous sources doesn't get it. You have to use them sometimes. But reporters need to recognize that they are undermining their credibility by using them with such profligacy."

Many journalists feel about anonymous sources the way peo-ple in troubled relationships feel about their partners: can't live with them, can't live without them. Today in newsrooms across the country there is a consensus that anonymous sources weaken credibility. Yet few news operations absolutely prohibit their use. Many have policies, written or unwritten, stressing that they should be used only as a last resort, but the policies are often ignored.

While sensational sagas often bring about a burst of anony-mous source stories, there is one place where unnamed officials are a journalism staple: Washington. "There's just a great deal more tolerance for people going nameless in the newspapers," said for-mer *Washington Post* ombudsman Joann Byrd. "I think there are more anonymous sources per capita in Washington than there are anywhere else in the world. Nobody has a name in Washington."

Deep Throat had a name—in fact, one that many in the Nixon White House knew well, which is why it was so vital that Wood-ward not betray his identity. Woodward had no intention of blab-bing the name; he just wanted to know what his covert source thought about *All the President's Men.*

In Woodward and Bernstein's archives, on a piece of discol-ored paper crammed with phone numbers, is Deep Throat's phone number. Woodward dialed it. When the famous source heard Woodward's voice, he slammed down the phone. "I can still hear the bang of his telephone and the sudden dial tone," wrote Wood-ward in *The Secret Man.* "Hanging up was worse than any words he might have uttered. I wanted to know what he was thinking, but I did not have the courage to phone him again."

For days, Woodward could only imagine the worst.

6

The Double-Edged Sword

Dear Carl and Bob:

I thought you should know that yesterday I saw a man standing on the corner of 58th and Lexington holding up copies of your book and shouting, "Get 'em while you can, The Final Days. Only five bucks." That's not as much as hookers in the same area get, but what the hell, they're not as famous.

Best,
Tom Brokaw
April 24, 1976

While Woodward feared that Deep Throat might do something drastic, like possibly take his own life, actor Robert Redford feared that the man would do something more benign, like go public. The famous movie star with his own production company wanted to make a movie of *All the President's Men*. To him, Deep Throat wasn't just a person with complicated motives: he was an essential plot device, a great theatrical character. The last thing Redford wanted was for the public to know the true identity of the mysterious character whom Woodward met at 2 a.m. in a dark parking garage.

From the first moment that Redford read about Woodward and Bernstein and their Watergate coverage in the summer of 1972, he thought their story would make a great movie. He wasn't much interested in a political story or the backstory of the Nixon White House. He found the pair of young, mismatched reporters most intriguing.

Redford had been following their reporting and was fascinated. In July 1972, he had just finished making *The Candidate*, and as a novel way to promote the comedy about American politics, Warner Bros. put Redford, who plays a liberal running for the U.S. Senate, aboard a whistle-stop campaign train heading toward Miami, the site of the 1972 Democratic convention. Also on board was a real-life press entourage. "I listened to the press talk about the break-in at the Democratic headquarters, three weeks before," Redford told reporters at the time. "I got into an argument. I don't want to sound like a Boy Scout, but I became inflamed by the abuse of public trust."

It was press indifference that really annoyed Redford. He saw the break-in as an outrage, whereas the press treated it as business as usual. Why were journalists wasting time tailing him, while hinting that something darker was behind the break-in? "They told me how naive I was," said Redford. "How I knew so little about the press. That nobody was going to go against Nixon. They told me I didn't know how newspapers worked."

"You mean to tell me there's more to this story?" Redford asked. "But nobody expects it to come out because there is such a grip on the community by Nixon, and nobody wants to be on the wrong side of Nixon?"

What further infuriated Redford were the crowds of three to four thousand that formed each time his train pulled into town. *The Candidate* showed how the American political system is based on cosmetics, how Americans vote with little regard to what a candidate thinks. When the crowds came, Redford reminded them that he had nothing to say. He was a movie star. They ought to pay attention to the real candidates.

A discouraged Redford returned home to Utah and continued to closely follow Watergate. He said he began to notice articles in the *Salt Lake Tribune* with the same names: Carl Bernstein and Bob Woodward. "I got really excited, thinking maybe this story won't go underground," recalled Redford. But still, he wondered, why were other papers strangely silent?

Then one day Redford stumbled across a profile of Woodward and Bernstein in an offbeat publication the name of which he can't remember. "I looked at the profile and saw Woodward and Bernstein," Redford told me. "It hit me. They were two guys on the low end of the totem pole. They couldn't be more different. Bernstein was radical, Jewish, intellectually inclined, very liberal. Woodward was bland, boring, a Waspy Republican. How in the hell could they work together? The tension intrigued me."

Redford wanted to make a character-driven movie about the press with Watergate as the backdrop. What did these two guys have to do to work together when they had such contrasting personalities? He began to think about a low-budget, black-and-white film that would explain how investigative reporting worked. He saw it as a kind of documentary.

He tried calling the men, but neither called back. First he tried Bernstein, leaving repeated messages. Redford figured (incorrectly) that as the more flamboyant one, Bernstein was likely to return his call, but the two reporters were too busy working Watergate to phone him.

In early December 1972, between the completion of his movie *The Way We Were* and the beginning of *The Sting*, Redford finally got Woodward on the phone. "I'm sorry I didn't call you back," Woodward told him. "We are a little paranoid. We didn't feel you were legitimate. We just feel like we are being set up on a lot of fronts."

This was no setup, though. Redford began to explain but got nowhere. Woodward was just too busy. "He blew me off," said Redford. "It was Bob's polite way of saying, 'Thank you, but no thanks.' Then I went off to make *The Sting* in Chicago." Redford hadn't yet started his Sundance Film Institute and was spending most of his time making movies. *The Way We Were* and *The Sting*, two successful movies, both came out in 1973.

Yet Redford never lost interest in making a movie about Woodward and Bernstein. After the Watergate burglars went on trial in January 1973 and the Senate Select Watergate Committee was formed in February, Watergate was often in the news. By late spring, the story was exploding as the White House was imploding. The way Redford saw it was that overnight, Woodward and Bernstein had been exonerated. He called Woodward again, saying he'd like to talk to him about a movie on their story. (At the time, they'd barely written a word on the book.)

"Just give me five minutes," Redford pleaded. "I'll do it however you want to do it."

Woodward agreed to meet Redford without Bernstein, who wasn't around. They planned to meet at a screening at the Motion Picture Association of America in D.C.

As Woodward was ready to hang up, Redford interjected, "How will I know what you look like?" In 1973, Woodward's face was largely unknown.

"Don't worry," said Woodward. "I'll find you."

Showing up unannounced at a screening for Washington political types, Redford recalled, made him an object of curiosity. "Me being there was clearly a weird thing," said Redford. "Then Bob showed up. 'Woodward here.' He was in my face."

Redford explained what he wanted to do. Woodward agreed in principle that he was interested in a movie, but he needed to talk to Bernstein—whose reaction was "First, let's get the damn book done." Later, the pair went to New York and spent a day holed up in Redford's apartment, telling him everything they knew about Watergate.

All three were excited by the story. It's just that they saw it differently. Woodward and Bernstein had conceived of writing the book *about* Watergate. They were journalists. They wanted to write on what they reported, what they could research, what they had observed. When they met at Redford's apartment, they asked him to wait until their book was finished.

"No. I'm really interested in your story," said Redford. "I don't need to wait for the book. I just need the rights. I want permission to make a film about what you guys did."

By the time Woodward and Bernstein turned in their manuscript for *All the President's Men* in December 1973, they had agreed with a handshake to sell Redford the rights.

Later, in June 1974, Bernstein told the *Los Angeles Times* that he never imagined the book would morph into anything else.

"For people who are supposedly sophisticated, we were totally unprepared for all this," Bernstein said. "When we were doing the book, we never even thought about a movie."

"I did," Woodward said.

"You did?" Bernstein asked.

"Yeah, I thought, you know, if somebody wanted to, they could probably make a movie out of it. I told you Robert Redford called me about it once. It was a long time before we started doing the book."

"He did?" Bernstein seemed surprised.

"Yeah," Woodward said. "I told you about it. I know I did."

"No, you didn't."

"You must have forgot."

"We were pretty busy then."

Redford told Jack Hirshberg, who wrote a quickie book in 1976 for Warner Books about making the movie, that he had liked both men right away. "The more you got to know them, the more interesting they became as individuals," said Redford. "Neither wastes much time with idle chatter."

Woodward and Bernstein agreed to a movie only because they implicitly trusted Redford. They believed that he would make a movie they could be proud of, a movie about journalism. "He'd ask questions that went to the subsurface of things," Woodward told Hirshberg. "He's got his antenna in the right place. It became clear to Carl and me that he could be trusted."

Redford promised to make a serious movie about reporting—not a Hollywood, flashy movie about the shifty Watergate figures surrounding Nixon or a screwball comedy about newspapering. Woodward and Bernstein wanted a movie that would honestly portray reporters. Redford had no intention of glamorizing either them or investigative reporting. He wanted to educate the public about the rigors of investigative journalism; to show how meticulous reporters need to be, how many dead ends they pursue, and how repetitive, sometimes downright boring, investigative reporting could be. Yet there also needed to be an element of comic byplay.

In May 1974, when the book had barely come out, Redford began research for the movie. He flew to Washington, D.C., to visit the *Post*, to observe. Redford and Woodward chatted for thirty minutes. The movie star began trying to figure out how to play the midwestern reporter. "He looks all over the place always seeming to be in time and alert while moving deceptively slow," Redford wrote in movie notes dated May 29, 1974. "He cuts you off. Makes you feel that what you are saying is unimportant or that he doesn't have time. (Bernstein does this too.) One wonders if there is ever a time Woodward can completely relax and focus for a long period of time."

Woodward later drove Redford past his old apartment, the one where he had moved a flower pot to attract Deep Throat's attention, and then took Redford to his new apartment, where Woodward showed Redford his files from the inception of Watergate. According to Redford's journal notes on May 29, 1974:

> His apartment is odd, a couple of oriental antiques. A shitty building with Musak and cheap plastic trimmings. A great black girl down the hall exchanged meaningful glances with either me or Bob (I don't know). The apartment had his unpublished manuscript. He doesn't like it; thinks it's embarrassing. All the newspapers containing every story he wrote (not just the clippings; the whole paper). It looks like a paper drive. A lot of classical music. This fits. He also reads a lot. We then went to the Ripon Society for young Republicans. Why do they all look so good? So healthy. He commented on this too. We spoke a bit. A good talk. He is at ease and works well with audiences. Then we went to the airport and I missed my plane. So we had a shitty meal at the airport restaurant and talked. He was catching a cold but was then going somewhere to see some people. Says he sometimes puts in $30 a day in cab fare.

On another sheet Redford noted "salient points about Woodward," including:

- He reads in spare time or goes out with women.
- He read a book in an hour and a half.
- He is sensitive and deceptively quick—appears to be slow and uninterested.
- He wants Bradlee's job and doesn't like writing. Seems very hip about success and its dangers and traps.
- Liked *Downhill Racer*. [1969]
- I like him. He is very congenial and refined.

It would take until September 1974 before an official movie deal was signed. By then, the book *All the President's Men* had succeeded in turning the pair into cultural icons. When they did ink the deal, Redford's Wildwood Production Company paid $450,000 (plus a percentage for film rentals) for the rights to the book. Of that amount, Woodward and Bernstein split $299,250 on September 19, 1974—after fees to their agent and their publisher Simon & Schuster were paid. With so much for rights and a nearly equal amount to A-list screenwriter William Goldman, Redford's plans for a small movie about investigative reporting were no longer possible. Nor, as Redford had wanted, could unknowns—which is how he thought of Woodward and Bernstein—play them. Redford would play Woodward and find another Big Name for Bernstein. He easily convinced Dustin Hoffman to play the long-haired Bernstein. (Coincidentally, Hoffman had tried to buy the movie rights at the suggestion of his brother, a Washington economist, but Redford beat him to it.)

Despite working nonstop, both Woodward and Bernstein managed to find time to fall in love with women whom they would marry during this heady period. Woodward first met Francie Barnard, a Washington correspondent for the *Ft. Worth Star-Telegram*, in October 1972, when she was twenty-six and he was twenty-nine. She had been married before to a general's son and was relegated to a life, she told director Alan J. Pakula, that included weekends with her in-laws among "stiff, powerful rich people who turned me off and tired me out." Barnard and her first husband got married in a Cecil B. DeMille–like wedding with six other generals in attendance. They then moved to Germany, where, as she put it, her then husband was in a tank and she was living in a stonecutter's attic. The marriage didn't last long. "I took him to work one morning," she said, "came back, packed my bag, wrote him a note that I was leaving, cashed a check, and flew back to New York." The military wasn't the life for her, and she took up reporting, which was not a stretch. She was the granddaughter of a Texas newspaper publisher and had grown up a Texas belle around the Lone Star State's newspaper world.

The couple began dating seriously in March 1973. Some nights, Barnard said, she and Woodward went out for dinner, and later, as they were getting ready for bed, the phone would ring around 11 p.m. and Woodward would leave. She'd fall asleep on the couch, sometimes waking up at 4 a.m. and still Woodward would be gone. "I stayed out of the way when Bob was working on the book," she told Redford.

On November 29, 1974, when Woodward was immersed in an intense period of reporting for his second book, he and Barnard quickly got married (it was a second marriage for both) in a civil ceremony in Washington, D.C. Only a handful of people were there, including Bernstein. Some of Woodward's friends say a false medical scare that Woodward was dying of leukemia motivated his sudden concern about mortality and his desire to marry Barnard.

"As I recall it, there were about six of us at the civil ceremony, which I think was in the chambers of [federal judge] Harold Greene," said Woodward's friend Scott Armstrong. "I remember Francie was unbelievably beautiful, literally aglow. Her mother was in a particularly good mood, constantly being kidded by Bob and returning the good humor."

The wedding almost didn't happen, as Barnard for a time had been courted by Delaware Democrat Senator Joseph R. Biden Jr., who had lost his wife and infant daughter in a car accident soon after his first election in 1972. Later Bernstein shared with Pakula that "when Francie left Woodward for a senator, Woodward said it was like going through all the same feelings of his mother leaving when he was a child."

It was Woodward whom Barnard married, though. Touting all that was good in Woodward's life in 1974 (a wildly successful first book, Robert Redford portraying him in a major motion picture, and Woodward's collecting almost $2 million before taxes), a Knight Ridder reporter wrote, "As if that were not enough, Francie Barnard, a cute, smart reporter and heiress to part of a Texas publishing fortune, threw over a U.S. senator to marry Bob Woodward in November 1974."

There was no time after the wedding for even a short honeymoon. Woodward and Bernstein were already hard at work on their next book. Barnard soon learned what she probably already suspected and Woodward's first wife, Kathleen, already knew: that Woodward was an incorrigible workaholic, incapable of relaxing for anything other than short periods. He loved his work.

While Barnard was married to Woodward, she left her $14,000-a-year newspaper job (by 1978, Woodward was earning $33,600 a year) and sued the *Ft. Worth Star-Telegram*, claiming sex discrimination for a decision not to make her bureau chief after the then chief died in his office. Newspaper archives show that she settled with the paper for $20,000 in 1977.

"Francie was very high strung," said Barbara Matusow, who wrote about Woodward for *Washingtonian* magazine. "I sort of knew her. She struck me as somebody who didn't know how to handle the limelight, wanted it but didn't know what to do when in it."

Bernstein, too, found someone. He met Nora Ephron, a talented, high-profile writer for *New York* magazine, at a party in the Big Apple in December 1973. They quickly clicked and began a long-distance relationship, even writing a never-published manuscript, *The Eastern Shuttle*, based on their commuter romance flying between cities on the New York–D.C. shuttle. Ephron was a winner. "Carl couldn't believe that this woman, who was so bright and so attractive, she had 'can't miss' written all over her, liked him," said Ben Bradlee, Bernstein's former boss. "It was a great catch for him."

Their budding romance even made it into the *Tampa Tribune*'s celebrities column on April 24, 1974: "[Carl Bernstein] is living the greatest romance of his life with New York Reporter Nora Ephron, ex of comic writer Dan Greenburg. Nora just gave Bernstein an old-fashioned ceiling fan for his birthday. Keep cool, Carl!"

Bernstein was smitten. Before Ephron, he had told Pakula that he didn't believe in monogamy. "I would go with a girl for about six months or a year," Bernstein said. "A year was about the time a relationship would last." His first wife was a newspaperwoman, noted Pakula. "And there was the girl who was rich, social. But pooh-poohing it, who dabbled with the *Post*, photography, horseback riding. That was who he was going out with through a big chunk of the Watergate story. And then there was Nora."

While the arrival of Ephron and Barnard enriched the two men, the departure of another major figure in their lives only seemed to make them richer.

Not long after *All the President's Men* came out, Nixon resigned on August 9, 1974. A chapter of Woodward and Bernstein's life officially ended. Their dogged reporting had helped to play a role in the resignation of one of the most criminally corrupt presidents in modern time. There was no gloating, however; instead, the Watergate partners watched the resignation speech on TV in the *Post* newsroom, while eating bologna sandwiches.

"I remember all kinds of feelings as I watched," Bernstein said later at a junior college commencement in Florida. "Empathy. Denial of having anything to do with it. Glad it was over. Interest. Fascination. And I was still covering the story that day. We had known for thirty-six hours, perhaps twenty-four hours that he was going to resign. The process that led to the decision still had to be covered. I never had a feeling of personal responsibility. We had our role, but Judge John Sirica had his, other newspapers had theirs."

Outside the *Post*, TV crews, aware that the paper was part of the drama, were clamoring to get inside. Bradlee refused to let them in. "When Nixon's resignation finally happened, the place was bombarded, invaded, surrounded by reporters," said Bradlee. "We kept all reporters out of the newsroom. We thought it would send a terrible picture of us being interviewed in the same room where we were trying to put out a newspaper. We wanted to protect ourselves."

The *Post*, its top editors, and its two star metro reporters had become as much a part of the story as the Nixon team was—a fate most journalists go out of their way to avoid.

Woodward later told Jack Hirshberg that neither he nor Bernstein celebrated that night. "I had no ax to grind with Nixon or the Republicans," Woodward said. "But as we watched him on TV rationalizing this resignation on a disintegration of support in the Congress, we felt no sense of triumph. If anything, we felt our role had been blown out of proportion. I suppose we were a contributing factor, but we didn't bring down the president. I think there must be an adversary situation in any case of investigative reporting. They kept saying we were liars. We had to prove them wrong. The only way we could do it was with solid facts."

Not long after Nixon got on Air Force One and flew home to California, Woodward and Bernstein realized that there was still much more of the story to tell. People who were once fiercely loyal to Nixon might now feel freer to tell what really happened in the days leading up to the unprecedented resignation of a sitting president. Woodward and Bernstein had reported pieces of it, but they knew there was a solid, compelling human story that no one else had written. Their second book, *The Final Days*, was Bernstein's idea. "I never, ever would have thought of it," Woodward said in a 1989 *Washington Post* magazine article. "It was his idea to do *All the President's Men*, too. I have enormous gaps and he filled them. I was at times able to capitalize on his gifts, probably more than he was."

Around the time that Nixon was resigning, screenwriter William Goldman gave Redford the first draft of a screenplay for *All the President's Men*. During the fall of 1974 and all of 1975, Woodward and Bernstein juggled helping Redford with the movie while trying to write their second book. It wasn't so bad, though. Money was rolling in. Woodward was thirty-one; Bernstein, thirty. They'd received $450,000 for the movie rights and a $300,000 advance for their second book, initially titled *The Last 100 Days*. Simon & Schuster kept the foreign rights, and Woodward and Bernstein owned the movie and the serial rights. (Again, Simon & Schuster was smarter. The movie that was made in 1989 was a barely watchable, made-for-TV dud with no-name actors. Nixon tried unsuccessfully to prevent ABC from airing it by threatening to sue if he didn't get script review.) Money was still flowing in from *All the President's Men*. "$600,000 minimum owed on old book," Bernstein jotted on a yellow legal pad about money paid through September 30, 1974. Of that $600,000, for example, the Book of the Month Club owed the duo $100,000 after selling 250,000 copies, according to Bernstein's Watergate archive notes. A year earlier, the men had barely written a word of *All the President's Men*. Such sudden, dizzying wealth was hard to fathom, especially for young reporters accustomed to washing laundry in coin-operated machines. Such wealth, too, was bound to change their personalities and lifestyles or, at the very least, alter how family, friends, and strangers responded to them.

To help the pair write *The Final Days*, the *Post* gave them an unpaid leave of absence but exacted a promise of 5 percent of all net royalties from their next book. The duo immediately set out to interview scores of people connected to Watergate, Congress, the courts, and the White House. They set up an office on the sixth floor of the *Washington Post* and began reconstructing every event that led to the resignation. They hired Woodward's close friend Scott Armstrong to help with research, paying him $13,832 in 1974, according to joint bank records in their Watergate archives. They hired Al Kamen, an Armstrong friend and a free-lance investigator, to do research and paid him $3,900 in the fall of 1974. Kamen, a former Peace Corps volunteer, developed a meticulous filing system while the authors and Armstrong spent six months reporting. Later, Kamen provided invaluable help with writing and editing the 480-page book.

The initial plan was to focus on the hundred days leading up to the resignation. Everyone quickly realized, however, that to do the book right, the authors and the investigative team would have to reconstruct all the events from the pivotal turning point when Nixon asked his top aides to resign on April 30, 1973.

In their Watergate archives is a note Woodward handwrote explaining how the book had been done. *The Final Days* was radically different from *All the President's Men*. That was *his and Bernstein's* story. This would be the untold story of Nixon's last fifteen months in office. The duo began reporting in September 1974 with a list of a hundred or so people who were most centrally involved, and then they set out to interview these key players. In October, according to a letter in their Watergate archives, Secretary of State Henry Kissinger agreed to talk to them.

"Over 700 interviews were conducted, all on background," wrote Woodward in an undated early draft of the foreword. "That is, they were on the record—we could use the information—but the source's identity was confidential. With this guarantee, those we talked to were willing to give us information we would never otherwise have been able to obtain." While they may have done 700 interviews (the book actually lists 394), equal weight was not given to each interview. According to a handwritten note, "The bulk of the information came from 65 people." Woodward and Bernstein called it "saturation reporting."

"In the course of over three years of reporting on the Nixon administration—two of them for the *Washington Post*," Woodward wrote by hand, "we had learned to place trust in the accuracy and candor of some individuals, and to distrust a slanted or self-serving version of events of certain others. We have attempted to verify every detail in the course of reconstructing events. In reporting big meetings, for example, we were able in almost all instances to talk to one or more of the participants. . . . No assumptions should be made about sources. It may appear that we definitely received information from certain persons when we did not."

Woodward noted in their Watergate archives that they would have preferred to conduct their interviews by naming their sources. Yet then, as now, Woodward believed that the only way you can get people to tell the truth is when they are not worrying about whether their names will be used.

This style of interviewing scores of players on background and then reconstructing events and conversations, even attributing thoughts and feelings, would become a hallmark of Woodward's later writing. Using an omniscient narrative to tell a complex story without ever stating where information came from became extremely controversial and drew heaps of stinging criticism. As he and Bernstein wrote *The Final Days*, they had no reason to expect the bumpy mix of praise and attacks that would come.

While Woodward and his investigative team geared up, though, Bernstein vanished, spending more and more time in New York City with Nora Ephron. That fall of 1974 was a hectic time. In addition to now having more complicated personal lives (Woodward was married and Bernstein virtually living with Ephron), the pair still gave speeches at colleges, dealt with Simon & Schuster, provided script advice to Redford, handled between fifty and a hundred letters a week, and tried to interview Nixon's men while everyone's memories were fresh. On top of that, they were deluged by requests for magazine, newspaper, and broadcast interviews and turned down literally scores of speaking invitations.

"Woodward and Bernstein were in big demand," said Robert Walker, who handled their speaking gigs at the time. "I turned away dates for them. They did a great job. It wasn't that they'd just collect their fees. People got their money's worth. They had Q&As and were very good with the college students."

There was a limit to what they could or wanted to do, though. Bernstein told *Parade* magazine in 1976, "Our first interest is in doing our work. When it's possible to accommodate somebody who seems to have a serious purpose in mind, we'll do it. But you can't spend all your life giving interviews."

Things had been crazy for so long that it was tough even for their assistant, Laura Quirk, to keep up. Their archives are stuffed with requests for their attention that clearly outweighed what they could handle; hundreds of letters went unanswered and attempts to speak to the two reporters were often ignored. On letter after letter, Quirk scrawled across the top: "You really should answer this."

> Dear Mr. Bernstein,
>
> I have been trying to get in touch with you for the past three months. I have phoned you, written you and have not received an answer yet. It has been five weeks since the last letter was written, and I have received no answer yet. The minute I do catch Mr. Woodward on the phone, he hangs up the first time I say Watergate. I must say I know what a hard time you had trying to talk to people; I have the same trouble trying to talk to you. Thank you for the little time you spent cooperating.
>
> Sharon A. Elam
> Pearl River, La.

The easily distracted Bernstein, in particular, had trouble handling all the demands on his time. As a result, the two men fought a lot, sometimes going for periods without speaking to each other. They tried not to argue in the presence of the women in their lives.

Bernstein's haphazard work habits had created long-term stress for Woodward, who may be one of the most disciplined writers in America. Woodward later admitted that during the end of 1974 and the beginning of 1975, his and Bernstein's friendship, such as it was, hit its lowest point. In January 1975, Woodward told Pakula, "Bernstein and I often don't like each other." Woodward had grown tired of Bernstein's disorganization and frustrated with always having to make sure things got done for both of them.

Underneath all the arguments, deep down they hated each other, Ephron told Pakula when he interviewed her in February 1975. Bernstein despised the way Woodward sucked up to people, Ephron said, but Bernstein knew that he needed to do it. "Bob needed Carl because Carl was pushy. Bob can formulate and Carl can draw conclusions," she said. After fights, Bernstein would be in tears, said Ephron, feeling like a frustrated puppy. Woodward often left him filled with tremendous feelings of impotence. Loyally, Ephron told Pakula that Woodward was stubborn, bull-headed, manipulative, and had no instinct for writing. She told of a $400 phone bill that she and Bernstein ran up while vacationing in Martinique during an edit of *All the President's Men*. The two men had fought long-distance over verb tenses.

The tension seeped into their second book. Bernstein admittedly was "awful about getting into gear" when they began. "I've always resisted the idea of anything obligatory," Bernstein told *Fame* magazine in 1989 about *The Final Days*. "I was always fighting the world." Eventually, however, the pair managed to mend things. Although they still fought, Woodward told *Parade* magazine in 1976, "the fights have become less bitter. Our relationship works, and it works because we disagree on so many things that we consider two different points of view, then resolve them."

Yet that friction over *The Final Days* meant that the far more organized Woodward shepherded the book. Their Watergate archives for *The Final Days* include twenty-seven boxes belonging to Woodward and thirteen boxes to Bernstein, with the curious note that "none of Bernstein's *Final Days* source files are currently open for research."

According to archivist Stephen Mielke's notes on *The Final Days*, "The early drafts include working files from both Bernstein and Woodward, with many of Woodward's files containing extensive input from research assistant Scott Armstrong." One file included the notation "Woodward rewrite of Armstrong rewrite of Woodward original."

It is clear that Armstrong did quite a bit of the research and writing of the book. Yet one of the book's most remarked-upon aspects, its omniscient narration, seems to have been thought up or, at least, enforced by their editor, Alice Mayhew.

In one section on Henry Kissinger, for example, Mayhew hand wrote that Armstrong's voice was coming through too strongly. "So far, we are seeing Henry Kissinger through Scott's eyes: We should never see that. Always must be through somebody else: Eagleburger, Scowcroft, Haig, Garment, etc. Never CB, BW, or SA! We can make some observations which are simple & immediately followed by examples and evidence. But no more."

Although Armstrong did a yeoman's job, there was no way that Bernstein's name would be dropped from the book or a third name added. By this point, the names Woodward and Bernstein were locked in the public's mind. There was one concession. The byline would not be alphabetical. Woodward's name would come first.

Bernstein spent more time shaping the book. Although he may not have written a lot of the first draft, he edited to mold it. On an undated yellow legal pad, he jotted notes that indicated he was not pleased after a close reading of the manuscript. "Incredible use of wrong words throughout. Tenses are awful. . . . The style is Alice's—not ours—and it is lousy. . . . Overall to this point (p. 185) is astounding sloppiness—not too hard to fix, tho. . . . Do we believe Haig that he recommended RMN turn over the tapes? . . . Pat Nixon—Great." Sprinkled on pages of the notes are references to Ephron. She had called, causing him to scrawl: "I miss you. I love you so much."

"You can see by reading it that Carl had a lot to do with it," said a good friend of both men. "It is better written than any Woodward book, and Armstrong was no writer. I felt Carl's voice in that book pretty strongly." While Woodward publicly acknowledged Bernstein's contribution, saying that his co-author edited the entire book and improved it, privately he has disputed that. "Over the years," wrote Walt Harrington in a 1989 *Post* piece, "Woodward has told intimates privately that he doesn't recall Bernstein running *The Final Days* through his typewriter, as Carl contends." But over time, that matters less.

By December 1975, Woodward and Bernstein turned *The Final Days* over to Mayhew. Whether or not they liked each other, Woodward and Bernstein were stuck with each other—at least until *The Final Days* and the movie were finished. In the middle of the book, they had to take breaks to work as advisers on the script and later on the set of *All the President's Men* when filming started in May 1975. Goldman's first script wasn't well received by anyone at the *Post*. Bernstein, in particular, hated it. "At every turn we insisted that it had to be factual, and that included a first draft of the screenplay that was disastrously unfactual and was horrifying," said Bernstein. "It was full of shtick."

Bernstein and Ephron, who was an editor at *Esquire* magazine, decided to work, unbeknownst to Goldman, on a second draft of his script to bring it closer to the real experience. They stuck with

Goldman's structure, but that was it. "It was Nora's first screen-writing effort, I believe," said Bernstein. "It didn't fictionalize any-thing about the reporting but did about some aspects of our characters to get at truths about our characters. Some might say that the truths of those characters might have been at Woodward's expense." (They did write some fiction. In actuality Bernstein never cleverly tricked the Miami secretary to sneak into the dis-trict attorney's office, as he did in the movie.) "In their version," wrote Jared Brown in a 2005 book, *Alan J. Pakula: His Films and His Life*, "Bernstein was portrayed as heroic and dashing, and Woodward as a passive, rather ineffective follower. The treatment also included several scenes of Bernstein as a romantic lady-killer. Woodward, who read the script, claims not to have been offended by it at all."

Goldman became irate when he saw how they'd changed his script. In a fall 1974 meeting with Woodward, Bernstein, and Redford, Goldman turned around and left Redford's apartment, furious at the breach of Hollywood etiquette.

Redford later said that it was a mistake to let Ephron and Bern-stein tackle Goldman's script because of the publicity that ensued—not because they did a poor job. In fact, Redford wasn't happy with the script either, and it was reworked many times before the movie came out. "Items were appearing in print all over the place that Bernstein and Ephron had revamped the script," Redford told Hirshberg. "We were hit with this kind of negativism before we even started shooting. It set the project back about ten weeks because Goldman was just reeled by it, and I could understand."

Years later, in 1983, Goldman wrote a book about his adven-tures in Hollywood and included a chapter on *All the President's Men*. He concluded that it was one of the worst experiences of his life, primarily because of the Bernstein-Ephron intrusion in a time-honored Hollywood process—nobody messes with the hired screenwriter's script without permission. "And if you were to ask me 'What would you change if you had your movie life to live over?' I'd tell you that I'd have written exactly the screenplays I've written. Only I wouldn't have come near *All the President's Men*." (Ironically, with that film Goldman won an Oscar for Best Screenplay.)

In December 1974, Redford hired director Alan Pakula for his movie. Pakula was best known then for producing the movie *To Kill a Mockingbird* and directing and producing *Klute* (1971) and *The Parallax View* (1974). Pakula was celebrated for his thoroughness. He insisted on spending a few months interviewing Woodward and Bernstein and the women in their lives, their friends, and *Washington Post* editors. While Goldman saw the film as a police story, Pakula imagined it as a personal saga as well. Moviegoers would learn not only how the Watergate scoopmeisters reported, but also of their personality quirks (Woodward was forever brushing his teeth in the men's room; Bernstein owned a Tiffany silver bike-pant clip with "Easy Writer" inscribed from a girlfriend).

"They were extremely cooperative," Redford told me. "They were terrific to work with. When I was having a struggle with the initial script, which they were extremely critical of, it looked like I was going to lose that package. They said, 'This is a piece of shit. It's shallow, like Hollywood.' The way I got the script written, prior to hiring Alan Pakula, was I worked with Bob and Carl. They showed me their notes while they were still pursuing the story. I couldn't have made the film without their cooperation. The script itself was mainly a result of their notes. William Goldman didn't work out. I just didn't have a screenwriter after that. Alan Pakula and I decided we would build the majority of it from their notes."

Bernstein and Woodward periodically wrote multipage memos commenting on and correcting the script: "At the bottom of the page where Bernstein goes on his fucking Bradlee routine, it might be tempered. Bernstein could not and would not rage openly like that. The *Post* is an organization that demands loyalty also." "One too many fuckings in the script." "Haldeman's name is not Robert; it's Harry Robbins." "One big thing: there should be women in this movie. They were in our lives, will be and should be."

In January 1975, Pakula, a Yale graduate like Woodward, arrived in Washington to begin interviewing. He talked with Bradlee, Rosenfeld, Ephron, Armstrong, and *Post* reporters Richard Cohen, Robert Kaiser, and Haynes Johnson. He spoke to Woodward and Bernstein alone, had dinner with Woodward and his wife, and had lunch with Bernstein and an old girlfriend. Pakula didn't want facts; he wanted to deeply understand both men, to capture their true characters and motivations. He wrote copious notes that his wife donated to the Academy of Motion Picture Arts and Sciences after his 1998 death. "Pakula was one of the world's loveliest men," said Bradlee. "He spent so much time with each of us. He knew all about my mother, brother, everything."

Pakula, known as an intuitive director, quickly drew a bead on each man. He noticed that Bernstein, while having a quick mind, could also be absentminded. "Forgets who he is calling—which woman he is calling, where he put anything," noted Pakula. Examples of his absentmindedness included the time that Bernstein ordered a box of cigars for a reporter friend's birthday. A week later the friend got a bill. Bernstein had forgotten to pay. There was the time that Bernstein and his first wife were in the lobby of their apartment building en route to work. She forgot something and went upstairs; when she came back, Bernstein was gone. A colleague had come by and asked whether he needed a lift. Bernstein, forgetting his wife, took the ride. It wasn't a hostile gesture; it was Bernstein. He was always late, always on the verge of being fired. Editors didn't trust him. He often hyped stories, Pakula wrote, and then they didn't pan out. "I don't know one quotation in the language," Bernstein told Pakula. "No matter how great the line is, I'll forget it."

Ephron told Pakula that her boyfriend was driven during Watergate because he wanted to prove everyone at the *Post* wrong; he was not lazy. He just had a "psychosis," she said, about being controlled. "All editors in his mind are out to control him."

He was wrong. They just wanted him to be reliable and consistent. "What made Carl in Watergate was that he retained focus," said his editor Harry Rosenfeld. "It wasn't that Carl all of a sudden acquired talents miraculously that he did not have on June 16, 1972. It was all of a sudden, he was in an enterprise that was very serious and he was working hard. He saw a very important career opportunity that he should do well on if he ever wanted to amount to anything. I think Woodward's personality helped Carl to bear down and settle down. Carl would focus before, but then he'd go off on some irresponsible tear, and he wouldn't do this and wouldn't do that. The consistency wasn't there." And it never would be. Bernstein would always be brilliant in spurts.

Woodward, on the other hand, was obsessive with a laserlike concentration. He was the deliberate one; he moved logically. He lived with an unfounded fear of being fired and a need to belong that fueled his workaholic lifestyle. Pakula wrote that Redford would have to scrap his "Redford charm" to play Woodward. "It's that square, straight, intense, decent quality of Woodward's that works," wrote Pakula. "Redford can get that compulsive drive. Can he get the hurt and vulnerability?"

Pakula quickly sensed what became common knowledge about the pair's partnership: there was a certain symbiosis that worked; neither one alone could have pulled off Watergate. They needed each other; they fed off each other. They were adversaries but were still dependent on each other. Each had strengths that supplemented and complemented the other. "Bernstein could be right intuitively—but dangerous left to himself," Pakula wrote. "Woodward cautiously would have to go from one step literally to another. And yet it was Bernstein's daring that was necessary."

In interviewing Woodward, Pakula discovered that other people's secrets fascinated and obsessed him. Woodward, always reluctant to talk about himself, kept things close to the chest. Yet as a reporter, he wanted to expose other people's secrets. The dichotomy intrigued Pakula.

After Pakula interviewed Ephron, his notes indicate that he had found a key to understanding Woodward and Bernstein. Both men initially felt that the other one was not loyal. Bernstein believed that Woodward would sell him out for an editor's approval, and Woodward felt that Bernstein would sell him out to anyone in the newsroom whom Bernstein preferred. Bernstein fit the "Naughty Boy Syndrome," and Woodward fit the "Good Boy Syndrome"—but they needed each other. Pakula determined that Woodward was eventually surprised to find that he could rely on Bernstein, that Bernstein was capable of hard work and worthy of his trust. Bernstein came to learn that Woodward was not who he thought. Woodward was not the Establishment or a straight-arrow WASP. In fact, he was funny, even a bit crazy, and full of surprises.

Pakula began to see similarities, while the rest of the world thought of them as oil and water. On the last page of his notes,

Pakula wrote, "The difference in the way their minds work is essential to the film. You mustn't blur that. Redford was told the exterior of Bernstein was the interior of Woodward and vice versa."

In May 1975, filming finally started in Washington, and then the cast flew to Los Angeles, where a crew had built an exact replica of the *Post* newsroom on a soundstage in Burbank for $200,000. For added authenticity, the *Post* shipped crates of newsroom trash, phone books, unopened mail, and government directories to clutter desks. Posties who visited the Burbank set experienced vertigo at the sight of the identical 35,000-square-foot newsroom. After much discussion, the *Post* had decided not to let Redford film inside the actual newsroom, even if it were in the wee hours when the newsroom was empty. It was just too disruptive. Every time Redford walked into the newsroom for "research," it caused a stir. Female reporters were seen grabbing their purses to pretty up. Some newsroom gawkers were subtle, but most were not. "Their behavior was so inane: There were all these people putting on makeup in the bathroom, then acting like they didn't care," Redford told *TV Guide* in 2002. Hoffman fit in, though. "Hoffman just hung around," said Leonard Downie Jr., a city desk editor in 1975. "I'd be having a meeting in some conference room and toward the end you would realize that during the whole meeting, Dustin Hoffman has been sitting on the floor. In the corner taking everything in. Or he'd be on the other end of the phone, listening."

Redford, too, felt that it was important for accuracy that he attend news meetings, hang out in the newsroom, and interview editors. Redford had a clear vision that this film would reveal the mysterious world of reporting. It would pay attention to detail. While Redford was clear on the story, Woodward posed a problem. Redford found him bland. Yet he was certain that underneath that mild exterior lay a quality he couldn't quite grasp. "Carl had no trouble letting you know how colorful he was," Redford said. "Bob was purposely more reserved and hidden." Redford peppered Woodward with questions. "He made it so hard," said Redford. "He was very open and friendly, but he revealed nothing."

"I'm just not interesting," Woodward told him. "Carl's more interesting."

Finally, Redford got it. Woodward possessed a killer instinct. "I felt that underneath that bland, polite exterior was a killer," said the movie star. "Someone who went for the jugular. I should say, someone who had a killer instinct as a journalist. That's when I felt comfortable that I knew what to try to play. I learned about the killer instinct because they had a routine where Bernstein would go after people and get them unsettled and nervous. Then Bob would come in and do the calming thing. People would look to Bob for comfort and then he would turn to zap them. I used that. In order to do his work, Bob tended to make people comfortable. Carl wasn't interested in making people comfortable; he rattled people. Until I found that out, I felt as if I had no idea how to play Bob."

Later, Redford told a reporter watching the Washington filming that Woodward had a short attention span. "He'll stay with you as long as you interest him, then he becomes very polite. The turnoff point is sometimes very transparent," said Redford. "Some reporters are just plain rude. He tends to maintain a relationship, but it's sort of clear that you cease to interest him in terms of what you're saying, what you can provide."

Hoffman spent nearly four months in the newsroom, trying to figure out how to play Bernstein and understand the news business. "I wasn't there to do a portrait of Bernstein," Hoffman told me. "But there were certain things that I picked up about him. I tried to emulate them, not imitate them. He was an avid smoker, so I would watch him smoke and try to emulate that. He had a habit of always getting a lot of cigarette ashes on his tie and shirt."

Hoffman even celebrated a Passover Seder with Bernstein and his parents in nearby Silver Spring, Maryland. "Carl's family always had a very nice Seder," said Barbara Cohen, then married to one of Bernstein's best friends, Richard Cohen. "They used a liberal Haggadah, the service that you say. Dustin Hoffman fit right in, just another person at the table. He was hanging out with Carl and studying him so he could do an accurate portrayal."

"Hoffman really did fit in well," said Mike Causey, a *Post* reporter in 1975. "He was literally breathing in the atmosphere. Redford was there, too. An older woman who was doing obits, who was sharp and all that, didn't have a clue who he was. Redford had come and sat beside her. 'Who is the skinny guy with bleached hair?' she asked. Redford was only in there a couple of times. Hoffman was a lot more. Bernstein used to have a habit. I had a corner office. Carl would walk by and give me the finger. That was just a joke, it was a guy thing. After about a week, Hoffman would walk by and give me the finger. Hoffman was just getting into the role."

Throughout the filming, if there was a question on how Woodward or Bernstein might react to something, Redford or Hoffman called either man. "It was the first film I ever made like this," said Hoffman. "I would either call Carl or Bob would call Woodward while we were doing a scene. We kept trying to adhere to the authenticity of what happened by almost talking to them on a daily basis. The set was brilliant because it was re-created. They literally tore the wall open and connected two soundstages. It was really extraordinary. It was the same newsroom that I had hung out in for four months back in Washington."

Whenever they could, Woodward and Bernstein visited the sets. No matter how often they watched the movie being shot, each time it proved surreal. Woodward stopped by as they filmed the break-in at the actual Watergate hotel. "It really grabbed me then," Woodward told Jack Hirshberg. "It got emotional. There were huge spotlights, loads of trucks, and it seemed like hundreds of people. They had watered down the streets, and the air was misty. I liked the feeling. And there was Baldwin—I mean, the actor playing him—out on the balcony at the Howard Johnson, doing his exercises. I felt like I was spying on the real thing, the bungled break-in three years earlier that somehow had brought us all together here this night. It was like something out of Alfred Hitchcock."

One midnight during filming in D.C., Bernstein watched as Pakula directed a scene. Hoffman was running down an empty, watered-down street chasing after Redford's gray Volvo as it pulled out of the *Washington Post* parking lot. He yelled, "Stop. . . . Woodward! Stop!" Nearby was Irwin Marcus, who slightly resembles Bernstein. Marcus was a stand-in for Hoffman.

"Big crowds were outside. I got there just as [Hoffman] broke from the building," Bernstein said in an October 1975 interview with Kaleidoscope Films. "It was one of the most incredible feel-ings that I've had in my life because, you know, it had been a long time since we had started to work on the story, and I didn't exactly know who I was or who he was—existentially, it was sort of a total mindfuck. He had the mannerisms. You're not used to seeing your actions. Yet I knew that it was right."

Hoffman dropped his notebook accidentally as he tried to jump into the car. That felt authentic to Bernstein. Even if it had not happened, it could have. An even more powerful feeling over-took Bernstein as he watched. Three years had passed since they had started reporting this story. Now it was June 1975. "I'm not really like that anymore," he said. "That happened a long time ago. Would I run like that again?"

7

When Are You Going to Screw Up?

I was very disappointed when my teacher told me that the two of you (you and Woodward) stopped writing together. If there is any way at all that I could help you, I would be delighted and flattered to do anything I could.

—Mary Kay Tittis, Mount Holly,
New Jersey, January 25, 1977

Sometime in the spring of 1976, Woodward and Bernstein, a handful of *Washington Post* editors, and publisher Katharine Graham filed into a special private screening at the Motion Picture Association of America in Washington, D.C., to watch a cut of *All the President's Men* before the world premiere on April 4, 1976. None of them sat together, save for Woodward and Bernstein.

"I know I was sitting absolutely alone. Kay was absolutely alone," said Ben Bradlee. "I wanted to reach my own conclusion. We were awfully scared of making asses of ourselves." He needn't have worried. Aside from almost daily double-checking scenes with Woodward and Bernstein during the filming, Redford's production company had hired two full-time fact-checkers in D.C. for the sole purpose of verifying all factual information in the script.

The lights went down, and up on the big screen appeared major Hollywood movie stars—Robert Redford, Dustin Hoffman, Jason Robards, Martin Balsam, and Jack Warden—playing

Woodward, Bernstein, Bradlee, Howard Simons, and Harry Rosenfeld, respectively—the same people who were sitting in that audience and who had personally lived through every stress-filled, frightening, intense, and thrilling minute of reporting the biggest story of their lives.

A long 138 minutes later, it was over. Two intense years crammed into a little more than two hours. The lights came back on. Nobody said a word.

"We were all apprehensive about what this would do to our reputations," said Rosenfeld, one of the four *Post* editors who had worked directly on Watergate. "Then the lights went up, and everybody's face was solemn; everybody was into themselves. I remember silence, silence."

Redford, the producer and co-star, finally couldn't take it. "For God's sake, someone say something."

For the most part, they were all pleasantly surprised to find that they approved of the movie about the *Post*'s finest hour. They had direly feared—to the point of legally trying to bar Redford from using the *Post*'s and their names—a Hollywood-hyped flick that turned them into laughingstocks and sacrificed the truth for entertainment. Liking a movie about yourself was embarrassing, though. They were uncomfortable admitting it. Bradlee actually thought it was a very good movie but was afraid to say anything because of how it would come off. The charismatic, brassy Robards—on the screen for only ten minutes total—had done a damn near perfect job of capturing the inimitable, larger-than-life Bradlee. (So on point was Robards's performance that he won an Oscar for Best Supporting Actor.) Bernstein later told a British newspaper that the experience of watching Hoffman portray him in a movie version of what he'd experienced was "existentially incomprehensible. Only at about four points did I have the feeling, 'Hey, this movie is about me.'"

Watching the preview was like reliving everything that had happened since five men in business suits broke into the Democratic national headquarters and permanently altered American history. During the scene where Woodward and Bernstein are ready to go with a story tying Nixon's chief of staff, H. R. Haldeman, to a secret slush fund, Bradlee orders them to get one more source as the paper's deadline is fast approaching. In a last-ditch effort, Bernstein calls a Justice Department lawyer as a fourth source. He runs the story by the lawyer, saying that he'll count to ten; the lawyer should hang up before ten if it's not true—an uncommon practice that pushes the limits of responsible journalism. They go with the story, learning the next day that it's incorrect. The lawyer didn't understand Bernstein's convoluted instructions. Woodward and Bernstein had just made their first and only major mistake. As the scene was reenacted on the big screen, Bernstein turned to watch Bradlee sitting behind him. "I could see Bradlee holding onto the edge of his chair, all ready to fire me just from watching the movie," Bernstein told the *Manchester Guardian*. He leaned back and whispered, "It's all right, Ben. It happened two years ago, and it came out all right."

What wasn't all right was how the movie did permanent psychic damage to two *Washington Post* editors—Barry Sussman and Howard Simons—who had both been instrumental in the early coverage of the break-in. Inside the paper, they were hailed as the two editors who early on grasped the significance of the story and pushed the reporting hard. Sussman, who made the early decision to call Woodward on the morning of the break-in and fought to keep Woodward and Bernstein on the story, wasn't even a character in the movie. Having three male editors was confusing enough, and for dramatic reasons he was written out of the story. Sussman was already miffed at his treatment concerning the book; the movie only widened the chasm of disgust he felt for Woodward and Bernstein. "When the celebrification of Watergate hit, Barry Sussman got cut out," said James Mann, a *Post* reporter during Watergate's early years. "If you take the hurt that Howard Simons felt, and you multiply that hurt by a thousand, you get to Barry Sussman. He was a central figure in the early coverage." *Post* movie critic Gary Arnold wrote that eliminating Sussman was what most *Post* staffers did not like about the movie. "Indeed, it has proved a more serious drawback than one might have guessed," wrote Arnold on April 4, 1976, "because the picture needs a rumpled, avuncular dogged editorial type to contrast with Robards' flamboyant Bradlee and to supply some lucid updating and recapping of information as we go along. I suppose it was unthinkable, but it appears to me that the supersource, 'Deep Throat,' might be more expendable." (He's correct: it is unthinkable to eliminate Deep Throat.)

Sussman, who was at the special screening, liked the movie certainly more than the book, which he hated, but that's because he felt that the first five minutes or so of the movie had been taken from his 1974 Watergate book.

Equally sad, though, is the story of Simons, a brilliant editor whose role in Watergate—the top editor who made certain the story happened—got flipped. In the movie, Bradlee gets the lion's share of the credit, when in reality Bradlee, a close friend of Simons's, did not really get involved until months after the June 1972 break-in. What hurt Simons was how the movie roles were handled: Martin Balsam plays Simons in a way that trivializes his role, especially in comparison to Robards's scene stealers as Bradlee. The impression is left, incorrectly, that Simons is a mere functionary to Bradlee. "I'm certain that Sussman was unhappy with the movie," said Rosenfeld, who liked how Jack Warden portrayed him. "But I gotta tell you, so was Howard Simons unhappy with the movie. He thought his character wasn't represented accurately. It ate at him." The fictional movie version of reality bent a few noses permanently out of joint. Bradlee and Simons had been such close friends that they had promised to take care of each other's children if anything ever happened to one of them. Yet Simons became so embittered by the movie version co-opting the truth that their friendship was never the same, though they did make peace before Simons died in 1989.

No embittered colleagues, however, could possibly diminish what lay ahead for Woodward and Bernstein. They had gotten a bounce from their first book, but it was nothing like what the movie would do. They were about to skyrocket into a stratosphere of fame and celebrity that few, if any, journalists had ever known, once *The Final Days* and the movie came out within a week of each other. There was no way to prepare for what was ahead. April 1976 cemented Woodward and Bernstein's status as two of the most famous journalists of the twentieth century. It was the month that would permanently alter their lives. In that April three decades ago, the pair performed a neat hat trick: they had the number one best-selling hardback with *The Final Days*, the number one movie, and the number one paperback with *All the President's Men*. They would make as much news as any candidate running for president in the spring of 1976.

National Woodstein Month officially began on March 27, 1976—sooner than planned—when the *Washington Post* and its sister publication, *Newsweek* magazine, began running explosive excerpts of *The Final Days*, shortly before publication of the hardback. A week later, on April 4, the film version of *All the President's Men* debuted before an audience of eleven hundred at the Kennedy Center, next door to the upscale Watergate hotel, where it all began, along the banks of the Potomac River.

For the *Post*, it was a no-brainer to plaster its star reporters' work on the top of the front page on Saturday, March 27, 1976, along with a companion piece by reporter Haynes Johnson heralding a week of Watergate revisited. For *Newsweek*, it was a first. The newsweekly had never before run a book excerpt in its pages. Five months earlier, *Newsweek*, *Esquire*, and *Playboy* had battled for the right to be the first to publish two 15,000-word excerpts from *The Final Days*. *Newsweek* won, paying $60,000 for exclusive rights.

Newsweek's hand, however, was forced by the enterprising young Kitty Kelley, today best known as the celebrity biographer of Frank Sinatra, Jackie Onassis, and Nancy Reagan. Kelley was slipped a prepublication copy of the *The Final Days* manuscript, which was supposed to have been a tightly held secret. Woodward and Bernstein had kept it locked up during the writing. Simon & Schuster had refused to send review copies ahead of publication because editors knew the contents would make news, which they did. "I got the manuscript and knew it was a great story because it had been under such wraps and there had been such secrecy," said Kelley, who at the time was a reporter for *New Times* in Washington, D.C. The manuscript was burning hot in her hands, but *New Times* had already closed its issue. So Kelley called Liz Smith, then a fledgling gossip columnist at the *New York Daily News*. Smith leaped at the chance to scoop *Newsweek*. She wanted to pay Kelley or send her a case of champagne or credit her, but Kelley refused. She feared that if her name were used, it would endanger her source. Kelley still won't tell her source's name. "When Liz ran her column, *Newsweek* had to rip up its issue and run it sooner than they wanted, and the same with the *Washington Post*," said Kelley, which explains why the *Post* ran its first excerpt on a Saturday when normally it would appear on Sunday, the paper's largest circulation day. "While it was a great story then, I didn't get to ride with it," added Kelley.

"The book was supposed to come out right after the movie," said David Obst, then Woodward and Bernstein's agent. "But somehow Kitty Kelley got a copy of the manuscript and leaked it to Liz Smith, and the revelations in the book made front-page news all over the place, sending paroxysms of anxiety and fear through Warner Bros. and Redford. They thought there would be a backlash of sympathy for Nixon. But the opposite happened. *The Final Days* outsold *All the President's Men* almost two-to-one in hardcover. It flew out of stores. Simon & Schuster didn't leak it. It wasn't in their interest to leak it either because books hadn't been shipped yet when the Liz Smith item ran."

The *New York Daily News* publicity didn't hurt. Plus, *Time* magazine too got hold of the highlights. When *Newsweek*'s first installment came out on April 5, 1976, it was the fastest-selling issue in *Newsweek*'s history. The magazine sold out within forty minutes of its delivery in D.C., according to a piece by *Post* columnist Mary McGrory. Woodward and Bernstein received this letter from Seymour Hersh of the *New York Times*, their arch-nemesis during the incipient Watergate reporting:

> Just wanted to say that I read the excerpt (Part 1) in *Newsweek* just now and it was terrific; I wished I had written it (which as I told David Obst, is the ultimate compliment anyone can get from me) . . . the last book I daydreamed about writing was *Humboldt's Gift*.
>
> And keep out of Las Vegas. Sy

Hersh's note was not the norm. Before the 175,000-word hardback even appeared in bookstores, critics were after Woodward and Bernstein. The reception was not nearly as warm as for *All the President's Men*. The attacks on their new book came quickly and ferociously. Few people disputed that *The Final Days* was a compelling, fast-paced narrative about the disintegration of a once-proud president fighting to stay in power, despite mounting evidence that made it impossible. Readers—and some reviewers—objected vehemently to the gossipy depiction of a depressed president careening through the White House, occasionally filled with booze, as his presidency fell apart. They accused the authors of piling on Nixon when he was down; he had ignominiously left office twenty months earlier. Part of the issue was the excerpts. ("The problem with most of the people who have been queuing up to attack *The Final Days* is that they don't seem to have read the book," wrote *Miami Herald* book critic Jonathan Yardley, who believed it to be a compassionate, fair portrayal.) What *Newsweek* ran, and nearly every paper in the country picked up, focused on the salacious details of a presidential family in crisis: a lonely Pat Nixon drinking on the sly, a presidential couple who hadn't had sexual relations in fourteen years, a brooding president talking of suicide, a despondent Nixon kneeling to pray in the Lincoln Bedroom in the White House with Secretary of State Henry Kissinger and sobbing as he banged the carpet, "What have I done? What has happened?" Nixon loyalists and disgusted Americans accused the authors of being petty and mean-spirited, invading the Nixon family's privacy for profit. They wrote their thoughts in letters to *Newsweek*, to the *Post*, and to the authors themselves. The tone was largely one of anger:

> "I, like millions of other Americans, applauded the journalistic and investigative efforts of Messrs. Woodward & Bernstein which led to the Watergate disclosures and the subsequent termination of the corrupt regime of Richard Nixon. Your front page display of 27 March, however, signals a new stage of Watergate disclosures. Gentlemen, you have now gone too far and should be ashamed."
>
> —N. C. Nicholas, Silver Spring, Maryland

> "I am completely repulsed and the two 'gentlemen' have lost their 'hero shine' for me. They are a pair of gossipy little men."
>
> —Mrs. L. E. Stevens of North Bergen, New Jersey

> "You two can be compared to Judas as you sold the heart and soul of a man for a few pieces of silver. May God forgive you for the sorrow you have caused Mr. Nixon and his family."
>
> —Cleveland man, May 4, 1976; the letter was cc'd to Nixon

Woodward and Bernstein responded to the vitriolic letters by saying that they had no negative intentions in writing the book. "Beyond this, I can only give you my personal assurance that our sole motivation in working on *The Final Days* was to report the truth: neither money nor any preconceived disposition regarding Mr. Nixon was a factor in our reporting," said a draft letter on *Washington Post* stationery, filled with typos and cross outs, that they asked their secretary to retype. "Incidentally, no suits have been filed against us in any of our Watergate reporting—for the paper, for *All the President's Men*, or for *The Final Days*."

The public objected to the tone of the book, criticizing it on grounds of questionable taste, but people read every word of the excerpts and bought the book. *The Final Days* became an instant best seller on the day of publication. It became known for a while as "The Book." One store in New York City reported that it was selling 100 copies a day. Other booksellers complained that they couldn't get enough copies in their stores to satisfy customer demand. The first press run was for 200,000 copies, according to Simon & Schuster president Richard E. Snyder. "The biggest initial printing in our history," Snyder told *Parade* on April 18, 1976. By the end of April, the book had gone into its sixth printing, making it one of the fastest sellers in publishing history. Eventually, "The Book" sold over 600,000 copies.

"Part of the problem, obviously, is that publication coincided with the release of *All the President's Men*, the filmed version of their cracking the Watergate case," explained the *Post*'s McGrory, in a column picked up by papers around the country. "Success, it is feared, perhaps, will spoil them. And Nixon is dead politically; they should not dance on his grave. Nobody is saying, if you listen closely to the howls, that what they have told us is not true. They are saying that Woodward and Bernstein should not be telling us. People hate themselves for reading this book, but they are doing it. Actually, it is on the whole sadder than it is sensational."

Members of the press, however, reacted differently from the way the public did. They generally found the book a remarkably fast turnaround of the mesmerizing story of a White House coming undone. "Bob Woodward and Carl Bernstein are being accused of practicing the worst sort of yellow journalism, when in point of fact they have written a sober, complex and ultimately

compassionate account of the fall of Richard Nixon," wrote Yardley. No one had to wait a decade before cool-headed historians
weighed in on this momentous time in America. The book was
dubbed "instant history." Woodward found that an acceptable
conclusion. He repelled criticisms by arguing in a rare interview
with *Newsweek* during the initial furor, "This is no laundered version of history. It includes material that is normally locked up for
50 years before being made public. It is an accurate account and
will stand the test of time." It has. Even, at the time, Kissinger,
who thought that writing about Nixon sobbing "showed an inde-
cent lack of compassion," conceded on NBC's *Today Show* that
the book was "essentially accurate." Kissinger's and Nixon's later
memoirs would confirm just how accurate the book was.

While *The Final Days* was valuable as a source that docu-
mented a significant slice of the biggest political scandal of our
time, many journalists, though not all, went after Woodward and
Bernstein for their methodology. They vehemently objected to the
authors' omniscient narrator approach, which omitted attribution
or footnotes. Basically, the pair compiled their notes, fed everything into the mix, and wrote about the last days inside the Nixon
White House like a nonfiction novel. That style, which they virtually invented and Woodward later perfected, is closely identified
with Woodward and rarely, if ever, was used by other journalists.
The pair used quotes from Nixon and people they hadn't directly
talked with, based on what other sources told them. More trou-
bling to reviewers such as Richard Reeves, however, was the way
that Woodward and Bernstein wrote about what Nixon and others were thinking and feeling, the way the authors authoritatively
got inside the heads of White House officials and the Nixon family. They wrote, for example, that Nixon's lawyer, Len Garment,
"felt the heat increase in his body," and that another Nixon
lawyer, James St. Clair, said to himself, "Dean's a smart little bas-
tard." It raised the obvious question: How did they know that
when everyone was denying having talked to them? As it turns
out, Woodward's handwritten and typed notes from interviewing
St. Clair are in their Watergate archives. But at the time, as people
read the book, a new kind of detective sleuthing came about: trying to figure out who told what to Woodward and Bernstein
became the rage.

Most reviewers felt that Woodward and Bernstein had crossed the line with their unorthodox "You are there" approach, which put the reader in the room with Nixon, his family, and his footmen. They objected to Woodward and Bernstein telling us what Nixon was thinking, when they had never spoken to the man.

"Journalistic narrative—'reconstructing events,' in the authors' foreword—is a tricky business," wrote Reeves in an April 18, 1976, review in the *New York Times*, titled "Lots of Footwork, No Footnotes." "Novelistic style served Woodward and Bernstein well in *All the President's Men*, their book about reporting on the Watergate break-in and its sleazy aftermath. But *The Final Days* is not about them, it is about other people's impressions of historic events, and narrative writing can reduce convincing reporting to a contract of trust between writers and readers who may not know each other."

In other words, many journalists pilloried Woodward and Bernstein for their "Trust me. I know this stuff is true" attitude. Reeves, a colleague and a friend, said that he trusted them but quibbled with their lack of attribution, saying that it unnecessarily raised questions about their credibility. "The reporters gave away too much," he wrote in a fairly uneven review, praising the terrific reporting but tearing apart the storytelling method. "I am uncomfortable with the two reporters' 'extraordinary trust in the accuracy and candor' of unnamed people who are assuredly as self-serving as the rest of us. . . . Woodward and Bernstein have been unfair—to their readers, to their sources and, foolishly, to themselves and their book."

After Reeves questioned their use of anonymous sources, he said, Woodward and Bernstein stopped talking to him for three years. Woodward's wife, Francie Barnard, was so angry, said Reeves, that she threatened to run over him when she bumped into him at a gas station in Georgetown. "I think she really meant it," said Reeves. (Almost thirty years later, Reeves said that when all three men were on a Watergate panel, Bernstein reminded him of the review, practically quoting it verbatim.)

John Osborne, an influential member of the White House press, wrote in the *New Republic* that the book, while fascinating, is "on the whole the worst job of nationally noted reporting that I've observed during 49 years in the business."

The book was pilloried not only for its contents, but also for its questionable timing—it debuted, as did the movie, in the middle of a contentious presidential primary season. Yet anyone who has written a book or made a movie knows that this was simply an unfortunate coincidence. Redford had wanted the movie to come out in 1975, but it had fallen far behind on the production schedule. Redford, who had been promised that the book would come out after the movie, was miffed.

Regardless of the criticism, the book flew off the bookshelves. As the national press started denouncing the book, Woodward and Bernstein faced another storm on the movie front. Friends were huffing that the pair had gotten too big for their reporter pants. *All the President's Men* was going to be shown for the first time on April 4, but *Post* reporters could not get tickets even though they had mailed in checks. Things were getting out of control. The cash-strapped Fund for Investigative Journalism, which was started in 1969, had suggested to Woodward and Bernstein that the movie premiere be used as a fund-raiser, and the pair agreed. "Redford came to town and I met him at the Kennedy Center," said Howard Bray, the fund's director. "He wanted to see the venue before the premiere. After that, we got his ultimate blessing on using the movie for a fund-raiser. But I didn't know how to do anything like this. I had no idea how much to even charge for tickets. I don't do many world premieres. So I let the Warner Bros. PR people jump in. A legion of them came to town." They took over, but not before Bray had decided to charge $25 a ticket and then worried that he wouldn't be able to sell enough tickets to fill the Eisenhower Theater's eleven hundred seats. He needn't have fretted. The demand for tickets was overwhelming. Bray was hounded by requests, but the PR folks were more interested in filling seats with Washington glitterati than with unkempt reporters, so they returned Postie ticket money and gave away their seats. When Bernstein learned of this, he was furious. If his fellow reporters couldn't go, neither would he. The *Post* reporters got their tickets, and a free sans-stars afternoon matinee was offered to the general public. (The fund netted $25,681, although it could have charged $100 a ticket and filled the theater. "I don't regret not charging more," said Bray. "A big grant for us then was $500 or $1,000.")

On the night of the glitzy event, limousines arrived at the Kennedy Center, a marble temple dedicated to President John F. Kennedy that had opened only five years earlier, in 1971. Out stepped Redford and his wife, Lola, Dustin Hoffman, Woodward, Bernstein, Bradlee, and his girlfriend, Sally Quinn. Famous news commentators and politicians also attended. A crowd of about fifteen hundred fans—including a couple hundred striking *Post* pressmen—watched from behind velvet ropes while WTOP radio broadcast live from the Kennedy Center and collared the stars. Earlier, Bernstein had threatened not to come if the event were black tie. It wasn't, but that didn't prevent Redford, who refused to even wear a tie, from playing a trick on *New York Times* reporter Sy Hersh. Redford made sure that Hersh's invite specified "black tie," but the notoriously disheveled Hersh didn't fall for it.

The event was another surreal moment for the *Washington Post* staff. Leonard Downie Jr., who started working on Watergate in 1973, recalled how distracting the movie was. "It wasn't just that Bob and Carl were done accurately, everything was done accurately," said Downie, now executive editor of the *Post*. "I had to watch the movie again another time to watch the movie because the first time I was so busy watching the newsroom." Added editor Harry Rosenfeld, "I remember the gala very well. We had a buffet dinner at the Kennedy Center. My youngest child was maybe ten or eleven. She was wearing a long skirt maybe for the first time in her life. As we go into dinner, Dustin Hoffman takes her arm and escorts her in. Well, she went berserk. That's what I remember. I was seeing the film for the second time, and I had too many drinks and was looking up at the screen bleary-eyed. I don't think I've seen it all together since."

It was bizarre for the principals to be sitting among hundreds who knew them well in the Kennedy Center, watching celebrated movie stars running around on a gigantic screen pretending to be them. "I thought Dustin Hoffman was so much like Bernstein," said Bradlee, "it made you cry." For Bradlee, the premiere was a defining event. He knew at that moment that he and Woodward and Bernstein had crossed over into another world. "Think about how amazing it was for Woodward and Bernstein," said Bradlee. "But it was for us, too. I had never before been a target of people's whispering and pointing. I was miserable. I hated it. And I couldn't pay any attention to the movie. The photographers were always trying to get me to pose with somebody. It was the first public event where I really understood that we were en route to becoming public figures at that time. The movie hammered home to me that there was an awful lot of fuss being made about us. I'm used to coping with the good run now. I wasn't used to it then."

Bradlee's predecessor, Russ Wiggins, had told him repeatedly that the job of a journalist was to stay off the stage. Yet that was becoming impossible because he and Woodward and Bernstein, in particular, were players in the story. "That was a learning process to me all throughout Watergate," said Bradlee. On the day the movie came out, though, Bradlee knew one thing for certain: life as they had known it was over. They were all stars, thanks to Robards, Redford, and Hoffman. The movie solidified Woodward and Bernstein's status as American folk heroes. "They had not been viewed as demigods in the newsroom," said Sally Quinn, a *Post* reporter at the time. "Only after the book, and really after the movie, did it become clear that their celebrity was a little over the top."

In an unusual twist, these newspapermen had become more famous than the people they wrote about. Television and radio commentators and some newspaper columnists enjoyed a certain degree of celebrity at the time, meaning that they or their names were known to the public. There were also famous newspaper names such as Walter Lippmann and H. L. Mencken. Yet never before had two regular-Joe newspaper reporters, not covering a war and with little seniority, become so well known. Woodward was then thirty-three; Bernstein, thirty-two. Once the movie was out, they were bona fide celebrities. Millions saw the film. Hundreds of thousands read their books. Their names defined the word *celebrity*, even though they dismissed suggestions that they were.

"I tend to reject the term *celebrity*," Woodward said at the time. "Celebrity is a fleeting thing, like the new hit TV show of the fall. There, and then it's gone. But what I really think you're asking me is 'When are you going to screw up?'"

It's what Americans expect of celebrities, and what they zealously watch for. Later, when they did screw up, their fellow reporters wrote the hell out of it. Their friend Richard Cohen knew they were celebrities. As a *Post* reporter close to both men, he fielded calls from *Time*, *Newsweek*, and *Parade*, pleading for Bernstein's unlisted phone number. "Being Bernstein's friend has some advantages," wrote Cohen in a column about the hubbub over his buddies. "I get taken to some fine restaurants by newspaper and magazine reporters doing stories about Woodward and Bernstein. I always tell them how neither one has been changed by celebrity or wealth, and if they don't believe me, the interviewer can check with Bernstein's secretary." (Even today, metro reporters don't have secretaries.)

"All of a sudden, Woodward and Bernstein are beautiful people," a *Post* reporter told a newspaper.

How could they not change? Ordinary reporters aren't buddy-buddy with movie stars. They don't dash up to New York City for a highly publicized movie opening benefiting Redford's wife's pet environmental group. They don't fly out to Los Angeles three days later for the West Coast premiere. They aren't constantly bombarded with questions about what they think of the movie made about them. "The feel of the movie is nice," Bernstein told *Parade* magazine. "It's understated; it's not about Batman and Robin." An ordinary reporter isn't the reason for a fund-raiser that nets $20,000 for a new addition for an Illinois hospital where his or her father (Woodward's in this case) is on the board. Woodward and Bernstein had arrived—even if that wasn't their goal. They were household names. They were now permanently etched in celluloid, their names forever ingrained in the American psyche. "What was happening seemed both normal and amazing," observed Robert Kaiser, who as a *Post* reporter and a good friend of Bernstein's since the late 1960s had watched the emotional shift. "It seemed normal because this was the era of the burgeoning celebrity journalists. This was when that was formed. Ben and Bob and Carl were in the avant-garde of that."

If one of the pair were likely to be rocked by the dizzying success, it was Bernstein, and his friends knew this. He was after all, dating Nora Ephron, who had fame of her own. "Dating Nora comes with the beat," said Richard Reeves in a 1974 magazine piece. "If you are Carl Bernstein, you get to date a witty, talented woman like that. Carl is an ornament to Nora and vice versa. Like

the money and the party invitations, it comes with the beat."
Ephron's earlier marriage to Daniel Greenburg, also an author of
a 1965 runaway best seller (*How to Be a Jewish Mother*), had
ended in divorce. Ephron's eighty-eight-year-old aunt was said to
have quipped while thanking Bernstein for an autographed copy
of *All the President's Men*, "You know, don't you, that Nora picks
her husbands from the best-seller list." Bernstein was the less sta-
ble, more iconoclastic of the two. Many of Bernstein's friends
commented that success had not, at first, turned him into an egotistical asshole. Success had made him bearable. Bernstein was less
abrasive and less likely to fight with editors now. Some said he
was calmer. "It would be ridiculous to pretend you can go through
this without changing," he told a newspaper reporter.

In October 1975, when director Alan Pakula asked how he
had changed, Bernstein said, "I think it's unavoidable. This kind
of experience has to affect you. I don't think I'm basically a different kind of person than I was. I think my values are still the same.
But you can't avoid having had so much attention, making a
movie about you, a lot of publicity. The trick is not to let it affect
your work. I think we've both been pretty successful at that."

In Pakula's movie notes, he observed after talking with Ephron
that "perhaps Carl has not changed much. Only the way people
view Carl has changed. Not always fucking up anymore."

In a way, that first week in April was a spectacular one-two
punch. While *The Final Days* reviews were glowering, the reviews
for the screen adaptation of their first book were glowing. Redford and Pakula had succeeded in doing what many people had
thought was impossible: making a movie about a serious issue that
was also entertaining. Its success was especially surprising because
every sentient human being knew the outcome, and polls showed
that the public was tired of Watergate. Not only was the movie
intelligent and riveting, but it also achieved what Woodward and
Bernstein had set out to do in their book—it explained the way the
news business operated. One woman who had never worked for a
newspaper confided during the movie to *Columbia Journalism
Review*'s Nat Hentoff, "I think I'm learning how to be an investigative reporter! I really had no idea how it was actually done."
The movie also, even more than the book, ennobled the field of

investigative journalism. Woodward and Bernstein had made the investigative reporter the new American hero.

The movie was a complete success, earning back its $7 million costs in the first week. By 2005, it had grossed $70.6 million worldwide, according to the Internet Movie Database. In 1977, it was nominated for eight Oscars, and it won four. *Rocky* beat out *All the President's Men* and *Taxi Driver* for Best Picture. When the American Film Institute compiled a list of its 50 greatest film heroes, Woodward and Bernstein were number 27. The names Woodward and Bernstein were famous, but their faces had morphed into those of Redford and Hoffman. In a small way, they had gotten back some of their anonymity. Years later, Woodward sometimes introduced himself to someone, and they'd reply, "You aren't Bob Woodward; that's not what you look like." They were expecting Redford.

The movie offset the pummeling they were taking for their new book. "If the image of the two Watergate reporters seems to be somewhat tarnished in recent weeks," said the *San Francisco Chronicle* on April 30, 1976, "their status as national heroes is alive and well and living in 604 movie theaters where the Hollywood version of *All the President's Men* has attracted ecstatic reviews and approximately $7 million in its first seven days." (Tickets were $3.)

Judging by their Watergate archives, the media could not get enough of Woodward and Bernstein in 1976. They wrote reams not only about the book and the movie, but also about the reporters' personal lives. They were, after all, celebrities, and journalists write about celebrities. Knight Ridder reporter Vera Glasser profiled the pair in an April 1976 story that appeared in newspapers around the country. She mentioned how rich they'd become—almost $2 million before taxes—with royalties and a slice of the movie profits to come.

Glasser wrote of how the pair's lives had undergone major changes:

> Bernstein's gaggle of new Manhattan friends include Nora Ephron with whom he has a "serious commuting relationship," he said. The Palm Restaurant keeps food warm for his 10 p.m. dinner. . . .

Bernstein, 32, bought an old co-op apartment in the inner city, then gutted and redesigned it with professional help. His new pad is done in air white, tan and neutrals. From the window, he looks down on where his parents lived when he was born. . . .

Woodward paid $140,000 in 1974 for a handsome white colonial house now valued in 1976 @ $200,000 off Foxhall Road. They are expecting their first child. Woodward, 33, drives an expensive BMW, but helps Francie with the dishes. A cleaning woman comes twice a week. They live quietly, read a lot and play tennis. Bob and Francie are now warm friends with Lola and Bob Redford. The two women are setting up 13 movie shows to benefit Redford's favorite environmental groups.

They were rich. They were famous. Everything they did made news. In the midst of this madness, Bernstein and Ephron, who been dating since December 1973, snuck off to New York City and quietly got married on April 14—ten days after the movie premiere and two days after Woodward and Bernstein got the news about the paperback rights for *The Final Days*. Seven publishers had competed in a telephone auction over three days. The paper rights sold for a dizzying $1,550,000—the highest sum ever paid for a nonfiction work at the time. The previous record had gone to *The Joy of Cooking*. Woodward and Bernstein would share 60 percent. Even with taxes and their agent's fee taken out, it was still a stunning amount in 1976 for reporters; Woodward had just turned thirty-three and Bernstein, thirty-two.

A justice of the peace performed the Bernstein-Ephron ceremony, attended by Woodward, a pregnant Barnard, and close friends Richard Cohen and his wife, *Washington Star* national editor Barbara Cohen. After the wedding, Bernstein rushed off to tape an interview for *Newsday*, and Ephron, a staunch New Yorker, announced that they would continue as a commuter couple. "This wedding has to be wedged in between interviews," Ephron told the *New York Times*, which announced the nuptials the next day. "Nobody is moving to the other person's town."

Bernstein really did fall for Ephron. She managed to adjust, for a while, how he previously had felt about a committed relationship. Originally he was opposed to the concept, he told a woman whom he dated pre-Watergate. He told her that sex with others wasn't a threat to a really good marriage. Shortly before Bernstein left the *Post*, they had another conversation. He had changed his mind about monogamy; maybe it was a good thing. "When he left the paper," she said, "he told me he was in a monogamous relationship with Nora and didn't have the same feelings he used to. He wanted to be monogamous." That change, however, would be temporary.

"You better sit down for this one, Earwigs," wrote Diana McClellan in her must-read stylish gossip column in the *Washington Star* known as "The Ear," the day after the marriage. "Everybody's talking about Carl Bernstein's sudden, super secret purchase of a co-op near 18th and Columbia Road. (That's where all the Marvy Media Ones with an ounce of hip live.) Now Ear's found out why: Carl married Nora Ephron, *Esquire* magazine's senior editor, yesterday in the Big Apple."

The London honeymoon would have to wait until June. Two days after the wedding, Woodward and Bernstein were scheduled to begin a back-breaking nineteen-day book tour that included Chicago, San Francisco, Los Angeles, and Boston.

The tour would kick off with a contentious April 18 appearance on NBC's vaunted *Meet the Press*, with moderator Bill Monroe. It had taken some persuading to get them on the Sunday show. The pair had been reluctant, knowing that the panelists would attack them—and they were right. (Coincidentally, on this same day the *New York Times* slashed their book, while *Parade* magazine hailed them on its cover for the movie.) The most impassioned denunciation of *The Final Days* came from the *Los Angeles Times*'s respected Washington reporter Jack Nelson. He had competed alongside Woodward and Bernstein during Watergate, distinguishing himself. Nelson knew the story intimately and had once greatly respected the young reporters, but he thought their reporting had crossed the boundaries of responsible journalism and had damaged the profession.

Nelson and two other panelists, NBC's Edwin Newman and United Features Syndicate writer John Lofton Jr., sat on one side of the stage, with Monroe in the middle and Woodward and Bernstein on the other side, as if they were on trial—which, in effect, they were. Right off the bat, Newman asked whether the only reason they'd written the book was to profit from Nixon. Woodward cleverly deflected the barbed question. "I think you know as a reporter yourself, you don't get into this business to make money. We certainly did not."

Next, their writing methods were impugned and accused of being "new journalism." "If there is anything this book is not, it's 'new journalism,'" Bernstein shot back. "It is not psychohistory. It is very simple reporting. The most basic, empirical type of reporting that you and I do every day. . . . We do use anonymous sources, just as you do in your daily stories about Washington. The difference is in this book we don't use the phrase 'according to informed sources' after every second or third paragraph." Woodward pointed out that there were not a lot of quotations in the book. Their goal, they said, had been to tell the exceedingly human story of Nixon and the people inside the White House during this extraordinary period. Woodward said that they were presenting the facts, that they'd made no judgments or analysis. This, too, would become a trademark in Woodward's later writing.

An angry Nelson didn't buy it.

"I think what disturbs a lot of journalists about the book is the methodology you used," said Nelson in an attack mode. "Both of you say that the book is journalism, and yet you have written it from an omniscient viewpoint. That is, you get into the minds of people. You said you made no judgments, but in fact you have made hundreds of judgments in the book about how people feel, about how they think, about whether they are sad or whether they are happy, and so forth, and you do all of this really from a very omniscient standpoint. What I wonder is, is this the full flowering of the new journalism and do you think this is healthy for journalism? Journalism already has a problem of creditability with the public, and if the public sees this as journalism, I wonder if it is healthy."

Their appearance on *Meet the Press* made good TV, but some of their fans didn't like it and took the time to write letters.

"I saw you on *Meet the Press* yesterday and I just wanted to write to tell you I'm behind you all the way! I'd go as far as to say it was the 'losers' quizzing the 'winners.' You stuck your necks

out during the Watergate mess while the rest of the media sat
back, thinking you'd make fools of yourself. Well, you didn't."
   —Connie Strand, journalism major, Kansas State University

"I just saw you on *Meet the Press* this afternoon and wish to
congratulate you on your 'performance.' You both handled the
situation very well and answered some of the questions I had
been wondering about due to some of the bad press that has
come your way over *The Final Days*. Let's face it, you are truly
American heroes, and I damn well think some of your question-
ers today are just plain jealous. . . . I personally thank you for
what you have done for America. God, how we need you."
   —John Malm, Commack, New York

"Your book was fantastic—stop—the movie was terrific—stop—
your interview on *Meet the Press* was 'cool'—stop—you guys
have done a helluva job—stop—and I'd love to meet you both—
stop. If you are ever in this area—stop!!!! I'd love to buy you a
drink."

   —Miss Eva Lupino, Utica, New York

"Congratulations on your marriage Carl and best of wishes. I
must say that I'm very attracted to you because you seem to be
a remarkable man, and Bob you are very fascinating yourself,
you seem to be a strong man. I really wrote this letter to boost
up your spirits. Relax because some of us are on your side. I said
this because it seems as though everyone seems to have disagreements about your books. But 'chin up,' ok?"
   —Sylvia Fisher, Houston, Texas

   The next day there was a slew of media interviews in D.C., followed by a flight to Chicago on Tuesday, then on to San Francisco
for back-to-back interviews. Midway through, with little explanation, Woodward and Bernstein canceled their book tour. Maybe
Bernstein missed his brand-new bride, or Woodward was worried
about his wife, who was expecting their first child in November,
or maybe it was the criticism. Or maybe it was true that they were
tired. This brief article appeared in a "Newsmakers" column in
the *Los Angeles Times* on April 23, 1976:

"Woodstein" have canceled the last half of a promotion tour for
their Watergate sequel, *The Final Days*. The two *Washington
Post* reporters, Bob Woodward and Carl Bernstein, "are really
exhausted," said a spokesman for publishers Simon & Schuster.

Asked if cancellations for Los Angeles, San Francisco and Boston were connected with criticism of the book, the spokesman said, "I don't think that had anything to do with it."

They did continue making speeches on college campuses, though. A month later, when Woodward spoke in Boston and was asked about quitting the tour, he told the *Herald*: "To be honest, we haven't been as successful as we should and could be in filtering that [celebrity scene] out. Right now, we've been successful in structuring work out. People want things."

People would continue to want things—autographs, books, favors, their time, money, and even help with school papers. The trick was to figure out the best way to handle that, and one of the pair would have an easier time than the other. Woodward returned to the *Post* as an investigative reporter on the national desk, a step up from metro. Bernstein, who had desperately wanted a slot on the national staff in 1972, now wasn't so sure. By December 1976, he had decided.

Tired of the judgments, the daily grind, the shouting bosses, and the high expectations, Bernstein decided to leave not just Woodward, but the *Post* and the world of newspapers altogether. It's not very often that a newspaper—and even other newspapers—runs a story when a reporter resigns. Reporters are always quitting to take another job, write a book, or try a different career—but this was Carl Bernstein. His leaving merited a staff-written story by his friend Bob Kaiser that got picked up by other newspapers around the country. Even the rival *New York Times* wrote about it. Kaiser wrote:

Carl Bernstein, who with Bob Woodward wrote the stories on Watergate that won a Pulitzer Prize for the *Washington Post* in 1973, is resigning from the newspaper effective Jan. 1, 1977.

Bernstein plans to write books and articles for magazines, he said yesterday. "It's very hard to leave the *Post*," said Bernstein, 32, "but I've worked for newspapers since I was 16-years-old—half my life—and I want to try other kinds of journalism."

Bernstein said his book project will be an account of Washington during the McCarthy era. "You've got to take risks," said Bernstein, explaining why he was leaving. "I took a risk when I quit school [he never completed college], and that was right.

We took risks in the way we covered Watergate, and that was right. Sure it's a risk to leave now, but it's also an opportunity."

"There's no way of ending a relationship like the one that Carl Bernstein and the *Washington Post* have enjoyed during the last four years," said *Washington Post* executive editor Ben Bradlee. "That was some ride, and no one even remotely involved in it will ever be quite the same."

Bradlee could not have spoken truer words. Bernstein's ride with the *Post* was coming to an end, and so was journalism's most famous pairing. They were no longer single guys willing to work around the clock on a story because there would never be another story like that, and they knew it. Besides, they had wives now who expected them to come home at decent hours. In November, Woodward's daughter, Mary Taliesin, was born, and Bernstein was spending more and more time in New York City.

"They came to a fork in the road," said Bradlee. "They were not natural friends. They were no Damon and Pythias. But who the hell among us is? After *The Final Days*, they just came apart."

The legendary partnership was over. The two men would barely speak for a year. On April 25, 1977, Woodward and Bernstein, who had opened a joint checking account to handle all their book and movie royalties, closed the account. The balance was $781.43.

8

Bernstein Unchaperoned

Carl is a lot like Reggie Jackson. He hits a lot of home runs, and he also strikes out a lot.

—Roone Arledge, who worked with Bernstein
in the early 1980s

When Bernstein left the *Post*, he walked away from all the constraints he hated, but he also walked away from the supervision that kept him in check. A rebel, after all, needs something to rebel against.

Woodward and Bernstein's historic and unorthodox partnership defined the word *synergy*. They had created something together that was greater than either one could have accomplished individually. It is doubtful that Woodward, the plodding reporter who moved logically from A to B to C, could have early on envisioned the Watergate story trajectory that Bernstein grasped so quickly. By fall 1972, Bernstein instinctively knew that the story went all the way to Nixon. Woodward would never have dared to think that big. Yet it is equally certain that the peripatetic Bernstein never could have done the story on his own without Woodward's discipline and laser focus.

"The thing you have to understand about Carl is that even in the middle of all this, Carl got bored," their good friend Richard Cohen said in the *Washington Post*.

Bernstein was quick at seeing a story and knowing what it should be; Woodward made sure it got done and done well. *Post* editors implicitly trusted Woodward, and this added a certain credibility that helped Bernstein's image of unreliability. "In some respects, Woodward is pure infantry, Carl is pure Air Force," said Cohen. "There's nothing glamorous about the way Bob reports. Bob keeps coming at you. He'll come back with two, three, four interviews. I don't think Carl can do that. Once Carl sees the story, that's it for him. The thing about Bob is, Bob is not just pure tenacity. Bob is really good, I think, brilliant in deconstruction or demolition. He knows how to take a story apart. I look at something and say something happened, and I think there's something wrong, and I have no idea who to call. Whereas Bob knows just how to do it. Sometimes it's just amazing to see. If Bob went into medicine, he would be a coroner." Bernstein had a history of letting his feelings run away with him; Woodward had served as anchor.

Now what would happen to Bernstein without Woodward? They both knew there would never be another story like Watergate, but they were still young. Woodward was only thirty-three and Bernstein thirty-two in January 1977 when they began to live separate lives and try out new career paths in separate cities. They had clearly recognizable roles carved from the mythology of Watergate. Their books and the movie had created a public image. Whether it was completely true or not, they had gained a reputation as journalistic icons, investigative reporters who had played a key role in taking down the president of the United States and had become millionaires in the process. The question became one of figuring out how next to play the roles of Carl Bernstein and Bob Woodward, post-Watergate. Although it was not a completely smooth transition for Woodward, it was easier than for his estranged erstwhile partner, Bernstein.

Seemingly overnight, in the space of four years, Bernstein had arrived. He was no longer the poorly dressed, long-haired, money-mooching metro reporter with a desk so littered with files, it could have been declared a fire hazard. He was leaving that Bernstein behind. He had lots of money in the bank and a hip, freshly decorated 2,700-square foot apartment in D.C., as well as another place in New York City with his new wife. He was a celebrity married to the celebrated New York writer Nora Ephron. They were a power couple. Photographers snapped their pictures; they were mentioned in newspaper columns for the benefits or the dinners they attended. Fans wrote to Bernstein, pleading for his autograph. Other than on-air television news personalities, the number of print reporters even today with a public clamoring for their autograph is next to none.

"Both Bob and I went along for a while with the fiction that our lives were unchanged by all this," Bernstein told *Vanity Fair* in 1989. "The fact is, it does affect you. I'd be ridiculous to say my life is the same now as it was before all this happened. It takes some getting used to, and it takes some adjustment."

The year 1977 began with more accolades. The National Society of Film Critics and the New York Film Critics Circle both named *All the President's Men* the best film of 1976. Each time the film was written about, there was the obligatory paragraph restating the true-life story of Woodward and Bernstein's reportorial accomplishments. This only ensured that they stayed household names. Now what would Bernstein do with his fame?

"What you really have to do is be very careful what you do next," said Ben Bradlee, Bernstein's former boss. "You can't do something for which you aren't qualified because it will eventually catch up with you."

Bernstein was ready to try something new. After years of playing the role, in public, of the "real writer" of the pair, he was ready to head off in a more literary direction.

Long simmering was the desire to write about his family's complicated path and relationship with the Communist Party. Although he wasn't sure his parents had been card-carrying members of the Communist Party, he knew that the federal government's persecution of his parents had pervaded the Bernsteins' lives as he was growing up. When the Watergate story first broke, Bernstein felt obligated to tell Bradlee about his parents. He was certain that if the Nixon administration put two and two together, it would accuse Bernstein of going after the president in retaliation for the government hounding his parents in the 1950s.

His parents' past is one of the first things he told Ephron about, and she was behind his decision to leave daily journalism and try the life of a writer. He began writing a magazine article about his family for the *New Yorker*, although it never got published. Along the way, Bernstein received $100,000 up front from a $400,000 book advance from Simon & Schuster, which was willing to take another chance on its best-selling author.

Bernstein and Ephron bought a country house called "The Trees" out in Bridgehampton, a beach community on Long Island where New York's elite gravitate to escape Manhattan summers. "It was a fantasy world for both of them," said Bernstein's friend Robert Kaiser. "Carl bought an old Cadillac convertible. I think it was 1941 or 1946, which he drove around the Hamptons with the top down. It was dark black or blue. It was worth a lot of money. It was a collector's car. Again, by my lights, he lived an irresponsible life. Spending money like water. But he had money." Kaiser was more the type to pay his mortgage off; Bernstein was the type to forget to pay his mortgage. He and Nora "went through amazing amounts of money," Bernstein told *Playboy* in 1986. "We bought a house. We traveled a lot. Both of us are way up there as major spenders, particularly when we were together. And I'm not very prudent about money. I don't invest it wisely. I don't pay much attention to it. I never set out to make a lot of money, and it's never been a guiding force in my life. I've always sort of lived off what I had, or a little bit above my means, perhaps." At this point in his life, though, he could afford to act like one of Gatsby's swells, spending money wantonly.

Living as a member of the landed gentry and writing in a cottage near his country house was not the dream Bernstein had imagined. He was uncomfortable and felt that he was living Ephron's dream more than his own. It was difficult to transition from breaking the story of the century to living by the Atlantic Ocean in self-imposed exile. He tried to write, but it just wasn't coming. He told friends that he hated it. Woodward and some *Post* friends had opposed his leaving the paper. They thought that Bernstein was too much under his wife's influence and was trying to become some kind of literary lion that he wasn't cut out to be. They knew him to be a beautiful writer and a brilliant street reporter. One of the best in the business. Why walk away now?

"I thought Carl made a mistake by leaving the *Post* and going to New York," Woodward told me. "We both needed the *Post*.

We'd done the stories on Watergate. We'd done two books. And the kind of opportunity I've had there to do what I wanted and still work for the paper was available to him. But he wanted to go to New York. He thought in terms of a more literary career for himself. I think it was Nora's influence, and I thought he was making a wrong turn in the road."

While Bernstein struggled to figure out how to write his parents' story, he took on an assignment from *Rolling Stone* that reportedly paid him an astronomical (for the time) $30,000 for an 11,890-word piece on the CIA's recruitment of journalists during the Cold War. It appeared in October 1977 and made a big splash after Bernstein wrote that as many as four hundred journalists had shared information and provided cover for the CIA, including some members of the *New York Times*. The article incensed the *Times*, which wrote about it, despite dismissing its findings as information that the *Times* and other publications had already reported. Bradlee criticized the article, claiming that Bernstein had gone too far, but the reporter was back in the buzz. Then he returned to his book about the McCarthy era and spent a year interviewing his parents, their friends, other Red Diaper babies, government officials, and people in the Communist Party.

During that time, his first son, Jacob, was born. In August 1978, according to court records, Ephron and Bernstein moved to Washington, D.C., although she never felt she fit into the Washington political scene, claiming to be the proverbial fish out of water. Her husband was working on the book, and yet he wasn't. It was far easier to talk about the book, as any writer will say, than to actually write it. This book was nothing like his other two. Those had been exciting tales, and he had cowritten them. Now he was working alone, leaving many people to wonder whether he could do it without Woodward. He was also digging up his past, encountering painful times that he'd long suppressed. His parents weren't much help; they resisted his questions. They didn't want him to write a book about them. Harry Rosenfeld, Bernstein's editor during Watergate, knew Bernstein's parents and was angry at him for writing this book. "His parents were lovely, lovely people," said Rosenfeld. "They were friends of friends of ours. I would never dream of writing a memoir about my parents. For what? Was this a story crying to be told? I know they didn't want that story told. I can't understand it."

In November 1979, Bernstein told the *Washington Post* that the book was "vaguely about the first witch hunts of the Cold War," and that he expected a fall 1980 publication. That wasn't going to happen, though. Unable to write, itching to once again be involved in daily journalism, and possibly to please his parents, Bernstein put the book aside. He began repaying Simon & Schuster the $100,000 it had advanced him.

Because Bernstein enjoyed his celebrity and lived lavishly, there was no shortage of people who delighted in his inability to finish the book. Bernstein had already experienced an undertone of resentment in the *Post* newsroom toward his and Woodward's triumph. "This kind of success alters everybody. It alters you and also your friends," Dustin Hoffman told Jack Hirshberg. "Unfortunately, too often we measure ourselves by comparison with those around us. If one of them shoots up suddenly and we remain the same height for the time being, we feel much smaller. And that alters our relationship. The price you pay for this sort of recognition is that what you have become in the eyes of other people, including friends, is not what you really are. And you are forced to live with that distortion."

This was happening to Bernstein. For some friends and observers, not finishing his book reinforced the notion that Bernstein couldn't succeed professionally without Woodward, and as time went on, there were would be some truth to that. Closer to the truth, however, was that Bernstein, with a new wife and a new baby, wasn't yet ready to write a book that would require him to dig deeply into his and his parents' lives. "I absolutely hated working on the book," Bernstein told me. "I was too young to do it. I was too young to write a memoir. I was only thirty-three. I stopped in the middle of it. It was too painful. I hated working on it. I felt like I was kind of the landed gentry up there living in Bridgehampton, without going to an office for the first time in my life. I missed daily newspapers. I'd worked for daily newspapers since I was sixteen."

Bernstein began talking to Woodward about going back to the *Post*, and Woodward listened. The two had been estranged, unfortunate especially for two men who had virtually lived and breathed the same air for years and were known interchangeably as Wood-stein. ("I did some shuttle diplomacy," said Cohen. "But it didn't work. They had very different work ethics.")

"Bob and I started talking about my coming back to the paper," Bernstein told me. "I wanted to come back. We came up with this idea that we would become co-metro editors and get in the race to succeed Ben Bradlee. Bradlee went for it. He took it to Katharine Graham, and she said, 'This is a very bad idea. You can't have a two-headed machine.' Katharine was probably right. Who knows? Out of that came the idea I would go to the style section and Woodward would go to metro. If it worked out as me as the assistant editor of style, then I would become the assistant M.E. for style, and Woodward was going on the city desk and would become the assistant M.E. for metro, and we would all be in this race for Bradlee's job. But I never was going to succeed Bradlee. Maybe in my heart I thought it was possible. But in my head I'm sure I must have realized I'm not quite the politic person to run that route."

Even if co–metro editors was a bad idea, Woodward still wanted to find a way to bring Bernstein back to the *Post*. "There was always some magnet that I was trying to dangle to get him back," said Woodward. "When he's focused and fully engaged and sees the possibilities in a story, there's no one equivalent."

In the spring of 1979, Bernstein ran into his friend Roone Arledge at a party in the Hamptons. Bernstein had always thought that print reporters were unwisely disdainful of TV journalists. He saw that television was becoming a more powerful medium. It hadn't played much of a role in Watergate—save for broadcasting the Watergate hearings—but Bernstein saw its potential. He asked Arledge whether he could try to do some stories for ABC before returning to his old newspaper. Arledge liked the idea, but he had something bigger and more complicated in mind.

Ever since moving over to the news division in 1977 from ABC Sports, where he'd had rip-roaring success, Arledge had big plans. He was determined to find someone high profile to raise the energy level in Washington and help ABC become a bigger player in the capital. When Bernstein and Arledge first talked, CNN was in the planning stages and ABC's news division was largely considered a joke, referred to as the Amateur Broadcast Network.

ABC had begun to show some promise but still struggled for parity with NBC and CBS. Many people teased that ABC was number 4 in a three-way network race. In 1979, ABC didn't hold a candle to CBS with Walter Cronkite or to NBC with John Chancellor. Arledge wasn't happy with the current bureau chief, George Watson. He wanted someone with pizzazz to beef up the three-hundred-plus D.C. bureau.

"Roone thought it would be a good thing to hire Carl," said Richard Wald, who was a senior vice president at ABC News. Arledge had envisioned Bernstein doing a documentary on Henry Kissinger, one of the few high-level Nixon appointees who was not ensnared in the Watergate prosecutorial net. Wald didn't like the idea. He did not think that Bernstein, with his near-shoulder-length hair, would look good on TV. "I didn't think he was the kind of person who would do well on-air either, which is how Roone though of him initially. Carl mumbled a lot," said Wald. "It would be a long process to get Carl up to broadcast quality." Since Wald and Arledge had been roommates in graduate school, Arledge listened to Wald. "We sat there discussing what we could do with Carl, who was interested in being hired," said Wald.

Then Wald uttered some fateful words that spring of 1979.

"Well, we are looking for a bureau chief, and Carl knows everybody in Washington," said Wald. "Why don't we think of him as a possible bureau chief?"

Arledge liked the idea, although he said later that he instantly regretted it. "To my utter surprise, I got a call the next week from Dick Wald to come in and see them," said Bernstein. "He said, 'We'd like you to be Washington bureau chief.' There was something very appealing about it. One, not getting into that race at the *Post*. And I thought it could be a great job."

Appealing, yes, but was it the right move? "I'll bet you Carl thought that was a perfectly natural next step for him," said Bradlee.

He did. Bernstein thought it a grand move, the logical maneuver for someone who had helped to topple a sitting president. He accepted the offer, getting a $150,000 salary with a $50,000 expense account. It was far more than he could earn at the *Post* in 1979. A $150,000 salary seemed commensurate with Bernstein's new status as a Watergate hero. His books *All the President's Men* and *The Final Days* continued to sell well. He appeared on news talk shows, on the lecture circuit, and on the social scene in Washington and New York. Other journalists hunted him down for quotes. He was married to another prominent journalist who was pregnant with their second child. Carl Bernstein, in the late 1970s, had come to be a person of consequence. Why shouldn't he, at age thirty-five, try on the mantle of ABC News's Washington bureau chief?

"Nora tried to turn Carl into a kind of Halberstamesque or Talesesque New York writer-thinker, which was just as silly as Carl being ABC bureau chief," said lifelong friend Robert Kaiser. "It just wasn't Carl."

While it might have seemed like a perfect life on the outside, things weren't going well inside the Ephron-Bernstein household. A true New Yorker, Ephron bristled at living in the nation's capital. "Nora and Carl were the unlikeliest couple," said Bradlee, who with his wife, Sally Quinn, befriended the New York City transplant. "Nora is a particular pal of ours. She's the godmother of our child. She and Sally are very, very close. I think it's obvious what Nora saw in him. It was a good ride. Nora had written a book of essays, which was quite wonderful and very promising. [Her collection, *Crazy Salad*, hit the best-seller list in 1975.] But it wasn't enough to make a career out of. I also think she was totally out of place in Washington. Politics bored her. She just didn't like Washington. It was the headiness of the times that made Carl attractive. I remember it was great having Nora down here. But Washington has this culture involving government and politicos. She didn't want to fit in and didn't fit in. She thought the politicians were boring and the people who covered them mostly were boring." Ephron thought of herself as a liberal New Yorker and was quick to deem Nixon guilty. "Washington was bland," she told Pakula. "You get used to the fact that every congressman you meet is dumber than you."

The marriage was wearing thin, Bernstein said, long before what happened next. It was a case of failed expectations, more possibly of Bernstein being unable to live up to Ephron's expectations of what their lives should be. If their marriage had been working,

Bernstein said, he would not have fallen in love with another woman. Yet he did—and he did as publicly as Prince Charles with Camilla Parker-Bowles. He fell in love with Margaret Jay, a mother of three, the daughter of former British prime minister James Callaghan, and the wife of the British ambassador, Peter Jay. At the time, Margaret Jay was a successful television producer and a fixture on the Washington party scene. Later, it was revealed that her marriage had its own set of problems. Jay's husband was having an affair with their nanny, who bore him a son. Ephron discovered her husband's infidelity when she was seven months pregnant with their second son, Max. Upon learning of the adultery, a humiliated, angry Ephron poured red wine over her husband at a dinner party at the Bradlee-Quinn house. "In October of 1979, when I was seven months pregnant with our second child, I discovered that my husband had for many months been carrying on an adulterous affair," Ephron wrote in her divorce papers. "I also learned that he and this woman were looking at houses in the Washington, DC area, which my husband intended to purchase for their joint household. I was shocked by the discovery and by my husband's claim that he was in love with this other woman. The affair continued, despite my husband's promises that he would stop seeing this woman."

In the midst of this soap opera, Bernstein was negotiating with ABC. On November 15, 1979, ABC announced its new Big Name hire. It made all the papers, but Bernstein had no time to celebrate. His life was disintegrating, and his wife was going into premature labor. In her divorce records, Ephron said, "The mental distress and emotional hurt that I experienced as a consequence of my husband's deception caused me to go into labor during my seventh month of pregnancy." Max Ephron Bernstein was born more than a month early by cesarean section on the same day that the *New York Times* was touting Bernstein's new job. For the next five weeks, Bernstein spent almost every day at the hospital, holding, feeding, and caring for his new son while Ephron recuperated from the cesarean.

The marriage was over, though. In her divorce papers, Ephron wrote, "My husband's adultery and cruelty, particularly that which was inflicted during my pregnancy, caused me such unhappiness, suffering and mental anguish that I no longer could reside with him. Almost immediately after the birth of our second child, I established separate residence for myself and our children in New York, New York."

Once there, Ephron decided to announce the end of her marriage in the newspapers. She called her pal New York gossip maven Liz Smith, telling her, "Carl is a rat." In *Natural Blonde*, Smith wrote that she knew of Bernstein's wandering eye for other women but believed—as had many—that he and Ephron were genuinely in love and had a happy marriage. "The stories about Carl's involvement with a married woman—Margaret Jay, the wife of the British ambassador—were epidemic but I discounted them," wrote Smith. "I couldn't bear the thought. One day Nora rang me up and said in her characteristic determined kind of way: 'Liz, I have a story for you. Carl and I are going to divorce! Please write it.' I gasped—Not Carl and Nora, not when they'd just had a baby! But I didn't ask too many questions, forgetting my reportorial duties, caught up in empathy. I did write on December 19, 1979: 'The four-year marriage of writer Nora Ephron and reporter Carl Bernstein . . . is over. But definitely—finis, the end and out. Writing this scoop makes me feel sick." Smith said that Bernstein called her later that day, insisting that the couple wasn't divorcing. That wasn't true, however; they were—but it would take five and a half years before the divorce was finalized.

During the breakup of Bernstein's marriage, Woodward reached out to his old buddy. Everyone was piling on Bernstein, calling him a heel for how he'd humiliated Ephron. Woodward, though, had never understood what everyone saw in Ephron and, like Kaiser, had thought the couple an odd match. "I just didn't have the natural connection with Nora," Woodward told me. "I remember I heard Nora talk about being at some dinner and holding a discourse on the kind of lettuce that had been served: 'Can you believe they served that lettuce?' There was just this sense that she had been offended. People agreed with her, and maybe I agreed with her, but it just wasn't the way I lived."

Woodward unnerved Ephron because they were so different. Neither was particularly fond of the other. She told Pakula about a time she and Woodward were at a party when she was dating

Bernstein and they were living apart. With no prelude, Woodward walked up to her and asked directly: "Isn't it tough living in another city than the man you're going with?" It threw her because that is exactly what she had been up late nights worrying about.

Woodward may not have understood Bernstein's relationship, but he did understand the hurt that comes with the dissolution of a marriage, especially a second failure. He, too, had gotten married during the heady days of Watergate, and that marriage had failed. One of the turning points in their friendship, said Woodward, was the unraveling of the four-star Ephron-Bernstein union. "I decided to be Carl's friend, and lots of other people called Nora and said: 'Can you believe what Carl has done and isn't this awful?' said Woodward. "And I didn't. I always wondered why she and Carl fell together, and I didn't see that that was a natural, long-lasting relationship. But Nora's smart, capable. Carl said something very important to me, which is true, that there are always two sides to every story and the breakup of every marriage. Meaning it was complicated. I'm not suggesting Nora's behavior or anything like that, but a relationship clicks or it doesn't click."

This one didn't. It was in this emotionally charged, vulnerable state that Bernstein walked into his new position of leadership at ABC. "My marriage blew up just before I was going to start the job," Bernstein told me. "In fact, I went to work earlier than I was going to because the marriage blew up, and I needed to go to work and focus on going to work. It was an extremely difficult time." Even if Bernstein had come equipped with the skills to be bureau chief, the odds were against him. His imploding personal life was getting as much attention as his new job. To the outside world, he appeared to be a real cad. He was drinking heavily. "The fear that was in his heart about trying to pretend to be the bureau chief must have aggravated all his other anxieties and problems," said Kaiser.

His new job, too, was not as Arledge had advertised. While bureau chief sounded glamorous, Bernstein was not moving into a welcoming environment. He was replacing the popular bureau chief George Watson, who, after four years in the role, was being forced out for Bernstein. Watson had been with ABC since 1962, and his ABC bureau peers considered him a solid journalist.

"Dick told me that Roone wanted to replace me with Carl, and I said, 'That's the craziest thing I've ever heard of,'" said Watson. "Wald said, 'Don't you ever say anything like that again.'"

Many people in the bureau resented Bernstein's new role before he even set foot in the office. "George's demise made me unhappy," said former ABC correspondent Bernard Shaw, who soon left for CNN to become its main news anchor in 1980. "When Carl came in, he was very restive. It was a quantum adjustment, as it would be for anyone. His lack of television experience raised eyebrows, but that was balanced by his sterling journalistic credentials. I was never told the reason why George was no longer bureau chief. It was clear to me that Roone wanted a sparkly name with social cachet. I think you'll find that a consensus feeling."

The old ABC headquarters on Connecticut Avenue was a grungy rabbit warren of offices with cigarette butts scattered about and mold growing on long-forgotten coffee cups. There was a big open area where the heartbeat of the operation sat, and a bunch of small, dirty offices against the walls. The bureau was growing so quickly that a $24-million renovation was in the works for a new location on DeSales Street. In the meantime, there weren't enough offices for everyone, and some correspondents had satellite digs away from the main newsroom. Bernstein would also have to oversee the renovation.

Bernstein's friends could not believe that he'd switch to a medium he knew absolutely nothing about. "It was just a completely cockamamy idea to have Carl be bureau chief," said Kaiser. "He was incapable of playing a leadership role. Carl is not what Ben Bradlee used to call a leader of men. He's got many wonderful qualities, but he's too disorganized and too helter-skelter. Therefore, he never would have been a successful leader or manager. It caused a distance to grow between Carl and me because he wanted me and everybody else to act as though, 'Shit, man, he's the bureau chief at ABC News.' I just knew he couldn't be and wasn't, and that it was phony." Prior to this, Bernstein's only TV experience had consisted of brief appearances during the whirlwind book tours with Woodward.

"Carl came to ABC in 1980. He was miscast there," said ABC News veteran Sam Donaldson. "There was a lot of resentment, though not from me. I knew Carl pretty well because I had worked on Watergate. But a lot of people at ABC didn't know him. The late Roone Arledge, whom we all mourned, was a genius. I'm not going to say the word out loud, but Roone was a star-blanker. Roone believed in the star system and believed that people who had made their mark and had some celebrity were the most desirable people. He hired Carl because, to Roone, he was a 'get.'"

For Arledge, it was perfect. Bernstein would bring panache to the bureau. His name alone—Carl Bernstein, one of the two most famous journalists in the country—would lend the bureau a star quality. Plus, he was a terrific investigative reporter. He had fantastic sources. He knew lots of people in Washington, where he'd grown up. Certainly, he would be breaking big stories for ABC. "Now that I'd all but given Carl the job, the casting seemed inspired," Arledge wrote in his book *Roone*. "He'd be the seal of approval on the worthiness of ABC News. Doors that had been closed would now swing open. Scoops would magically tumble through them."

Bernstein envisioned himself directing the D.C. coverage and working closely with reporters. What he did not realize was that the job was largely administrative—and if Bernstein lacked any skills, it was as an administrator, something he had never done and wasn't personally suited for. This was the guy who couldn't even handle his expense accounts. Now he was going to run a bureau with three hundred people, including correspondents, technicians, cameramen, secretaries, and a sales force. Fortunately for Bernstein, Watson agreed to stay on for eight weeks to train him. "The more I thought about it, the more annoyed I got," said Watson, then forty-three. "Carl had no qualifications to be the Washington bureau chief of ABC News, however one regarded him as a reporter. Roone Arledge neglected to investigate Carl's capacity for running anything. I discovered quickly that he didn't keep regular hours. If you expected to see him in the morning, you were lucky to find him in the afternoon." Instead of sticking around to help Bernstein, Watson jumped at an offer from CNN. Watson's deputy bureau chief left as well.

Bernstein was on his own in hostile territory. He reached out to Bill Knowles, an old ABC hand who had worked in the bureau and was Southern bureau chief in Atlanta. Bernstein flew down to take Knowles out to dinner and offer him the number 2 spot. "I'm in the editing room, and he walks into the bureau, and I think: 'My God, it's Dustin Hoffman,'" recalled Knowles. Bernstein made his pitch. Knowles was an administrator. He knew how television equipment worked. In the D.C. bureau, it had been Knowles's job to get the evening news show on the air every night under enormous pressure. He knew everything Bernstein didn't—but Knowles turned Bernstein down. "It occurred to me when Roone put him in this situation that if Bernstein became a raging success, he'd get all the credit," said Knowles. "If he failed, I would get all the blame. Why go back and be number two to a guy who doesn't know what he's doing?"

Bernstein, by his own admission, failed miserably. "It turned out not to be a great job," said Bernstein. "But whatever the job I was permitted to do, I was lousy at it."

At the time, the job involved handling a lot of details. Things like making sure the New York bosses' orders were carried out. The bureau chief was responsible for dealing with the White House and handling travel plans if the president were going abroad. "Too much was laid on Carl's desk that was extraneous to what Carl did best, which was report," said Robert Zelnick, who worked in the ABC bureau. "A couple of months into it, it was clear to me that Carl wasn't going to make it."

Bernstein never deluded himself either. "Certainly, as an administrator, I'm hopeless. It's just not what I do. So it was disastrous." He joined the bureau six years after Nixon resigned, and his star status was losing its glimmer with time. He did not help himself by coming to work late, sometimes being missing in action, and taking long lunches. He promised to do things and didn't follow through. Nor did he seem to take much interest in television. "The collaborative nature of television is unparalleled," said Patrick Cullen, a former ABC News desk editor. "You are as dependent on the courier as on the correspondent. Carl, coming from print, was a loner."

"All I can say is, this was a terrible time in my life," said Bernstein. "My marriage was falling apart. I was drinking too much. I was not a happy character. It became clear to me within weeks that the producers of the broadcast really controlled what went on the air. The bureau chief really had no power in terms of content. None. None. I began a battle with them to try and get control of the editorial content of the broadcasts, particularly with *World News Tonight*. It was an impossible battle."

It was also one that Bernstein would ultimately lose, although he appealed to Arledge several times for support, asking him to come to D.C. In Arledge's autobiography, he says that he gave up after the fourth request. "Carl, I can't make these people respect you. You have to earn it from them." Yet Bernstein never did. He was never able to build a bridge between the stalwart old-timers and Arledge's crowd. Nor did he learn the television business or how to turn around a slow-moving bureau. He had wanted to create new editorial concepts, change the news product, and build the bureau into a showpiece, but he had reached too high. "I failed at it," said Bernstein. "I certainly was unable to do it the way I wanted to do it."

Sixteen months after the Watergate hero came aboard as bureau chief, he was replaced by Bill Knowles, the technical guy who actually knew how to run the place.

"It wasn't just that his personal life was falling apart," said Richard Wald. "That happens to a lot of people. It was that it was falling apart in public. A lot of the influence that you have in any newsroom comes from the perception that you are a person of consequence. If you become a person of gossip and amusement, things don't work out so well."

By the end of his tenure as bureau chief, Bernstein had ceased to be a person of consequence. He would have to work hard, once again, to achieve the stratospheric success he'd earned in Watergate. "After Carl left the bureau-chief job, Ted Koppel tried to turn him into a television correspondent on *Nightline*. But Carl didn't quite work on television, either—behind or in front of the camera," said Watson. "This was a really stressful time in Carl's personal life. Nora was around for a while, then the former British ambassador Peter Jay's wife was involved with him, and I think his socializing was taking precedence over his professional activities." He stayed with ABC until the spring of 1984 as an on-air reporter for both ABC News and *Nightline*, occasionally distinguishing himself covering the Falklands War and the Israeli invasion of Lebanon under Ariel Sharon's command. Yet several people who watched him said that Bernstein was never quite comfortable on television. He'd sweat and get nervous.

"I covered the war in Lebanon from Israel," said Bernstein. "I covered the Falklands War from London for ABC. I did some national security pieces for *Nightline*. The pieces were good. I would say that my work was probably erratic."

Almost everything about his life in the early 1980s was erratic, but things truly hit the nadir in 1983, when he was living in D.C., flying up to New York to see his kids, and working as a correspondent for ABC. In the spring of 1983, Ephron exacted literary revenge. She wrote her first novel, *Heartburn*, a 178-page roman à clef about the breakup of a marriage. She reminded Bernstein why one should never marry anyone who is witty and can touch-type.

Heartburn was the thinly disguised story about the ugly end of their marriage—only it was just her version, and in it, her former husband was an unprincipled cur. The most famous, oft-repeated line came when "Rachel" described her wanton husband as "capable of having sex with a Venetian blind." (*Playboy* once asked Bernstein if that was true. Bernstein wouldn't answer.) *Heartburn* is written from the standpoint of cookbook author Rachel Samstat (Ephron) whose husband, Mark Feldman (Bernstein), is a "fairly short" womanizing newspaper columnist who has an affair with an elegant, long-necked socialite (Margaret Jay), which Rachel discovers while pregnant with her second child. The acerbic Ephron even got in the red wine dousing, only in the novel, Rachel threw a key lime pie at her husband. "If I tell the story, I control the version," Ephron wrote in her novel, which was excerpted in *Vanity Fair*. The celebrated media mating was once again fodder for the gossip columns. The first printing had forty thousand copies and was widely reviewed and written about.

"How awfully lucky for those who treat them badly . . . that when journalists get mad they reach for a typewriter instead of a gun," wrote Grace Glueck in the *New York Times Book Review* about *Heartburn*. Ephron was criticized for turning their lives into a bigger soap opera than it already was, but writing cleverly about her life had become Ephron's trademark as she penned confessional essays for *Esquire*. She had warned Bernstein ahead of time that anything and everything in life is potential copy. "If you can turn a disaster into a funny story, then it's not as if the disaster happened to you, it's as if you happened to it," Ephron said in an April 1983 *Washington Post* profile.

She added that although the public breakup "was the most awful thing I've ever been through, it was by far the most interesting."

Bernstein, for the most part, kept his opinion about *Heartburn* to himself, as it became a runaway best seller. "Obviously, I wish Nora hadn't written the book. But I've always known she writes about her life. Nora goes to the supermarket, and she uses it for material." He was having enough problems of his own. As Ephron thrived in her new life without Bernstein—working on the script for the movie *Silkwood*, directed by Mike Nichols—Bernstein's life was declining. "Carl was consumed by his personal problems. Carl's problems were monumental. They were in the press," said Richard Cohen. "Woodward and Bernstein were two of the most famous people in the world at that time. It was an amazing thing to watch. They weren't just famous journalists, they were celebrities. Especially for print. So when Carl had problems, these were terribly magnified by his own celebrity. Most of us go through things on a more private level. Everything that Carl did, the separation, the divorce, the thing with Margaret Jay, was all very public." And painful.

"My whole life was in turmoil," said Bernstein. "In retrospect, it's hard to separate one thing from another. I think also the attention on my personal life was so unexpected and so unrelenting."

In July 1983, at his rock bottom, Bernstein made news—again. This time it was after the D.C. police stopped him at 3:15 a.m. in his 1977 Toyota only a few blocks from his home. They arrested him for drunk driving and then released him. "When he got arrested one night, he called me, and it was a real low point," Woodward told me. "I went down to the police station and brought him back." Later that day, Bernstein wrecked his Toyota. His life was falling apart and he knew it, so he checked himself into a Washington hospital to be treated for depression and exhaustion for four days. He was under so much pressure that the migraines he'd had in his twenties had returned. His drinking was clearly a problem. During Watergate, he rarely drank. He was too

busy, too absorbed by the story. "Drinking had never been a problem for me, it really hadn't," said Bernstein. "I resumed drinking
during *The Final Days*. But I could see after a while, it didn't
work. It wasn't fun anymore. It didn't do anything for me." He
drank to relieve the tension, and to dull the pain of a life spinning
out of control. His friends knew that he drank, but they didn't see
him as a falling-down drunk because he wasn't. "I guess I was just
terribly naive," said Cohen. "If you said alcoholic, I thought it
was someone with a bottle in a drawer. I never saw Carl doing
that. We were virtually roommates. We went on vacation together.
His problem was of a different nature. I could see the consequences
of his drinking, and obviously, sometimes there were the effects
from his drinking."

The alcoholism helped to dull the fact that Bernstein's life had
turned into a three-ring circus, devoid of any privacy and filled
with a distinct feeling of schadenfreude from the public.

"Carl was damaged by that book Nora wrote," said his former editor Harry Rosenfeld. "I'm not saying she was wrong about
that, but that contributes to his public image. I think you can say
that he has not been his own best friend." Not only had Ephron's
Heartburn stayed on the *New York Times* best-seller list, but in
May, Pocket Books paid an unusually high $341,000 for the
paperback rights. That wasn't the worst of it, though. The worst
was that director Mike Nichols wanted to turn the book into a
movie. Ephron and her sister would write the screenplay.

When Ephron's book came out in 1983, she and Bernstein
were still legally married, although they had separated four years
earlier. She had filed for divorce in June 1980 in New York, but
the case languished. Ephron told the court that she had not gone
through with the divorce because she feared a trial. "I was still
traumatized by the injury of my husband's open, flagrant infidelity
and I remained upset by the effects of extensive media coverage of
the breakup of our marriage," wrote Ephron in court papers. "The
prospect of court appearances, and of having to retell openly the
details of the breakup of our marriage frightened me." Although
she sought the divorce, Ephron wanted to work things out without a trial. Negotiations had stopped around the time of Bernstein's arrest. "It was my understanding and belief that he had a
nervous breakdown," she told the court. "I also learned that his

employment contract at ABC was in jeopardy and was not going to be renewed. In addition, my husband informed me that he was in financial difficulty, he was attempting to sell the house in Bridge-hampton, and his financial affairs had been turned over to [an attorney]. Beginning in August 1983, and for eight months there-after, he failed to make child support payments. Negotiations were temporarily discontinued during that period as an accommoda-tion to my husband's delicate emotional condition. As soon as my husband's emotional and financial difficulties began to improve in early 1984, negotiations resumed."

By spring 1984, Bernstein had left ABC and was intending to move to New York to be closer to his boys. Since 1973, when he first met Ephron, he had commuted between two cities—three, including Bridgehampton—and now he wanted to live in one place. He had also returned to the book about his parents at the suggestion of his friend the author Joan Didion. He asked her to read the fifty or so pages that he'd written. She did and called him the next morning, encouraging him to finish. It was the impetus Bernstein needed.

But first he wanted to get his divorce over with. What ensued was dreadful and, again, very public. In June 1984, Bernstein filed for divorce in Washington, D.C., hiring the divorce attorney his pal Woodward had used. Ephron claimed that he was trying to cash in on her success with *Heartburn* because he was having financial difficulties. That wasn't it at all, said Bernstein. He could handle the book, but he feared that a movie, which millions would see, might hurt his sons, who in 1984 were barely school age. Ephron didn't agree, she said, given their young ages, but Bern-stein didn't buy it. In August, he threatened Paramount with legal action if the novel were turned into a movie. He even issued a press statement. Ephron countered publicly that she had deep con-cerns about a father who would use his children as "pawns in a nuisance suit." Yet the ugliness could last only so long. By Decem-ber, they had compromised. They would have joint custody, he would pay $1,180 a month in child support, and they would share private-school costs. Under no circumstances, if she were to remarry, could the boys give up their surname.

That part was pretty standard, but the final agreement went on for pages about *Heartburn*. As part of an unusual settlement,

Bernstein won the right to read Ephron's screenplay, read subsequent drafts, see a first cut, *and* register his concerns. Ephron could not write about him or her children in the future, and she agreed to put 5 percent of the book's profits and 15 percent of the rights sale into a trust for their children. The agreement spelled out that Bernstein must be portrayed as a loving father in the film. Ephron had concluded that he was a lousy husband, but she agreed that he was a good father and would portray him so. The agreement went even further: the screenplay could have no references to Bernstein's parents and the boys could not visit the movie set without his permission and they could not attend any movie-related events.

In June 1985, the divorce was finalized. While Bernstein had some script rights, Paramount included a letter stating that Bernstein should not infer that he had rights to control the film's final cut or distribution. Of course, the divorce settlement—like every other part of the marriage—became public. "The truth was, today our divorce would get four minutes in *People* magazine; then it got almost four years," Bernstein told me. "That you have a celebrity culture now is what's different. In a celebrity culture all of that stuff is catalogued and gets about three or four minutes, and they go on to the next stuff. But at that time, it was the cusp of the celebrity culture, and it was my good luck to be self-selected to ride the wave and get inundated. I hope you put in there that I laughed. So it was awful. It was terrible." He was also racked with guilt. "The way I blew that marriage. Our marriage. It's not something I feel good about."

Nichols was about to begin shooting, and Bernstein worried that script changes that he wanted would not be made. "Be forewarned," he threatened Ephron in a fourteen-page letter on July 18, 1985, "that as long as the *Heartburn* screenplay continues to reflect a false and self-serving version of our marriage and its breakup I will continue to pursue action against you in the courts. . . . Finishing your screenplay I feel exactly like I did when I first read the book. You're very clever. But this time, as you may have gathered, I'm not going to play dead."

Bernstein had many objections, but chief among them was that Ephron had made him look like a lousy father. "Sophie," their daughter, appears on screen about twenty times. "Following the day of her birth, her father does not touch her through the entire course of the movie. He does not speak a single word to her," wrote Bernstein. "In no subsequent scene in the whole movie does he express or demonstrate either love or feeling or affection for his child. That role is left entirely to Rachel (Ephron). . . . (Maybe once, before the shit hits the fan, dear old Dad could tuck his child in? A peck on the cheek? Come on, Nora.)" The maid, he observed, spends more time on screen with the baby than her father does.

Bernstein had another objection. In the fictionalized marriage, the husband inexplicably leaves for the other woman, but that's not what happened in real life. "The other basic deficiency (and equally dishonest aspect) of the screenplay," wrote Bernstein, "is that it is premised upon an egregious falsehood about the circumstances of the breakup of our marriage: i.e., the notion that—until I undertook a loving relationship with another woman—ours was an almost perfect marriage . . . blissful, peaceful, satisfying, always loving and respectful. As you well know, this was not the case; that it took both of us to wreck our marriage—me in my way, you in your fashion; and that the disintegration of our marriage was well underway by the time alluded to in your screenplay.

"Perhaps I can give you a piece of help here: Instead of always thinking that a stranger is going to be reading and/or seeing this work, and instead of viewing this episode in your life as a never-ending struggle with me, think of our kids reading it or seeing it or hearing about it—either now or five years from now: Will it make them angry? Make them feel hurt? Used? Try finding a way to write this that does the least damage to any of us—you, me or the children, our family. Which reflects the fact that, in a marriage of two people who once loved each other, some things went horribly and successively wrong. That we both fucked up. That our expectations of a marriage were unreasonable and could have never been fulfilled. That instead of having just a good or ordinary or dull or plodding marriage—the kind that people work on day in and out—we insisted on having it all, always reaching for the illusory brass ring instead of being content with touching real life and each other. That you couldn't handle your expectations and, eventually, neither could I. That your attitude toward me changed.

That eventually I gave up—on you and the marriage. That eventually you gave up too—on me and the marriage."

Bernstein's friends say that Ephron married an idealized version of Bernstein, the one lionized in the press when the *Post* won the Pulitzer in 1973, the one in much demand on the lecture circuit, the one profiled in the press, the one Dustin Hoffman played in a smash hit. "This [marrying Carl] was very hard for Nora," said Bob Kaiser. "I'm full of sympathy for Nora. She bought into something that she didn't fully understand when she made the purchase. When she began to understand how complicated it was, she got nervous and tried to cope, and part of the coping pattern that she hit on was to hold Carl close and create a new world for him. But it didn't work."

Eventually, Ephron made modifications that satisfied Bernstein, and the film was shot with Jack Nicholson playing the Bernstein role and Meryl Streep as the Ephron character. Dustin Hoffman was offered the Bernstein part first. "Nichols asked me to play Carl in *Heartburn*, but I didn't want to do it," said Hoffman. "I have children, and I didn't want to be a part of a project where I had to portray an actual person who had actual children who would grow up and have this distorted view of their father." Years later, Hoffman worked with Ephron and found that his presence confused her. "Nora and I were working on another project that Nichols was going to direct," said Hoffman. "It was about a divorce lawyer. We were having these meetings and fighting about things. One time I said: 'Why are you so angry at me, Nora? I'm not Carl Bernstein—I just played him.'"

A decade after he had married for the second time, Carl Bernstein, the freckle-faced kid from Silver Spring, Maryland, who used to look like Howdy Doody, had by age forty-two been portrayed in two major motion pictures by two A-list actors. It wasn't the last time, either. Although he still hadn't figured out what to do as a successful encore after Watergate, he had stopped drinking (by 1987). "I stopped because it was not working anymore," Bernstein said in 2003. "I don't think other people recognized I had a problem. But I could see I did. I just stopped. I never talk about what I do to maintain my sobriety. I don't go into it. But I don't drink."

With a clearer head and a marriage no longer fodder for gossip, Bernstein went back to his book and tried to figure out his next act. As Watergate's luster receded, Carl Bernstein came to epitomize Daniel J. Boorstin's definition of celebrity. Bernstein was now known for his well-knownness. There would be more tabloid headlines and more famous women, but he would stick with the book and surprise both his friends and his detractors. "Carl realized that his life had been transformed," said Kaiser. "His status in the world had changed. In principle, it was all a great thing. But what do you do with it? How do you take advantage of it? Bob came up with a good answer. Go back and do good work. Do original journalism."

9

Mr. Carte Blanche

Woodward is very tough. He can have a real cutting edge but he looks like such a good old boy, so low key. You'd be sitting there at an interview and I'd be sort of trying to butter them up and trying to slow it down, let them talk a while before we came to the hard questions, and suddenly Woodward, very early, would say, "Why did you take the money?" I mean, he can be almost brutal.

> —Bernstein on Woodward to David Halberstam
> in the mid-1970s

Neither Woodward's nor Bernstein's second marriage survived during the intoxicating years of Watergate. The pressures and the demands on both men proved too enormous to get through the rocky first years of any marriage. Both unions lasted about three and a half years before the couples separated. While Bernstein's divorce was public, painful, and ugly, Woodward managed to end his marriage of thirty-nine months to former newspaper reporter Francie Barnard Woodward fairly quietly. Woodward has always been good at steering attention away from himself in a way that Bernstein has not. Not comfortable with people focusing on him, Woodward has worked hard to live a life outside the spotlight, getting under its glare only when it is necessary to promote books.

"Bob became a little bit reclusive," said high school pal Scott Armstrong. "There's certain things Bob's never liked the accoutrements of. I think he learned a lot from Redford. He admired Redford's ability to avoid publicity. Woodward was immediately wary

of fame, whereas Carl embraced it. Francie came from a prominent family and was used to being a big fish in a big pond. One of
her buddies was Ethel Kennedy. She didn't dislike the fame. In her
world, you would use it for things like charity or some other
cause. Bob didn't use it for anything but journalism. There weren't
big parties. We would all go out to Gibson Island. They were just
different people. Bob's very intense and wants very much to get
back to his work. Francie had kind of given up her journalistic
career to be a mom, and that was fine. But she didn't want to not
go out to dinner or have him work all the time. Bob has often said
that young, single people have opportunities in journalism that
nobody else has, because they can go out and see people every
night. That's harmful to a relationship." While clearly Woodward's Calvinist work ethic played a role in the demise of the marriage, he told David Halberstam that while he was married to
Barnard his methodical vacuuming and cleaning almost drove her
crazy.

Woodward and Frances Barnard Woodward separated in February 1978, not terribly long after their only child, a daughter,
Mary Taliesin (known as Tali) Woodward, was born in November
1976. Barnard claimed in her September 1978 divorce filings that
she could not afford to support herself and her daughter. She
wanted Woodward to give her $5,000 a month because he "is able
to earn substantial sums of money as a self-employed writer and
lecturer and earned in excess of $840,000 in 1977." Woodward
conceded that he had earned a lot in 1977, but he was already giving Barnard $2,400 a month. He countered that the $840,000
income was a one-time fluke and did not constitute his annual
income. He could not promise that he'd earn that much again. In
December 1978, he told the court he was earning $33,600 as a
national reporter for the *Post*. The couple had assets totaling
$1 million, with net assets of $555,000.

The second Mrs. Woodward came from a wealthy Texas family and wasn't granted alimony, but she was given the right to
restore her maiden name to Frances Roderick Barnard. She got the
1976 Mercedes; he took the 1979 Honda. They owned two pieces
of property, one the 1868 Georgetown house on Q Street in Washington that Woodward has lived in most of his adult life. The other

was outside Washington on Gibson Island. Woodward kept the Q Street house, and Barnard got the Gibson Island property. The two properties were considered of equal value. Court records indicate that Woodward made a smart deal. In 1978, the Q Street property was valued at $100,000, with $97,000 owed and a monthly payment of $839. In 2006, that property was assessed at $2.5 million, according to D.C. tax records. The divorce settlement lingered for a year, with the common accusations of poor parenting flying back and forth, until it was settled in September 1979. Joint custody was awarded, although Tali would live primarily with her mother. Woodward was ordered to pay $1,500 a month in child support, as well as medical and school expenses. He was thirty-six and had failed twice at marriage, largely because of his driving ambition and intense work ethic. It would be ten years before Woodward tried again.

After the Woodwards separated, Bernstein reached out to his friend, although their relationship had been rocky for a while. "Now, when we did fight like cats and dogs was around the period when I left the paper [December 1976]," Bernstein told me. "We wanted to do different books. I wanted to do a book on a corporation. He wanted to do a book on the government. He proceeded to do a book on the Supreme Court. I wanted to do a book actually on the Rockwell Corp. and corporate life. Then when Bob's marriage broke up, I called him and said, 'Are you all right?' I think I was in Washington, actually. We hadn't talked in a while. I think that he was glad to hear from me. No, no, he didn't say that. That is what I'm saying. We then became extraordinarily close again and have been since." (When Bernstein later needed $16,000, Woodward lent it to him, and Bernstein paid it back.)

Woodward accepted the olive branch but refused to work with Bernstein again, although the two would briefly take a victory lap together, arms raised high, in 2005 when Deep Throat was revealed. If they worked together again, it would be on Woodward's terms. Working together caused Woodward too much anxiety. He needed a partner he could rely on. They could try friendship, although, in their midthirties, even the friendship was tenuous. They knew they were forever linked together in history, but neither one knew where the friendship was headed or whether it would stand the test of time. Scores of journalists do two-man investigative projects, but the majority split up and move on. The exception is the preeminent investigative team of Donald L. Bartlett and James B. Steele, who have worked together for decades, are renowned in journalism circles, but don't have the name cachet of Woodward and Bernstein. "We started working on Watergate when he was twenty-eight and I was twenty-nine," Woodward told me. "Carl and I had a foxhole experience that ties us together for life. We realized that. Interestingly enough, I think he realized that more than I did over time. Because Carl has been a really good friend and a strong friend and kept—at least in the 1970s, when he moved to New York and went his way, and I stayed here at the *Post*—he kept the connection open. He talked about it and had a natural intuitive sense that we could help each other and mean something to each other."

Woodward knew better than most people did that there were two Bernsteins: one of them, Woodward considered one of the best reporters in the business. The other desired to become a New York personality. Woodward didn't want any part of the latter's world, and he couldn't trust the former. "Bob is certainly as interesting as Carl. I remember Bob and Carl having lunch with Truman Capote years before that and how fascinated Bob and Capote were with each other," said Armstrong. "Bob could certainly have become a New York intellectual, gone to New York, and written books. But he didn't really want to do that. Carl couldn't be gotten away from the party. If there were seven parties in a week, Carl had a really tough schedule." Their lifestyles clearly diverged, but Woodward was not ready to venture out on his own yet. He asked Armstrong, then a reporter at the *Post*, to work on his next project. He wanted to pull back the curtain—a lifelong theme—on the highly secretive U.S. Supreme Court.

Woodward's previous book, *The Final Days*, was based on anonymous sources. His next book on the Supreme Court would be no different. One main source was Justice Potter Stewart, whom Woodward met at a party at *Washington Post* publisher Katharine Graham's house in the spring of 1977. Woodward's interest in the nation's top court was piqued during the fight over Nixon's tapes. He tried to talk to Stewart while reporting for *The Final Days* but got nowhere. Now Stewart would talk. He invited Woodward to his Washington home and agreed to explain the court to Woodward on background—meaning that Stewart's name would never appear as a source. As is sometimes his practice, Woodward didn't take out a notebook. Instead, when he got home, he told *Playboy* magazine in February 1989, he typed up a two-and-a-half-page, single-spaced memo about the encounter. (Woodward is so trustworthy in doing this after every key encounter that his boss Ben Bradlee relied on Woodward's memos years later when he wrote his own memoir. "Bob Woodward is a machine on this kind of stuff," said Bradlee. "If I went to look for my notes, I'd start in my basement in Georgetown and work up. I just don't know where anything is, but he does. They are thoughtfully annotated. He can put his finger on anything.")

That night Stewart basically outlined Woodward's next book. "As I drove home," he told *Playboy*, "I realized that either I could write a really interesting article with a little bit more work or here was the next book." By now, book writing had become more attractive to Woodward, and he negotiated another deal with Simon & Schuster. He'd write it with Armstrong, and it would explain in detail how the court worked from the inside, even the personal and philosophical conflicts exacerbated by Chief Justice Warren Burger's attempts to manipulate and control the court. They got a $350,000 advance and began working on *The Brethren* in the summer of 1977, writing parts at the *Post* on the eighth floor next to Don Graham's office and parts at Woodward's Gibson Island place on the water. Armstrong said that they had enough information for four books. Midway through, Al Kamen, their researcher on *The Final Days*, came to help with the editing and the rewriting, as did Ben Weiser.

"Woodward and I would often get completely tangled up," said Armstrong. "Bob likes very stark portrayals, and I like long, nuanced cases. I don't want to miss a twist or turn or a detail. Bob's the opposite. Here's the rabbi and the priest going to see the minister. Here's what was said, and the joke. I wanted to tell you the history of all three, and about the sunlight coming through the altar window, and the way they walked. Bob would put it through his typewriter, and bam, it was done. Often, it seemed to me that it missed showing the nuance of the legal structure of the court or overstated the subtle drama of the justices' unique approaches to the law, and we would have a big set-to. Al became the arbitrator, if that was possible."

But their disagreements were minor. For one thing, Woodward completely trusted Armstrong. He knew he'd do the reporting and get the writing done on time. But in 1979, as Bernstein's marriage was publicly unraveling, Woodward's life started to become hectic. He was finishing writing *The Brethren*. He was in the midst of a divorce. And on May 1, 1979, having just turned thirty-six, Woodward became assistant managing editor for metropolitan news. He'd been at the *Post*, including generous book leaves, for eight years. But Woodward had never even been an editor or managed people since he was in the navy. Now he would be in charge of a staff of 108 journalists, who, by their skeptical, truculent nature, were famously hard to manage. Herding cats is not for rookies.

"He had such an aura of leadership about him," Bradlee told me. "He was looking for something to do. I think he must have been thinking: Should he be, could he be, would he be editor of the *Post*? I wondered that, too. Although very casually. So I said, 'Let's put him on the management track.'"

The job may have been the logical next step for a journalistic Babe Ruth, but it was also a step toward the Establishment. One could argue that the Woodward who grew up in a Republican enclave, attended Yale, and served in the navy had already secured a spot there. During Watergate, however, he and Bernstein had developed the reputation of being outsiders who refused to play the game of mouthpiece journalism, rewriting press releases and quizzing government officials. They eschewed "access journalism." Now Woodward was moving into a position of power. He was ignoring Bernstein's Cassandra-like warnings: "Watch out, Woodward. Don't listen to them. Be careful of that establishment and the way they will incorporate you and get you to do something different than you have been doing." But Woodward wanted the challenge.

The Brethren came out in December 1979, and, like *The Final Days*, it became a highly controversial best seller, eventually selling 600,000 copies. Again, it wasn't the content; people found the stories fascinating. It was the omniscient narrator approach—interviewing scores of people, re-creating scenes, and giving people's thoughts and motivations as if the reader was in the room. The authors' confidential source relationship didn't work for Renata Adler, a high-profile essayist who did a take-down of the book in the *New York Times*. She objected to the anonymity because it "makes stories almost impossible to verify. It suppresses a major element of almost every investigative story: who wanted it known." Why was the source talking to him? What angle did the source want public? What was the source's motivation? Was it malevolent or public spirited? This was the second time that Woodward's reporting style came under attack. With *The Final Days*, Woodward had calmly refuted the criticism, but occasionally he debated the critic's competence. Adler, who has a Yale law degree, was no exception. "Adler didn't understand how the Court worked," he told *Playboy*. "And she has a kind of infantile ignorance about the way reporters work, because she's not a practicing journalist. Specifically, she doesn't understand what we were doing in that book. It is verifiable. We had documents, we had diaries." Later, Armstrong said that he wished they had used footnotes.

Ten years after *The Brethren* appeared, Woodward revealed to *Playboy* magazine that Stewart was a key source, which immediately made news. "I'll tell you the source who started that whole project, because he's dead," said Woodward. "I'm revealing his name now, for the first time, because it's worth showing that there really are sources, people really do talk. It's not some reporter's imagination or some letter that comes in the mail with no address, typed on a standard typewritten paper. You have relationships, you nurture them and they pay off."

Overall, the book received positive reviews, being one of the first of its kind to reveal the inner workings of such a secretive entity. An article in *Newsweek* on December 10, 1979, stated:

> The book goes beyond describing superficial judicial blemishes. Indeed, the book's emphatically serious tone should defuse some of the more predictable criticism. Nevertheless, several pointed issues are likely to dominate the coming debate. The book's critics will argue that its dramatic disclosures about sitting Justices and what they think of one another may chill their future deliberations and skew the development of unsettled legal doctrines.

Some readers will mistrust the book's omniscient voice and un-attributed declarations of what the Justices did, said and felt in their private deliberations. Some will question whether the initial undifferentiated hype and headlines surrounding the publication make the Court seem even worse than the authors' descriptions.

Such questions make Bob Woodward and Scott Armstrong uncomfortable. All they were trying to do, they say, is report on Washington's great secret story. "The Court was a sitting target," Woodward says. In the past, other Washington reporters tried to pry open the Court and came away with little more than tantalizing anecdotes. The difference this time, apart from the team's Watergate-sharpened skills, was time and money. Armed with a $350,000 advance from Simon and Schuster, plus a paid leave from the *Washington Post*, Woodward and Armstrong set out in the summer of 1977 to talk with Justices and former law clerks scattered around the country.

After they finished *The Brethren*, Armstrong says, they flirted with the idea of buying the *San Francisco Chronicle* by selling off its television properties and turning it into a better newspaper, but nothing came of it. With his new job as assistant managing editor for metropolitan news, Woodward barely had time to do a full-fledged Simon & Schuster book tour. He needed to jump right in, as the learning curve was high for someone with no management experience. He would be master over a kingdom consisting of one-quarter of the entire *Post* news staff. It included the District of Columbia, plus Maryland and Virginia suburban and state coverage, at a time when the *Post* wanted to expand into the suburbs. It was the wrong job for him.

Not long after Woodward started, he assigned a complicated investigative story about Mobil Oil Corp. to one of his brightest and most aggressive young reporters, Patrick Tyler, who was twenty-seven and had been at the *Post* for only a year. In 1976, when Woodward was on the national staff, he had gotten an anonymous tip about a top Mobil executive improperly using the company's money and influence. He checked it out and did not think it worth pursuing. In 1979, the tip came around again, this time from a reporter named Sandy Golden, who had worked at a local paper and wanted a job at the *Post*. The paper hired Golden temporarily as a special correspondent to help Tyler investigate the Mobil tip. The eventual story, which Woodward edited, stated that Mobil's president, William P. Tavoulareas, had used his influence and Mobil assets in 1974 to help his son, Peter, twenty-four, become the principal owner of a London-based shipping management company that did millions of dollars in business with Mobil under no-bid contracts. As Mobil was the nation's second-largest oil company, this was a Big Story. It was just the kind of "Holy shit!" story that Woodward was known to love and encourage among his staff. Tyler's opus—MOBIL CHIEF SETS UP SON IN VENTURE—ran on the front page in the November 30, 1979, paper. A second story followed the next day about a congressman investigating Tavoulareas. Within days, the senior Tavoulareas was in Bradlee's office demanding a retraction, insisting that he had never played an active role in his son's company and that the story damaged his reputation as an industry titan.

A newspaper lives and dies by the veracity of what it publishes. A journalist's only currency is the truth, and a paper's only asset is the accumulated trust of its readers. It is the fundamental contract between a publication and its subscribers, and once it is broken, it takes a long time to repair. So the *Post*, certain it had accurately reported the story, refused to back down. A year later, in November 1980, the Tavoulareases filed a $50 million libel suit against the *Post*, Bradlee, Tyler, Tyler's editor, Bob Woodward, and Sandy Golden.

The lawsuit became like *Bleak House*'s Jarndyce and Jarndyce, costing the *Post* almost $1 million in legal fees and Tavoulareas $2 million before it was resolved nearly eight years after the first story ran.

The trial began in federal court in July 1982, with Woodward and Tyler spending hours on the witness stand. Woodward sat through most of the three-week trial. The judge had determined that Tavoulareas, as the head of a major company, was a public figure. This meant that the jury had to decide whether the *Post* knowingly or recklessly printed a proven falsehood. Golden also testified, and one of his remarks was considered highly damaging to the *Post*. He told the court that after he had introduced Tyler to his source and it looked like the story would play out, Tyler had commented, "It's not every day you knock off one of the seven sisters," referring to Mobil as one of the seven largest international oil firms. At the trial's end, the jury said that the *Post* had libeled Tavoulareas, and it awarded him $2 million.

The jury did not find Woodward or Bradlee at fault, but that didn't really matter. It was still Woodward and Tyler's story. The story dogged Woodward when he occasionally went out on the lecture circuit. "I think the story is a model of responsible journalism," Woodward said at Webster College in St. Louis in September 1982, and he stood by the story. The following May, the *Post* got good news. The judge threw out the $2 million verdict, saying there was no evidence that the *Post* had acted recklessly or with malice, and that Tyler had obviously spent a lot of time and effort on the story. The case didn't end, however; Tavoulareas appealed. It would take more than two years before a decision was handed down.

This one was a stunner. In April 1985, a three-judge panel on the U.S. Court of Appeals sided with Tavoulareas. The judges figured that if Woodward, the super-sleuth of Watergate, were involved in the story, then the *Post* must have been out to get the Mobil president. In an eighty-eight-page opinion, Judge George E. MacKinnon said that some *Post* employees "deliberately slanted, rejected and ignored evidence contrary to the false premise of the story." The attack on Woodward was unprecedented. "A reasonable inference is that Woodward, as editor, wanted from his reporters the same kind of stories on which he built his own reputation: high-impact investigative stories of wrongdoing," wrote Judge MacKinnon.

Of course, by this time Tavoulareas still had not gotten a dime. Even if he had, it all would have gone toward legal fees—but the *Post* refused to pay. It was not about the money; it was about the repercussions of such a verdict. The *Post* could well afford the $2 million, but not every news outlet could. If the libel verdict stood, it would have a chilling effect on the news media, possibly making journalists think twice before they tried to expose wrongdoing. The *Post* appealed to the full Court of Appeals. It took another two years for an answer. The *Post* eventually won and the court overturned the $2 million verdict. The full court wrote that the *Post*'s story was "substantially true," and the record "abounds with uncontradicted evidence of nepotism in favor of

Peter Tavoulareas." It was a huge victory for the media, and especially for the *Washington Post*.

Woodward believes that this legal decision is more important,
in the long run, for journalism than Watergate or the Pentagon
Papers were. Bradlee doesn't agree. If Bradlee had known that the
story would cost $1 million and take eight years, he said, he would
not have run it. "I argued with Ben about that," Woodward told
the *American Journalism Review* in 1998, "saying if someone
comes to you with all the facts and says, 'You are going to pay a
million dollars in legal fees and, yes, have some ups and downs
but get this final opinion,' that's definitely worth the money and
some of the agony. If you get constitutional law that is the law forever in the District of Columbia that enshrines investigative
reporting—now that's one million dollars for a license. It's the
biggest bargain the *Washington Post* ever got."

The story was solid, but it was also the first Big Story under
Woodward the Editor. It was definitely his kind of story. So was
the Big Story that eventually did him in as an editor, knocking him
off the track to be the next executive editor after Bradlee retired.
Woodward certainly had a good shot. Bradlee adored Woodward,
who was clearly an heir apparent. The job of metro editor would
give Woodward a chance to prove himself—only it was not to be.
Janet Cooke made sure of that.

Cooke was a dazzling young black woman from Toledo, who
at twenty-six was fueled by the same burning ambition as Woodward. Her resume said she had graduated magna cum laude from
Vassar College in 1976, studied at the Sorbonne, and spoke four
languages. After two years at the *Toledo Blade*, she was ready to
move to a bigger paper. The *Post* hired her in January 1980 to
report for the *District Weekly*, a once-a-week section that's a standard starting ground for green reporters. She had a flair for writing and was a big presence in the newsroom because of the
fashionable way she dressed and how she carried herself. "In
many ways, we were all seduced by both her charm and intelligence and our own good intentions," said Ted Gup, then a metro
reporter. "We all wanted this brilliant, naturally talented, beautiful black woman to reach her full potential and open the door for
so many others. Under those circumstances, it was all too easy to
suspend critical judgment. We were all enamored of her."

Everyone knew she was ambitious and wanted off the less glamorous *District Weekly* and on to the daily metro staff. She let Woodward know her plans. She confided to metro reporter Karlyn Barker that she wanted to win a Pulitzer and get on the national staff—a trajectory similar to Woodward's. Editors were impressed with her eagerness. "It did appear that most of the editors at the *Post* were taken in by her," said a former metro reporter. "It was not just one editor. It was most of the editors. I never really understood why. Somebody becomes a real favorite, a golden person, and you don't understand why. Not only me, but most of the reporters didn't understand. Usually, you see it associated with stories the reporter does, but that wasn't the case with Janet."

Editors, including Woodward, were excited when Cooke mentioned that she had found an eight-year-old heroin addict—especially Woodward's city editor, Milton Coleman. "I talked over Janet's materials with her," Coleman said at the time. "She talked about hundreds of people being hooked. And at one point she mentioned an 8-year-old addict. I stopped her and said, 'That's the story. Go after it. It's a front-page story.'" This was the kind of story that got noticed. It was just the kind of "Holy shit!" story that Woodward loved. (Pressure for such stories came ultimately from Bradlee, said former *Post* editor and media critic Ben Bagdikian. "Bradlee wanted something lively every single day," he told the *Columbia Journalism Review* in 2002. "He used to say at editorial meetings, 'I want people to pick up this fucking paper every morning and look at it and say, *Holy shit!*'")

Cooke was given time and freedom to report the story. She handed in a beautifully written narrative piece of journalism destined for the front page. Her compelling story "Jimmy's World" appeared on September 28, 1980. It would permanently scar journalism.

> Jimmy is 8 years old and a third-generation heroin addict, a precocious little boy with sandy hair, velvety brown eyes and needle marks freckling the baby-smooth skin of his thin brown arms.
>
> He nestles in a large, beige reclining chair in the living room of his comfortably furnished home in Southeast Washington. There is an almost cherubic expression on his small, round face

as he talks about life—clothes, money, the Baltimore Orioles and heroin. He has been an addict since the age of 5.

His hands are clasped behind his head, fancy running shoes adorn his feet, and a striped Izod T-shirt hangs over his thin frame. "Bad, ain't it," he boasts to a reporter visiting recently. "I got me six of these."

Jimmy's is a world of hard drugs, fast money and the good life he believes both can bring. Every day, junkies casually buy heroin from Ron, his mother's live-in lover, in the dining room of Jimmy's home. They "cook" it in the kitchen and "fire up" in the bedrooms. And every day, Ron or someone else fires up Jimmy, plunging a needle into his bony arm, sending the fourth grader into a hypnotic nod.

The story was a stunner, or a bacon burner, as they are called, meaning that once you started reading, you forgot what was on the stove. The particular paragraph that lives on, for many who read the story, was when Cooke vividly, brilliantly—and nauseatingly—described in meticulous detail Jimmy shooting heroin as if she were an eyewitness. Ron "grabs Jimmy's left arm just above the elbow, his massive hand tightly encircling the child's small limb. The needle slides into the boy's soft skin like a straw pushing into the center of a freshly baked cake. Liquid ebbs out of the syringe, replaced by bright red blood. The blood is then re-injected into the child."

The day after "Jimmy's World" ran, Woodward walked over to Cooke's boss on the *District Weekly* and told her that Cooke now worked for him. Janet Cooke had reached her goal faster than even she expected. She had arrived. It had taken only nine months to write a "Holy shit!" story that reverberated across the country. Not only was it a gripping account, but Cooke had bolstered her reputation as a first-class writer. Woodward had been at the *Post* for only nine months when he started on Watergate, but he was known as a terrible writer. Cooke had exceeded even Woodward.

Like Woodward's Watergate reporting, Cooke had relied on anonymity. Coleman and Woodward trusted her, a crucial component in any successful newsroom. "She had been a reporter that we'd never received a complaint about," Woodward told the *New York Times* in April 1981. "In fact, just the opposite. She'd written about things, and people had called and said she got it exactly right and captured the essence of it. She was a trusted reporter with a reputation that had no footnote to it." The quite reasonable newsroom thinking went that pervasive heroin use in D.C. was an important story and best told if it could be proven that even kids were shooting up. Editors let Cooke write the story without using the boy's real name.

"Post Watergate, we were on cloud nine," said Leonard Downie Jr., now the executive editor. "I don't think there was this sense of worry about whether or not you are doing things right. Also, systemically, it was just a different newsroom. Lots of stuff that is now in place wasn't there then." The use of anonymous sources in the post-Watergate era had become so prevalent that no *Post* editor demanded that Cooke prove Jimmy actually existed or even reveal his name. Some outside editors later questioned the *Post*'s trusting a reporter with only nine months' experience on such an important story and never checking her sources. "You have to build a chain of trust with your reporters," Woodward told *Time* in April 1981. "If you attempt to re-report stories, you erect a barrier. I was sympathetic."

Everyone was talking about "Jimmy's World." Some people publicly praised it. Others at the *Post* whispered their concerns. "The day the story appeared," said Thomas Lippman, a metro reporter when the story ran, "I sat in my kitchen and read it and said, 'I don't know any sandy-haired black kid.' The story just didn't ring true to me from the first minute I read it."

About a dozen reporters called each other at home. They didn't believe the story, either. There were no real locations. Nothing was attributed. It read like great fiction. They wondered how their paper could publish such a story. "A group of about six of us went out and tried to find the schoolyard and places she wrote about and tried to document the story," said one *Post* reporter. "Our goal was to protect our newspaper. We couldn't confirm anything. We talked to all the editors at the *Post* about it. Woodward didn't like the fact that we were doing that. The editors thought we shouldn't be doing that."

Anyone who doubted the story's veracity or voiced objections was labeled jealous. "Bob's reaction was that he assigned each of us a motive about why we were doing it," said one suspicious reporter.

City officials and social workers, concerned for the boy's welfare, were equally suspicious when the *Post* refused to share his name. They set out to find Jimmy but never could. The mayor and others viciously attacked the *Post* for being more concerned about the story than about an endangered child, as the mayor actually believed such a child existed. "We went into Watergate mode: protect the source and back the reporter," Woodward said.

Eventually, as happens with any sizzling story, the buzz died down. The story was filed away. In November 1980, a *Post* official asked which stories the paper should nominate for a Pulitzer Prize—a yearly process at newspapers. At the time, the paper had won sixteen of the vaunted prize. Despite strong misgivings from some metro staffers, "Jimmy's World" was nominated. Woodward had heard the mutterings but dismissed them. When he and Bernstein were working on Watergate, several reporters and even the national editor at the time, Richard Harwood, had grumbled that they didn't believe Woodward and Bernstein's stories.

Woodward's attitude was "in for a dime, in for a dollar," said William Prochnau, who was a *Post* national staffer then and played poker with Woodward. Woodward had edited the story and put his stamp on it when it first ran; why should he pull back now? Some reporters had tried to warn Woodward about Cooke, but no one had proven that Jimmy did not exist.

On April 13, 1981, a proud Bradlee announced that Cooke's story had won the Pulitzer for feature writing. Bradlee had loved the story; it was just what he wanted to see in his pages. The judges wrote that the story "was met by a wave of shock and disbelief."

The *Post*'s triumph was short-lived. One day after a wave of ecstasy flooded the newsroom, Bradlee got an unnerving phone call. The *Toledo Blade* had noticed a discrepancy in Cooke's resume. Cooke had not graduated from Vassar, as she had told the *Post*. She had spent only a year there. Much of Cooke's resume was a lie. What else had she lied about?

Post editors jumped on Cooke. Was the Jimmy story true? After ten hours of off and on grilling, Cooke broke down. There was no Jimmy. She had made him up. She resigned immediately.

The *Post* faced the humiliation of giving back a Pulitzer Prize on April 15, 1981. No paper had ever returned a Pulitzer because of a discredited story in the prize's then sixty-four-year history. The paper had to admit to the world that it had printed and stood firmly by a false story. "I think Bob was devastated," said reporter Ted Gup. "But you've got to understand when that landmine went off, we were all equally hit by the shrapnel. All of our hearts were collectively broken."

Cooke had tricked Woodward and everyone else. "In a way, both she and the story were almost too good to be true," said Woodward in the *Post* on April 19, 1981. "I had seen her go out on a complicated story and an hour later turn in a beautifully written piece. This story was so well-written and tied together so well that my alarm bells simply did not go off. My skepticism left me. I was personally negligent." (Later, Woodward would beat himself up for not putting the child's safety first.)

Woodward, at the top of metro's chain of command, offered to resign, although it was not accepted. Woodward alone was not negligent. He had company from other editors, above and below in the hierarchical editorial structure. Later, the *Post* investigated exactly how its system fell apart. "Milton Coleman and Bob Woodward try to take the blame, and well they should. They had primary responsibility," wrote the *Post*'s ombudsman in an unprecedented fourteen-thousand-word piece, four days after the fraud was discovered, that explained how the Cooke fiasco unfolded. "But to place all the burden on them is a huge mistake. . . . It was a complete systems failure, and there's no excuse for it."

Almost a year later, Cooke talked for the first time on the *Phil Donahue Show*. "My whole mind-set was pretty much in the *Washington Post* mentality, which was that [a child heroin addict] must be there and it's being covered up," she said, adding that she felt newsroom pressure "to be first, to be flashiest, to be sensational. I simply wanted to write a story I had been working on so that I would not have to go back and say I cannot do it. I did not want to fail."

Intense competition in a newsroom goes with the territory; Cooke's failings were her own. In the end, she received the punishment that fit the crime: she would never be trusted as a reporter again. Her name became a cautionary tale for ambitious young journalists.

Woodward, the navy man, assumed responsibility for the Cooke deception and invited his staff to his home to talk with him and other editors. Nearly thirty-five staffers showed up, stunned and angry. "This was definitely a low point for Woodward," said metro reporter Karlyn Barker. "But then Woodward did an amazing thing. He had this really frank discussion and took questions about this whole incident. I remember it was extraordinary to be sitting there in Woodward's living room while he made an effort to be accountable to his staff."

It was a smart move, but not calculated. It was just Woodward's way of stepping up to the plate. "I did not get the impression that he was damaged goods after Cooke," said Armstrong. "It was a lesson learned and a blemish on the Golden Boy. But it didn't make a whit of difference in Bradlee's opinion."

The incident, though, had far-ranging consequences for journalism. It was one of the worst blows to press credibility, and Woodward had been directly involved, unlike Bradlee, who knew little about internal skepticism about the story. "There is no question that the biggest journalistic failure in the *Post*'s history blew up on Woodward's watch," said Howard Kurtz, the *Post*'s long-time media critic. "It was a failure that contrasted with the dogged success of Watergate. But I don't think people viewed Woodward at the time as someone who had failed terribly. The paper had failed." Watergate had elevated the *Post*'s and all of journalism's reputations. So it was not surprising that the Cooke hoax not only severely injured the *Post*'s hard-won trustworthiness, but it wounded journalism as well.

For the first time, Woodward was tasting the downside of fame, as there was a certain element of glee among colleagues inside and outside the paper who were happy to see Woodward fall from glory. "When you damage the credibility of the *Post*, you damage the credibility of the *Des Moines Register* and every other paper in the country," commented Michael Gartner, the *Register*'s editor in 1981. Editors of other papers came down hard on the *Post*, mad that they, too, would be tarred by the *Post*'s sloppy editing. The *Virginian-Pilot* of Norfolk, Virginia, accused *Post* editors of allowing "their love of a good story to overcome the duty to nail down the facts." "I think it was pretty badly handled," said John McMullan, then the editor of the *Miami Herald*, "on the part of the *Washington Post* editors. I think there's been too much reliance on the part of some newspapers on using confidential sources."

For a while, Janet Cooke cooled the use of anonymous sources in journalism, but that restraint was short-lived. For Woodward, confidential sources remained essential.

The Cooke imbroglio ended any chance of the thirty-eight-year-old Woodward becoming executive editor, although it was not the only reason. "The Cooke affair was devastating for Bob," said Ted Gup, a former investigative reporter under Woodward. "Bob was at the helm. If you are at the helm, you get the credit, you get the blame. Bob championed her in ways that were not only excusable but commendable. Maybe it did spell the end of his aspirations to be executive editor."

Woodward was not cut out for management, however, which is not all that unusual in the news business. It's a common mistake for terrific reporters to believe that management is the next obvious step, although a talented reporter does not necessarily have the right skill set to be a great editor. "It turned out he wasn't very good at that," said Bradlee. "So that experiment didn't last very long. He showed no great skills there. There's nothing wrong with that. I always think it's totally amazing that I showed any skills in that. If you want to scare me, talk about work schedules and vacation relief. I can't stand that."

Neither, it seems, could Woodward. He wasn't good at managing a large, complex staff. Nor did he have the temperament or patience for it, say many people who watched him as metro editor. "He doesn't deal with lots of other people well at the same time," said a *Post* editor who has known him for three decades. "When he has a lot of people working for him, he's just not going to be interested in all of them and what they are all doing. And talk to them all and floor walk. It's just not what he does. He deals with people one on one. That's the great virtue of his reporting. It's also why he works well with research assistants, because they do a lot of the other stuff that he's not so good at."

Leaving the metro desk would make things easier on Woodward's love life. Around the time Cooke was hired, Woodward, thirty-seven, had hired another young ambitious woman for the *Weekly* staff. Her name was Elsa Walsh. She was twenty-three and a UC Berkeley graduate, and she fell for Woodward the first time she met him—but not as quickly as Woodward fell for her. A friend, Jim Wooten, asked *Post* reporter Sally Quinn to have coffee with Walsh, who was living in Wooten's basement apartment while babysitting his cats and sometimes his kids. Quinn instantly liked Walsh, who is often described as a tall, dark-haired Irish beauty. She arranged for Walsh to meet the metro editor and took Walsh to Woodward's office. Walsh, fourteen years younger than Woodward, was about to meet a journalistic legend. She had been seventeen when Nixon resigned, but she'd read *All the President's Men*. She was nervous. "Elsa walked into Bob's office and sat down," said Quinn. "Bob's jaw dropped to the floor. He fell madly in love with her that very minute. I watched it happen. It was just extraordinary. He knew that very minute. So I was standing there and Elsa was all nervous with her hands clasped on her lap. Bob was standing there with his mouth opened. So I said, 'I guess I'll just leave you two together,' and closed the door."

Walsh was hired. Yet newsroom relationships are complicated, and none more so than when a reporter is dating her editor. The imbalance in the relationship, the obvious newsroom gossip, and suspicion that Walsh might get favorable treatment slowed the progress of what would become, by all accounts, a great love affair. Ironically, Walsh became part of the Janet Cooke drama. She and Cooke, who had become friendly while working, began sharing an apartment a few months before Cooke was exposed. "Janet was hard to live with, very high-strung," Walsh recalled in the ombudsman piece. "She bought clothes lavishly. Every day she talked about her ambitions. She had no sense of the past or even the present, except for its consequences for the future. She always looked to the future, and she didn't care about the people she left behind." Walsh had never believed the Jimmy story but also never said anything to Woodward, highlighting the complexity of a reporter and editor dating. "Janet Cooke is every editor's nightmare," said a longtime *Post* editor. "Isn't it ironic, though, that the most suspicious guy in the newsroom wasn't suspicious of his girlfriend's roommate? The *Post's* most dogged reporter got snookered by

Janet Cooke. Some people would say he didn't suffer. Well, he did. As a journalist, I think it pains him today."

After the Cooke incident, Woodward found a job better suited for him. Bradlee created a special investigative unit, known as the SWAT team, for Woodward. He retained the title of assistant managing editor, which included coming in on weekends several times a year to get out the all-important Sunday paper. (Woodward continued a rotation as an editor in charge of putting out the Sunday paper for two decades after this.) In his new job, Woodward had the freedom to investigate whatever he wanted. He was given eight full-time reporters and editors, and a healthy budget. In the early 1980s, it was unusual for a newspaper to have such a big investigative unit since the payoff is generally not a wise economic investment—often reporters spend weeks, months, or even a year working on one story. After Watergate, though, it became popular for TV and newspapers to have an investigative unit or individual reporters specifically designated as "investigative reporters."

Woodward had almost left the *Post*. After the Cooke incident, in 1982 CBS News execs wooed Woodward, offering him far more money than he was making at the *Post* and a chance to run his own investigative unit and appear on air. It was tempting. Ten years after Watergate, Woodward's salary was only $45,000, according to a 1987 article in *Washingtonian* magazine. CBS promised several hundred thousand dollars. Woodward, having seen his friend Sally Quinn bomb as a coanchor at *CBS Morning News* in 1973 and having watched Bernstein struggle at ABC, decided to stay put. The *Post* and Bradlee provided Woodward with an immeasurable sense of security.

For Woodward's next project, he ventured out of his comfort zone. This time it was a book that chose him. In 1982, Woodward started looking into what had happened to the beloved master of physical comedy John Belushi, who died at thirty-three in a Los Angeles hotel after a toxic injection of cocaine and heroin. Why would Woodward set aside his Washington status to take on a Hollywood story? It's hard not to read deeply into the choice. Like Woodward, Belushi was a strongly driven man who had reached the highest professional heights while still in his twenties. Belushi had also grown up in Wheaton, Illinois, Woodward's hometown, although they had not known each other. Woodward had watched Belushi as an early cast member on *Saturday Night Live* and had seen the 1978 smash hit *Animal House*, and he loved the talented man.

Four months after the manic comedian's tragic death, his widow, Judy Jacklin Belushi, contacted Woodward, the country's premier investigative reporter. She had not been with her husband the night he died. She thought that the Los Angeles Police Department was covering something up. Belushi's story intrigued Woodward on a personal level and provided a respite from digging in government. He felt an odd connection to Belushi. Like Woodward, Belushi had experienced sudden dizzying success. At the time, *Animal House* was the top-grossing comedy in Hollywood history. After one season on *SNL*, Belushi's salary jumped from $750 a week to $100,000 a year. "I was kind of angry that somebody I never met," Woodward said, "somebody clearly so talented, was essentially allowed to kill himself." Woodward wanted to know more about the failure of success.

Judy Belushi opened up her heart and her diaries to Woodward. She encouraged John's friends and Hollywood associates to talk to the famous Watergate reporter. She alone talked with him thirty-two times. He spent nearly two years on the book and talked to 267 sources—getting 217 on the record, according to *Wired: The Short Life and Fast Times of John Belushi*, which debuted in June 1984. What was unusual about *Wired* was that for the first and only time, Woodward used detailed endnotes, and nearly everything was on the record.

Once again, Simon & Schuster rolled out the red carpet for another Woodward extravaganza—the super-sleuth's first book without a partner. *Wired* was excerpted in *Playboy* and some fifty newspapers, and the Post ran eight installments in late May 1984. Some people considered eight days excessive, claiming that the paper was shilling for Woodward's publisher on the *Post*'s front pages. Bradlee disagreed. Belushi was a tragic, popular cultural figure emblematic of the times, he said. Besides, anything with Woodward's name on it "has an impact other names wouldn't have." The *Washington Post* had special rules for its star reporter.

Over time, they would earn Woodward the nickname Mr. Carte Blanche.

Woodward's fourth book got mediocre reviews. Most critics decried the dispassionate writing style where he flatly laid out well-reported sordid fact after sordid fact. "The same dogged investigative ability that has served Mr. Woodward and his readers so well in earlier works seems oddly inappropriate here. Page after page is dense with irrelevant detail," wrote Joe McGinniss in a *New York Times* review. "Perhaps a writer with a different sensibility could have imbued this story with tragic dimension, or at least he might have aroused empathy in us." Nonetheless, the book became a best seller, with 300,000 copies printed.

Yet the one person who had most wanted Woodward to write a book—Judy Belushi—hated it. She even sued unsuccessfully to stop publication of the first 175,000 copies, claiming that Woodward illegally used photographs. She and John Belushi's Hollywood friends accused Woodward of taking advantage of their grief and trust. "I only ever read about six pages of *Wired* and found it despicable," Belushi friend and actor Bill Murray, who had participated in the book, told the *Times* of London in 1988. "I mean, this is America's foremost journalist? He should be put to death."

Woodward had written in painstaking detail about the rampant use of drugs in Hollywood, and he had named names. He took notes right in front of actors and directors as they confessed to using drugs or told lurid tales. "Everyone talked at great length," Woodward told me. "[Actor] Dan Aykroyd about using heroin. Judy Belushi about her episodes, and walking this nightmare road. It's a very grim story. Yeah, unrelenting, but that's the way it was. It's all reported. There was no friendship and a safety net in that circle to save him. I think it would have been morally offensive for me to try to please."

Belushi's friends hated it, but no one successfully proved Woodward to be inaccurate. They accused him of being tone deaf, of writing the words without the music. "I hated Woodward's book because I don't believe he made an honest attempt to understand John, who despite his sometimes gruff exterior was a gentle soul," wrote friend and comedian Al Franken in *Variety* in 1999. "My former partner Tom Davis put it this way: 'It's as if someone did your college yearbook and called it 'Puked.' And all it did was say who puked, when they puked and what they puked. But no one learned any history, read Dostoevsky for the first time, or fell in love.'"

The backlash intrigued a young *Rolling Stone* reporter, Lynn Hirschberg, who at twenty-two was assigned to write a cover story. She was dazzled, she admits, by the "great Bob Woodward." She would get the chance to meet and interview him. She got the Woodward treatment and in the process, she said two decades later, learned a valuable journalistic lesson.

"[Publisher] Jann Wenner was friends with Judy Belushi and gave Judy quote approval without telling me," said Hirschberg, editor at large for the *New York Times* magazine. "Here's where I got really stupid. I thought Bob Woodward was my protector. I started confiding in Bob Woodward about the Judy thing. At the time, my refrigerator was broken. He was calling me so often that he was asking me if I had gotten it fixed yet. He seemed to have an enormous interest in my life, which, of course, was very flattering. What I didn't realize was that he was taking notes on every one of our phone conversations. He wrote this letter to Jann, quoting me at length, and said the ethics of this piece are in question. Bob Woodward also sent the letter to Liz Smith and all the gossip columnists. It was my fault for confiding in him. I've never been surprised when someone said something to him that seemed highly classified because I had the experience of being caught in his high beams."

Woodward, though, was caught off guard by the vicious Hollywood attacks, especially since most of the book was on the record. "My books are true," Woodward told me. "It's not that they turn out to be true. *Wired* was heavily footnoted and I still get, 'Well, you don't show that having drugs can be fun.' These were the people who were Belushi's friends. I guess I say: 'Where was the remorse?' Because I felt it. I felt it on their behalf. Look, I'm in the business of writing about controversial subjects or things that are going on contemporaneous. There are going to be people who aren't going to like it."

Around this time, Bernstein couldn't help notice that others seemed to delight in the dynamic duo's woes. "So Bob writes *Wired* and gets the s— kicked out of him by the critics; my marriage falls apart and it becomes a national soap opera," Bernstein said in a 1986 *Playboy* interview. "Some of this goes with the territory, and some we've helped along ourselves. Some has been helped along by other people, some of whom wish you ill. We've had plenty of shots taken at us, some deserved, some self-inflicted, some wild-assed, and you get used to occupying that territory."

After *Wired*, Woodward spent more time with his SWAT team. His tenure there was mixed. Woodward was in charge, but he wasn't always around. Some reporters wanted more of his attention; others didn't like how intense he was. "If you needed handholding, or you were wasteful of your time, or didn't keep your end in sight over a long stretch of time, then you were not someone who was going to benefit from Woodward," said Ted Gup, who worked on the SWAT team at its inception and remains fond of him. "The people who prospered under him were people like him who were single-minded." But there was another complaint. Ronald Kessler was part of the original team. Woodward had been best man at Kessler's 1979 wedding. But their styles clashed. "He would try to become a substitute for the reporter," said Kessler, who left the paper in 1985, and has written several books about the intelligence community. "He didn't know how to edit in a sensitive way. I think he felt a certain competitiveness with other investigative reporters at that time. There seemed to be a lot of emphasis on sociological stories that were not really what I would consider investigative. He seemed to like that. I had trouble working with him. There wasn't the finesse there that was needed as an editor." He and Woodward are no longer friends.

10

Loyalties

People think Carl is sloppy. He is not. He is very meticulous. Very professional. [But] you never know with Carl, when he is going to be working very hard or not working at all. There is a kind of arrogance to him. It's as if he's convinced that six hours of his work is worth twenty hours of someone else's. And he's probably right.

— Woodward on Bernstein, talking to David Halberstam
in the mid-1970s

Woodward was able to keep his bearings despite a thunderstorm of criticism after the Belushi book. It was nothing like the criticism he and Bernstein had weathered during Watergate. He had learned how to categorize the attacks as being about his work and not take them personally. Besides, he possessed a great deal of confidence about the accuracy of his work. It was hard to unhinge Woodward.

For Bernstein, however, life in the spotlight was more difficult. In the decade after Watergate, he didn't have much, if anything, to show for his early successes. He'd blown through hundreds of thousands of dollars, produced a few strong pieces at ABC, but still had not finished the book on his parents. In fact, Bernstein's "writing a book" had become somewhat of a joke in literary circles and among friends. "I worried that he wouldn't finish it," said *Post* buddy Robert Kaiser. By 1989, Woodward had written a TV miniseries, dozens of newspaper articles, and three best-selling books without Bernstein. He had finessed his way past the potentially career-ending Janet Cooke debacle into a role as respected head of the *Post*'s investigative unit and had maintained the title assistant managing editor.

Woodward was still winning accolades for his work; Bernstein got attention for the women he squired. Bernstein's womanizing has always been legendary—before Watergate, after Watergate, while married, and long after he was no longer somebody's husband. While Woodward was getting rave book reviews, public attention focused laserlike on Bernstein's messy personal life.

Bernstein had stopped drinking and smoking but not carousing. He still showed up regularly in the gossip columns because of the flashy women he dated. Once while living in New York, he was seen enough in 1985 to be written about with the much-married Elizabeth Taylor. When he famously told ex-wife Ephron about Taylor—twelve years his senior—Ephron told him he had to leave her apartment immediately because she needed to call her friends. When Bernstein's sister Mary was getting married, she told her older brother that under no condition was he to bring Elizabeth Taylor to her wedding; she did not want to be upstaged on her wedding day.

In 1988, he made news, though not the kind he liked, when he started showing up at New York hot spots with Bianca Jagger, Rolling Stones legend Mick Jagger's long-ago wife, and then with actress Shirley MacLaine. Bernstein's name appeared in the news more than his byline did. In the 1980s, he was still famous for Watergate, but he had gained another persona, as a party animal better known for spending beyond his means, dining with the glitterati at Elaine's, and dating the stars the paparazzi got paid to shoot. He was famous just for being Carl Bernstein.

"People notice Carl," said his friend songwriter Judy Collins. "He's a legendary person. His work or whatever he does is going to be watched, because he is a legendary person. It's an important piece of his life. So when he goes to a party, he gets noticed and it's great." Or not. When he got behind on rent for his $4,000-a-month Upper East Side apartment in 1986, it made the newspapers. The attention also confirmed that he had arrived; he was one of New York City's beautiful people. Woodward was not, nor did he want to be. "Bob is bulletproof. You can't turn his head easily," said a longtime friend of both men, Richard Cohen. "He's not the kind of guy who craves celebrity or has to go to every party. Carl did. I can't say honestly it didn't change him. He clearly had a lot of money. He had access to people and fame. And he also had authority. He was going to meet people I read about. All of a sudden, he went from the no-list to the A-list. All of a sudden, I heard these names coming out of his mouth. You know him? You know her? Carl didn't go up the ladder; he just took a rocket. But he could always laugh at himself. He never got to be a pompous idiot."

He sometimes appeared that way in print, though. In April 1988, *Spy* magazine, the irreverent now-defunct monthly, poked fun at Bernstein's bon vivant lifestyle by creating a tongue-in-cheek Ironman Nightlife Decathlon. The magazine chose two other carousing Casanovas and shadowed them and Bernstein clubbing in New York City on a weeknight: "March 29, 2:40 AM: From our position outside the club we see Bernstein depart with Lauren Hutton. Apparently eager to continue his relentless questioning for a possible profile of one of America's former top models, America's top journalist attempts to slip into her cab. She prevents this by slamming the door. He hails his own cab." *Spy* used to refer to Bernstein as a "coaster," that is, someone who once did something great and now is coasting.

"Carl and a couple of other people were these sort of ubiquitous party animals—he would turn up at an envelope opening," said Kurt Andersen, *Spy*'s former editor. "We would get in pictures that a photographer took at a party, and he would appear in them again and again. There were a few others like him—Jay McInerney, Anthony Haden-Guest. So we decided to create a mocking notion of a competition among these party guys of a certain age. We began collecting these pictures as if they were engaged in this competition, which we called the Nightlife Ironman Decathlon."

Bernstein didn't win, but he came in second.

"It is a tale of two cities," Woodward told the now-defunct *Fame* magazine in 1989. "There's a Carl of Washington, who is associated with work. And there's a Carl of New York, who is associated with social life. And for a long time, all many people saw was the Carl of New York."

In New York, Bernstein stayed on the A-list in the 1980s and began to count A-list names as close friends, such as Judy Collins, the writer Joan Didion, the playwright Eve Ensler, and the actor Alec Baldwin, all of whom he suggested I call when I first interviewed him. "New York is somewhere you can go after you've done something and become famous, and even if you never do anything again, you can be famous for that," said Karlyn Barker, a *Post* reporter who dated Bernstein briefly before Watergate. "In Washington, it's always 'What have you done lately?'—particularly in the journalism world. I don't think Carl could have hobnobbed with famous people as much if he had stayed in Washington."

Part of hobnobbing includes becoming fodder for gossip columnists, and Bernstein was easy prey. When George Rush was working for the *New York Post*'s hungry Page Six, he pursued what he considered a delicious Bernstein story. While Bernstein was dancing in clubs and squiring gorgeous women, he was also often broke. "It is not a secret that finances are not my strong suit," Bernstein said, acknowledging that he blew through a lot of money without much thought to saving. "Some might judge it profligate. I didn't see the need to invest for the future."

Rush once got a call from an exasperated Upper East Side deli owner, at whose store Bernstein often bought sandwiches and coffee. "He complained that Carl hadn't paid his bill. I don't remember how much the bill was, maybe just under $1,000," said Rush. "It was in that period when people were asking, 'Whatever happened to Carl Bernstein?'—even before the book on his parents. So we called Carl. He said, 'I want to deal with this. I'm on the other line. Let me call you right back.'" Bernstein never called back, but the deli man did. Bernstein had come in to pay his bill. "Around that time we also did a story about his feud with his landlord," said Rush. "The landlord's lawyer supplied us letters. You would see these letters complaining about the ceiling cracks and the plaster falling. It was the full energy of the guy who cracked Watergate fighting with his landlord." Yet it was telling— if someone had a beef with Bernstein, they could take it to ravenous gossip writers who would spit something out because it was Carl Bernstein.

"You can't control what everybody says about you, particularly if you are somewhat of a public person," Bernstein told me. "I don't see myself [as a public person], but I am aware that I am. I mean, I'd be naive to say I'm not aware of it. But if you can't have some irony about yourself or laugh at yourself, take some of this a little lightly. There've been times I'm sure I haven't. By it, I mean the attention. Times when I probably haven't had enough detachment or irony." Gradually, however, he came to see the benefit of being more detached.

Not only was Bernstein criticized for living an indolent lifestyle, but because of it, and because of his famous association with Woodward, he was constantly held up to the hyperproductive Woodward and shown wanting. In 1986, Bernstein sat down with *Playboy* for a fairly brutal Q&A by Tony Schwartz.

> PLAYBOY: You've had a lot of bad press, some of it about how little you seem to have done in the decade since Watergate. What do you think of your output?
>
> BERNSTEIN: I've got my life. I've got my children. I've got my work. I don't make sausages. I don't measure my work by sheer output. I'm more interested in the quality of what goes into it, the continuing quality of the product. I'm proud of the work I've done since I was 16 years old. I'd be glad to hold it up against any standard. Would I like to see more? Sure, I'd always like to see more.
>
> PLAYBOY: Still, you have one of the two most famous names in journalism. And the perception is that Woodward has been, and continues to be, a major success.
>
> BERNSTEIN: He should be. He's the best journalist in the business.
>
> PLAYBOY: And the perception of you is much more mixed.
>
> BERNSTEIN: I totally agree.

In his forties, Bernstein wrestled with the desire for, and the meaning of, fame and tried to come out the other end to structure a life with import and respect. What he faced at forty-two was typical for any middle-aged man, but he had to deal with it in celebrity magazines. "Like many other men his age, he has had women problems and career problems," wrote Graydon Carter in a 1986 *GQ* piece. "In gossip columns he is often portrayed as a philandering husband and a clam-handed nitwit who outrages hostesses by dragging his elbow through the dip or having a run-in with an ex-girlfriend's paramour." One woman, with no celebrity pedigree, who had dated him around this time, said that he pursued her ardently with flowers, chicken soup, and extravagant gestures that didn't befit a budding relationship. Once she slept with him, he stopped calling.

Gradually, Bernstein began to think seriously about his unfinished book—partly because he also needed the money. "I really have seen him change. I probably started to be more friendly with him around the early '80s," said singer Judy Collins. "I didn't know him personally during the low period, but as he came out of it, I got to know him. Getting your life cleared up is a big start. I must say, like Carl, I too had great outward success while my life was a mess. That's an interesting thing to contemplate. How does that happen? It's living two lives, and to have the discipline to do that and keep trying to destroy yourself at the same time, that's a big job."

Bernstein eventually grew tired of a divided life and settled into finally finishing *Progressive People*. He had started this book about his parents in 1977 while living the landed gentry life in Bridgehampton with Ephron in their $240,000 turn-of-the-century country house. So much had happened since then; he no longer had the money he once did or the house, but he had another decade of life experience to work with.

"You know, we're all fighting our demons," Woodward told me, "and I have the utmost respect and admiration for the way he has learned to control his." Bernstein's friend Joan Didion helped him get back to the book, but he also said that he felt freer to return to his manuscript after he'd forced Ephron to modify the movie version of *Heartburn*.

Bernstein's choice of books said as much about his methods as Woodward's did. Woodward always chose institutions—the press, the White House, the Supreme Court—cloaked in mystery, so that he could expose them. Bernstein was more drawn to people, so he started his first solo book with a story he felt truly passionate about: his own.

If, in the past, Bernstein had been accused of not following Woodward's example, he'd make up for it with this book. In 1986, he spent a lot of time flying to Washington and working on his book on the third floor of Woodward's house known affectionately as the Factory, because that's where the prolific Woodward continues to churn out copy. Woodward was a good influence on Bernstein, who realized that he needed to get away from New York to write. "Bob is incredibly disciplined. If he says he is going to write ten pages a day, he's going to write ten pages," said Barbara Feinman, Woodward's assistant during this period. "He's not distracted by normal human temptations. He's just single-minded like nobody I've ever known. He won't be tempted by phone calls or hunger or people stopping by, or anything. The way he set up his writing life, there are very few interruptions." Feinman would arrive at 8:30 a.m. and Woodward would already be at his computer. Long after she left at night, Woodward was still at work. Food was an inconvenient distraction. "We'd break for lunch, when I reminded him it was time to eat," said Feinman. "We'd break for dinner when Elsa would remind him. If it weren't for Elsa, I probably wouldn't have eaten." Walsh said her husband regularly gets up at 4:30 a.m.

For a few months, Feinman worked as an assistant for Bernstein, trying to help him stay on track whenever Woodward wasn't telling him: "Work! Work!" Feinman is one of the rare people, after Watergate, who got a front-row seat as the former partners once again worked side by side, off and on, reading each other's copy on their separate books. "They are very close in their own unique way," she said. "They have enormous affection for each other, and they both understand each other's shortcomings and accept those shortcomings. They are loyal to each other, like brothers. And like brothers, they have their differences. They have a lifelong bond; they went through something together that was so big and that they alone share. They probably would not have become or stayed friends had Watergate not happened, because they are so different and they order their universes so differently. But Watergate did happen, and they are inextricably a part of each other's history."

In this way, Woodward, who some say feels a perverse loyalty to Bernstein, not unlike survivor's guilt, helped push his friend to finish his 260-page book called *Loyalties: A Son's Memoir*. It would be three more years before it appeared in print—twelve years after he had started. His parents still did not want him to write the book, but he felt he had to. Along the way, when Bernstein got stuck, Woodward was there. (Besides dedicating the book to his parents and his two sons, Bernstein dedicated it to Woodward and another friend.) Once, before the book was published in 1989, Bernstein sat in Woodward's car as Woodward interviewed him. Bernstein told the story of how he'd gotten into a playground fight with a kid who had called Bernstein's mother a communist. He was ten. He didn't know what a communist was, but the taunting tone convinced him that it was not good. He tore the kid's clothes and banged his head in the dirt, shoving sand into his mouth. As he told the story, the memory was so vivid that Bernstein, shaking, began to cry. He couldn't continue until he had taken several deep breaths. When Bernstein regained his composure, Woodward asked, "Did you go after him because you thought it was false, or because you were worried it was true?"

Bernstein didn't know. "I don't think you have any ability to know," he wrote in *Loyalties*. "I don't know if it was my anger with him, anger with my mother, with my parents, who knows? It just kind of ignited a rod, a flare of fury."

The book is a memoir about growing up with communist parents in the 1950s. Bernstein tells of his parents' ordeal as party members and how it affected the family, particularly him. As a freckle-faced adolescent known as "Chips," he had no idea really what it all meant. He was a red-blooded patriot who sold Defense Bond stamps and was the class air-raid warden, but he always wondered about his parents' political leanings. At eight, he asked his father if he was a communist. "I remember the silence that followed and my not daring to look at him. . . . My question offered no escape; there is no Fifth Amendment for eight-year-olds." The next time Bernstein asked, he was thirty-three and had begun to think about writing the book. Part of the reason it took so long was not his own admitted lack of discipline, but rather that he found it so emotionally painful to mine the memories. "Probably it was [my parents' friends] the Gellers' descriptions of the chaos and tensions in [my] house—the excavation of that part of our lives—that, as much as anything, led me to abandon the book and sent me scurrying back to the safer precincts of conventional journalism," he wrote. Aside from revisiting the turmoil he'd grown up with, he dreaded what he might find. "There was always the fear that I would stumble onto something," he wrote, "fall upon some parental Pumpkin Paper that would forever close me off to my parents." To write the book, Bernstein filed Freedom of Information requests and received 2,500 pages of FBI documents on his parents, who had been under surveillance for communist activities. They formed a pile of paper two feet high.

Bernstein's father, Alfred, a lawyer, was emotionally unavailable to him after he lost his union job for representing more than five hundred people who refused to sign Harry Truman's 1947 loyalty oath. On July 14, 1954, when he was ten, his mother, Sylvia, was called to testify before the House Committee on Un-American Activities. She refused, taking the Fifth Amendment; the next day her picture was on the front page of the *Washington Daily News*. The fallout was immediate. Bernstein's play date with a local florist's son was canceled. The boy's mother saw Bernstein in the front yard and told him, "Your mother's a communist," and said that her son could not play with Bernstein. His sister, Mary, was thrown out of nursery school, and his mother's sister stopped speaking to the family. Her husband had told her to choose between him and her sister, Sylvia. She did not choose Sylvia. Bernstein never knew why the two families stopped seeing one another. When Julius and Ethel Rosenberg were executed in June 1953, the nine-year-old Bernstein wept hysterically, for them and out of an indefinable fear that this could happen to his parents.

The book is a mixture of memories, interviews with his parents and their friends, FBI documents, and historical research. Walter Isaacson, writing in *Time* magazine, called it an "investigative memoir." "A good memoir should produce shocks of recognition that are both intimate and historical, revealing truths about a person and about his times," he wrote. "Bernstein provides both, in abundance. It combines the journalistic thrill of Watergate with the emotional punch of that most basic of literary themes, a boy's search to understand his father."

Loyalties went a long way toward explaining Bernstein's sometimes manic energy, his distrust and dislike of authority, and why he had battled his editors at every turn. What he had unearthed was revealing to Bernstein himself; the FBI, he discovered, had kept his family under surveillance for years. They had even infiltrated his bar mitzvah.

"The context of Carl's own life hasn't been paid adequate attention to by the people who write about him," said his friend Robert Kaiser. "Growing up in this left-wing Jewish atheistic milieu, where his father is persecuted by the government and makes a living defending other victims of the persecution, had to have an effect. [Richard] Cohen and I went to the funeral of some relative—maternal grandparents or one of Carl's grandparents. It was a wildly revelatory moment for me. It was before *Loyalties* came out. Carl had joked about the fact that his family was divided between the Stalinists and the Trotskyites. There were these factions that barely abided each other's politics but personally got along. Suddenly before us in this Jewish funeral home, there they were. The Trotskyites and the Stalinists. It suddenly hit me what a huge thing it was for this family that their Carl had played this central role in bringing down what, for them, was one of the leading villains of the twentieth century. It was a miracle really that Nixon or Mitchell or anybody never managed to smear Carl with his parents' past."

It *was* a miracle, considering how mean-spirited and vindictive Nixon proved to be. In 1973, managing editor Howard Simons told Bernstein when he and Woodward interviewed Simons for *All the President's Men*, that he and Ben Bradlee had briefly worried that the administration would try to compromise the paper.

> CB: Did the business with my parents' background ever bother you at all? I mean, what you knew about it.
>
> HS: Oh, yeah. That came very late, Carl. It came very late when we were told that your mother, that they knew your mother was a communist.
>
> CB: Well, that she had been named by Nixon's subcommittee. [In 1973, Bernstein did not know for sure that his mother had been a Communist Party member.]
>
> HS: Right. Whatever it is. But you had harbored a resentment all your childhood and beyond to get even with him. That didn't bother us. No, up until that point, that never crossed our minds.

What Bernstein learned as he pushed his parents to dredge up the past that they wanted to forget was that, yes, they were communists, but they were not anarchists advocating the overthrow of the government. They were idealists, more like civil rights activists, who wanted to transform society—not unlike what their son would do decades later, although he had never set out to overthrow a criminal American president. Yet it's significant that Bernstein was determined to reveal his family's secret past in print, even though his parents continued to ask him not to. In the book's postscript, Bernstein admits that his father refused to read the final manuscript, resigned to the inevitability that his son would betray his request. "Nevertheless, he wanted to register his disapproval in the strongest terms," Bernstein wrote. Somehow, though, in the process of writing the book, Bernstein found a sense of peace that helped him to resolve the tumult of his past. His mother and his father, like any parents who adore their son, did not disown him after the book came out but reached resolution and forgiveness. In the end, Bernstein's book brought him closer to his mother and father, who remained married for sixty-three years until his father died at age ninety-two in February 2003 and his mother nine months later at eighty-eight.

"Long before I ever knew what Carl looked like, I knew his parents," said Harry Rosenfeld, the former *Post* Watergate editor. "Whatever his good contributions to the *Post* were, he was sort of a prankster and a pain in the neck, and they knew that. But I liked his parents. They were nice, warm-hearted, decent people. I knew they were left-liberal, but I didn't know if they were specifically communist. Many people thought Carl shouldn't have written *Loyalties*, that it was unkind to his parents. I am a parent, and I had difficulty with his book. There was no one holding a gun to his head, saying to tell the truth about whether his parents were communist." Loyal Woodward had only praise. "People for too long have been reviewing Carl's life and not his work," Woodward told *Vanity Fair* in a 1989 profile of Bernstein. "This book is a powerful way to get a dose of history. His father and mother come out heroes, but you see the concealment that they've had to live, and the pressure that's generated. I've never read anything quite like it."

Loyalties came out to mixed reviews and had disappointing sales, but it was finished.

"It was really hard, really hard to write, partly because of my parents' obvious disapproval," Bernstein said. "You've got to let books speak for themselves. I can't say whether it's self-conscious or not. I've never gone back to reread a book that I've written. But I occasionally will look inside one, and usually it's *Loyalties* for a few pages. It seems to me that every once in a while in *Loyalties*, I see a tone that may border on, not usually, but occasionally, a moment that could use a little irony and a little less self-absorption. And even at one moment or so, perhaps self-pity. So I blanch a little when I read that. But basically, I think it's the best writing I've ever done." After a hard fight, Bernstein, at forty-five, had completed his first book alone. Its debut brought renewed interest in Bernstein. Profilers in *Vanity Fair*, *New York*, *Vogue*, *Rolling Stone*, *Fame*, the *Washington Post* magazine, and dozens of newspaper stories could not help but describe *Loyalties* as the long-awaited return of the Watergate legend. Much was made of the acknowledgments. He thanks, among others: Elizabeth Taylor, Joan Didion, Lillian Hellman, Alec Baldwin, Eve Ensler, Shirley MacLaine, Nora Ephron (yes!), Margaret Jay (yes!), Hendrik Hertzberg, and Victor Navasky. "It's a 'Who's Who' of who he's dated," said an old friend. "The acknowledgments say everything about Carl."

Each profile rehashed the stunning achievement of Watergate, followed by Bernstein's slip into the whirlpool of fame. In a thorough *Washington Post* magazine piece, it was mentioned that among various public humiliations Bernstein had suffered, one particularly smarted. Bernstein, who had once brought such honor to the *Post*, was not invited to publisher Katharine Graham's seventieth birthday extravaganza in 1987, while Woodward was.

In 1990, shortly after Bernstein rode the wave of attention from his book—appearing on *David Letterman*, *Good Morning, America*, and other shows—he signed a contract to write for *Time* magazine. When he was sent over to Iraq to cover the unrest there several weeks before the outbreak of the first Gulf War, he reportedly took along copies of *All the President's Men* to pass out to sources. He wrote one piece about how the Iraqis loathed their leader Saddam Hussein, which got him kicked out of the country, but not before he picked up a pair of camel saddlebags to decorate his eclectically designed New York apartment. It was a 1992 story that Bernstein wrote for *Time*, however, that led to his next book project, though it was not one he would write alone. In the story, Bernstein took on an even more powerful leader than the president of the United States: Pope John Paul II.

His controversial fifty-four-hundred-word *Time* cover story claimed that a secret alliance between the pope, President Ronald Reagan, and the CIA had played a crucial role in bringing down Poland's communist regime. As the head of the worldwide Catholic Church, the pope is supposed to be a spiritual leader, not a calculating politician, as Bernstein claimed in his story. A Vatican spokesman, without denying the story, simply said that it was "bizarre." Bernstein made the case that in the 1980s, Reagan and the pope had secretly joined forces to keep the Solidarity union alive in Poland toward the end of the Cold War. In a 1982 meeting between Reagan and the pope at the Vatican, the pair "agreed to undertake a clandestine campaign to hasten the dissolution of the communist empire," wrote Bernstein. "Both the Pope and the President were convinced that Poland could be broken out of the Soviet orbit if the Vatican and the U.S. committed their resources to destabilizing the Polish government and keeping the outlawed Solidarity movement alive after the declaration of martial law in 1981. Until Solidarity's legal status was restored in 1989 it flourished underground, supplied, nurtured and advised largely by the network established under the auspices of Reagan and John Paul II."

After Bernstein's contract with *Time* ended in 1992, he wrote a piece for the *New Republic* on the contemporary media culture, which would become a theme he has used during hundreds of speeches to colleges, conferences, and Jewish organizations. He had grown disgusted with the media, blaming it for promoting the cult of celebrity and gossip—the very same thing that he'd been ensnared in. He attacked the media—especially gossip columns—for its shallowness. "I always liked Carl," said Liz Smith, the gossip columnist with the *New York Post*. "He used to be very sexy. And fun. But after he took out after me as the devil incarnate of gossip, we didn't see each other. Then later we did. He has pretty much been on his uppers since his jobs with ABC and *Time* ended. I tried to help him by writing about the book he did on the fifties and the Red scare, but nothing could help that."

It wasn't just gossip writers he was after, though; he took on the mainstream media and the twenty-four-hour cable shows.

"We are in the process of creating, in sum, what deserves to be called the idiot culture," Bernstein wrote on the twentieth anniversary of the Watergate break-in. "Not an idiot subculture, which every society has bubbling beneath the surface and which can provide harmless fun; but the culture itself. For the first time in our history the weird and the stupid and the coarse are becoming our cultural norm, even our cultural ideal. . . . Yes, we have always had a sensational, popular, yellow tabloid press; and we have always had gossip columns, even powerful ones like Hedda Hopper's and Walter Winchell's. But never before have we had anything like today's situation in which supposedly serious people—I mean the so-called intellectual and social elites of this country— live and die by (and actually believe!) these columns and these shows and millions more rely upon them for their primary source of information." Bernstein continued to riff on this theme, decrying the media's fascination with sleaze whenever he spoke. Unlike Woodward, who kept his opinions to himself, Bernstein felt an obligation to criticize the media in hopes of changing it.

Because of his *Time* assignment on the pope, Bernstein was offered a chance to expand his much-disputed cover story into a book. He took it, working on the manuscript over the next two years. During this period, he turned fifty and threw a party to celebrate the half-century mark at his loft in the West Village. Woodward came; so did his good friend Shirley MacLaine (who had accompanied him to Liz Taylor's sixtieth birthday party at Disneyland) and the playwright Eve Ensler, author of *The Vagina Monologues*. "At Carl's fiftieth birthday, Shirley MacLaine was there and we were kvelling about how wonderful Carl is," said Ensler. "There are a lot of people who love Carl. I just remember at his birthday party that Jacob, his son, who is a doll, was telling wonderful stories and saying how deeply his father accepted him as a gay man. He's totally been there for Jacob. Carl's one of those rare men who actually learned something from his own behavior and history, and he's transformed. I can tell you he is a great friend."

Bernstein's book on the pope's role in the collapse of communism came out in 1996, when he was fifty-two. "Like the Nixon White House, here was an amazingly powerful institution sitting under our noses that no one had really looked at," Bernstein told *Publishers Weekly* in September 1996. "To me that was a great story. It's about power. All my books are about power." Because Bernstein had not spent years covering the pope, nor did he know the Vatican's internal machinations, he turned to a well-respected Vatican correspondent, Marco Politi, for the Rome newspaper *La Repubblica*, to coauthor the book. Although he had initially signed a two-book contract with Simon & Schuster when he wrote *Loyalties*, that house did not publish Bernstein's pope book. In fact, Bernstein had said publicly after he finished *Loyalties* that he intended to write a book about the press, but that never came about.

His Holiness: John Paul II and the Hidden History of Our Time was considered a political biography of Pope John Paul II. The pope did not grant the authors an interview, but several of his close advisers did. For the book, the pair did more than three hundred interviews and pored over scores of documents. They used few anonymous sources. "If you had told me 25 years ago that one of the great figures of our time would be the pope of Rome, and that I'd be writing about him," Bernstein told *Publishers Weekly*, "I would have said you're smoking something." The book got fairly good reviews, and *Reader's Digest* paid the pair $100,000 for the first exclusive worldwide rights to excerpt the book, according to the *International Herald Tribune* on June 19, 1996. "The papal preview will come out in 12 languages in mid-September [1996], several weeks before the book is due in stores," *Publishers Weekly* reported.

Somewhere along the line, though, no doubt from the public perception of Bernstein's work ethic, rumors started to circulate that his coauthor, Politi, had really authored the book. Politi had covered the Vatican for fifteen years, more than a quarter of his life. The *New York Times*'s respected religion writer Peter Steinfels interviewed Politi in September 1996 and wrote, "There are rumors, however, that Mr. Politi is responsible for much of the biography, with Mr. Bernstein concentrating on the long chapter that expands a 1992 *Time* magazine cover story asserting that Pope John Paul II formed a close working alliance with the CIA to bring down the communist government in Poland." Five days after that story ran, the *Times* was forced to apologize. It's highly unorthodox for a newspaper to print rumors. The *Times* had never asked Bernstein. Publisher Doubleday wrote a letter that the *Times* reprinted: "Mr. Bernstein, as the primary author, masterminded the project and was responsible for, and delivered, the complete typewritten manuscript." Yet that did not prevent the venerated book reviewer Garry Wills from repeating the assertion. In his review in the December 1996 *New Yorker*, Wills, who called the book "schizophrenic," wrote that *His Holiness* was "written in part by Carl Bernstein but mainly by Marco Politi, a journalist who covers the Vatican for *La Repubblica*. The result is a two-headed book, one head only slightly connected to the body and babbling the *Time* story again, while the other head quietly brings up aspects of the Pope's life." Even today, rumors swirl that Politi wrote most of the biography, although he has denied that. But it reveals that even when Bernstein does serious work, he is not always taken seriously, as Woodward would be.

A few years later, a young man would worry that Bernstein was too serious before deciding to hire him for an online venture during the dot-com boom of the late 1990s, when venture capitalists were throwing money at new-wave, high-tech business concepts as if it were confetti tossed at a political convention. A friend of Bernstein's was a minor investor in a startup called Voter.com that aimed to become the definitive Web site for politics and campaign races. It was being run by a young man in his early twenties, Justin Dangel, from Boston. Dangel, the chief executive, wanted someone with a strong journalistic background to make the site a success. Bernstein had the journalistic skills and saw the Internet's potential to provide detailed, useful information to voters.

In early 2000, Dangel and a colleague met Bernstein for lunch in Washington. Dangel was twenty-five; Bernstein, fifty-six, old enough to be Dangel's father. Dangel was interested in Bernstein. He knew his name, knew of his Watergate reputation, but worried that Bernstein might be too stodgy for a hip, fast-paced Internet venture. Dangel and his colleague decided that they'd ask Bernstein about the movie *Dick*, and based on Bernstein's reaction, they could gauge whether Bernstein would fit in. "We came up with that question as a perfect way to figure out if he had a sense of humor or whether he was open to new things," said Dangel. The 1999 movie *Dick* marked the third time in twenty-three years that Bernstein was portrayed in a feature-length Hollywood film. This time, the movie was a spoof about two high school girls visiting the White House who wander off from their tour group, meet Nixon, and become his official dog walkers. By accident, the two ditzy girls witness G. Gordon Liddy's gang burglarizing the Democratic national headquarters at the Watergate hotel and become Woodward and Bernstein's mysterious source, Deep Throat. The comedian Will Ferrell played Woodward, and Bruce McCulloch played Bernstein in the $13 million movie.

When Dangel asked Bernstein what he thought of *Dick*, Bernstein laughed. ("I love that movie," he later told me. "I think it is so funny. C'mon. How can you not like it?") Dangel was relieved. "We were afraid if we hired someone who was too egotistical, we would be in trouble," he said. "We'd heard that Carl was not like that but wanted to find out for ourselves. From the first moment, we had a great laugh about the movie *Dick*, and the fact that he was willing to laugh about a caricature put us all at ease." Bernstein was hired as an executive editor in charge of content, a job he did from New York while Voter.com operated from Boston and Washington. When Bernstein started in April 2000, he said, the Web site had 120 employees and was spending money as if it came from a Monopoly game.

"When I got there," said Bernstein, "what I did was really to revamp the site in terms of content. Totally. What I realized was that you could produce a better daily political report on the Web than any newspaper in the world because you could link to all the best stories of the day from wherever you wanted, from the *Jerusalem Post* to the *Washington Post*. Then you'd add your own content." For Bernstein, it was fun to be back in the daily mix.

The site won press praise. *Forbes* magazine listed it as one of the best political sites on the Web, said Bernstein. In November 2000, it received 3 million unique visitors. Like other Internet start-ups at the turn of the century, however, Voter.com didn't have a strong business model. In February 2001 the site had dwindled to forty-five employees, including Bernstein, and went belly-up. According to a December 2001 article in the *Boston Herald*. "Voter.com boasted legendary Watergate journalist Carl Bernstein as its $185,000-a-year editor," according to a December 2001 article in the *Boston Herald*. "And the site had a huge presence at both the Republican and Democratic national conventions in 2000. But once the historic presidential election was over, Voter.com found its hoped-for audience of lobbyists, activists, consultants and political junkies unresponsive and unprofitable."

Bernstein bought the URL for Voter.com and had plans to try to turn it into a nonprofit site that would drill deep and provide political information. Five years later, nothing had happened with the Web site. One reason is that in early 1999, Bernstein signed a contract with Knopf to write his next book, a detailed Bernstein-investigative look at Hillary Rodham Clinton's life. Around the same time, author Gail Sheehy had written a lengthy piece on Mrs. Clinton for *Vanity Fair*, a publication for which Bernstein writes, and his name appears on its masthead. By November 1999, Sheehy had *Hillary's Choice* in print. In June 2003, Clinton came out with her own book, *Living History*.

"I think," Bernstein said, "that what you will see with my book is certainly a much more realistic portrait of her than *Living History*, her book, which is really a self-portrait as she would like to be seen. The way she portrays herself, there are some real omissions. My book will be a more balanced, realistic look at who she is." The book was due out in 2003. Aside from Bernstein's usual reasons, the Hillary book, as it's called, might have gotten delayed because Bernstein got engaged to a tall, blond former model, Christine Kuehbeck, who had been an administrative director of the American Academy in Berlin and is only a few years younger. Twenty-seven years after marrying Ephron, Bernstein married for the third time, on July 4, 2003, in Reykjavik, Iceland.

In February 2006, when Woodward and Bernstein appeared on CNN's *Larry King Live*, King asked Bernstein about his Clinton book. "End of this year, or early next year," he told King. In November 1979, Bernstein had told the *Washington Post* that he expected a fall 1980 publication date for the book about his parents. It came out a decade later. "Carl always had trouble finishing a project, always had trouble sticking with anything," said Robert Kaiser.

11

Piercing the Veil

"Why do you need to deal with this in the book?" [Bush] asked. "What's this got to do about it?"

I said that I had to cover the aftermath of the war. This was a key question.

The president said he wanted to make sure that his acknowledgment that no weapons of mass destruction had been found so far would not be published in The Washington Post *until the book was released. "In other words, I'm not going to read a headline, 'Bush says No Weapons.'"*

I promised that he would not.

—Woodward interviewing President George W. Bush
in December 2003 for *Plan of Attack*, 2004

Publishing *Wired* proved to be an anomaly for Woodward. For one thing, he provided copious chapter notes and attributed his work, something he would not do again. For another, Hollywood was alien ground for Woodward. The stars, who had willingly opened up to the famed Watergate reporter, turned venomously on him after *Wired* was published, in a way that both hurt and surprised Woodward.

For his next book, he went back to the more comfortable land of government, where the signposts and the players had a familiar feel. His fifth book set the pattern for all the others to follow and established Bob Woodward as one of the most phenomenally successful nonfiction writers in the country. It also established him as a human brand. When a Woodward book rolled out, people knew just what to expect. It would sizzle. It would be controversial. It would be full of revelations. It would make news. The *Post* and its corporate sister *Newsweek* would publish exclusive excerpts and bask in its reflected glory. It would be a best seller, most likely a number-one *New York Times* best seller. It would continue to seal his reputation as the most famous and influential reporter in the country.

His next book would be about the CIA, and after that he would go on to expose the inner workings of the Pentagon, the Federal Reserve, a presidential campaign, and both the Clinton and the Bush White Houses. Each book benefited from unprecedented access to sources at the highest level, and each suffered from a certain narrowness because of this. Critics have attacked each book for a lack of analysis, a dearth of attribution, and a penchant for highly detailed, novelistic re-creations of scenes that were unrecorded, except in the memory of participants.

If Woodward's whole career has been built on the trust he earned from readers, the holy grail of his critics is to find that one important piece of information he got wrong, to bring the whole mammoth Woodward oeuvre into question. Yet ever since he wrongly reported that Sloan had named Haldeman before the grand jury, he's managed never to make a serious mistake again.

Still, although Woodward has never been shown to get his facts wrong, there have been times when he missed the most important facts or nuances altogether. Relying on high-level sources telling him the truth means relying on them to tell the whole truth, even when it's not in their interest.

It was Woodward's mentor, Ben Bradlee, who suggested in 1984 that Woodward's next book focus on the Central Intelligence Agency. As the most secretive agency in the U.S. government, it particularly appealed to Woodward, who loved secrets.

To write the book that would become *Veil*, Woodward reached out to the equally secret-obsessed CIA director William Casey. Over the course of reporting on the CIA for the *Washington Post* and for the book, Woodward met with Casey more than four dozen times, dining at his house, seeing him in his office, traveling with him on an airplane, and inevitably developing a close professional relationship with him.

Yet over the years that Woodward courted the CIA director as a confidential source for *Washington Post* articles and for his book, it turned out that Casey had deftly steered Woodward away from one of the biggest scandals to befall a presidential administration after Watergate. The story that Woodward missed was Iran-contra, a debacle that might have brought down Ronald Reagan's presidency had Reagan not been the skilled and wildly popular politician that Nixon never was.

Iran-contra was an elaborate scheme by Reagan's National Security Council to finance the right-wing Nicaraguan contras with money raised by illegally selling sophisticated weapons to Iran, an avowed U.S. enemy, during the years it was at war with Iraq. The naive hope had been that if the United States sold arms to Iran, that country would pressure Lebanon into releasing its U.S. hostages. Since it was illegal to sell weapons to Iran, the people running the operation had to do something with the profits, so the money was funneled to the Nicaraguan rebels to fight the socialist government in Nicaragua. It wasn't just Woodward who missed this blockbuster story; no one in the American media broke it. Instead, a small Lebanese magazine, *Al-Shiraa*, first exposed the complicated arrangement on November 3, 1986.

"I would have preferred to have found out about the Iran arms sales before that rag in Beirut, and I didn't," Woodward told *Playboy*. "I failed and I should have got it, and I am really critical of myself. [Casey] knew about it and he didn't tell me. So was I being co-opted? I don't know. I didn't get anyone else to tell me about it." By talking so much with Woodward, it appears that Casey successfully steered the reporter away from Iran-contra by offering him bits of other stories.

Later that month, on November 25, 1986, Attorney General Edwin Meese III told the press that the national security advisor, John M. Poindexter, had resigned, and his assistant, Lieutenant Colonel Oliver North, was fired. He also confirmed that $10 million to $30 million dollars had been diverted to the Nicaraguan contras.

The biggest scandal since Watergate had eluded the famous Watergate reporter while he was in the middle of ongoing conversations with the head of the CIA. Woodward had come close to Iran-contra with some front-page stories he wrote in 1984, but he still missed it. An April 13, 1984, Woodward story reads, "Director William J. Casey is considering the possibility of asking another country, such as Saudi Arabia, to send money to the contras until the funding problem is solved, according to one well-placed source, but no decisions have been made."

In October 1986, Leonard Downie Jr., then the *Washington Post*'s managing editor, suspected that there was a good story to pursue when a C-123 cargo plane supplying arms to U.S.-backed contra rebels was shot down over Nicaragua. The Sandinistas captured the only survivor, American crew member Eugene Hasenfus, raising the question: was the U.S. providing military aid to the Nicaraguan contras in defiance of Congress? "I went to see Woodward and I said, 'I really think this is significant. I think something has happened here,'" said Downie, now the *Post*'s executive editor. "I couldn't really stir Woodward's interest in it. He later acknowledged that he just didn't get it. You never know when he's going to react positively and connect up to what you are trying to talk about or what kind of a rope-a-dope he'll use to keep you at bay and pursue his own agenda."

Woodward was too busy writing his book on the CIA to make the connection that the CIA might be involved. "The Hasenfus plane, we now know, was like the Watergate burglary," Woodward told the *Washingtonian* in September 1987. "There was a body caught red-handed, phone records of calls to government officials, an official denial, and the mother's milk of American politics—money. It all fit. I knew the CIA was desperate for money in 1984, and suddenly they had plenty of it."

Editor Steve Luxenberg worked closely with Woodward during this period. While Woodward was the titular head of the investigative unit, Luxenberg ran it day to day. He noted that another *Post* reporter had written some contra stories. "No one seemed to care," he said. "They thought her story wasn't going anywhere. Then Iran-contra occurred. Suddenly, it was Watergate all over again for some people and for a limited amount of time. It seemed like the second time in fifteen years that the presidency itself was in question. Not that it was corrupt, but is this an impeachable offense or not? If you hadn't had Watergate, would you have had the same attitude toward Iran-contra? I would argue not. Woodward, I think, would argue not."

When Iran-contra became public in November 1986, Woodward had almost finished his CIA book. He quickly updated it with information that came out during the subsequent Iran-contra congressional hearings. *Veil* was published on a crash cycle that took about a month to convert the finished, edited manuscript into the hardback, instead of the normal nine months, according to Simon & Schuster. (Though, it should be said, some kind of crash cycle has now become the norm for Woodward's books.) When the book came out, the publisher and the *Post* gave it what would become the full Woodward treatment. Other journalists write books and pray that they get reviewed or even written about. Woodward's book roll-outs become events. The star reporter can count on an all-out effort that guarantees a best seller.

No advance copies of *Veil* were sent to reviewers. In fact, to guarantee secrecy, only the *Post* and *Newsweek* got copies before publication. The *Post* planned to run an excerpt in its Sunday magazine, followed by five days of front-page excerpts. *Newsweek* paid $75,000 for exclusive rights to run an 11,000-word, 18-page illustrated excerpt as a cover story. "Exclusive Book Excerpts: The Secret Wars of the CIA by Bob Woodward," trumpeted *Newsweek*. Forty-six other newspapers carried the excerpts. A news report said that Woodward got almost $1 million for a television movie based on *Veil*. In addition, CBS's *60 Minutes* did a segment on the new five-hundred-page book that told the story of how Casey aggressively pushed the CIA into bigger and more daring secret rogue worldwide operations.

The top-secret book, which Simon & Schuster had worked hard to keep a mystery, somehow got out ahead of schedule. Days before the *Post*'s big roll-out on Sunday September 27, 1987, *U.S. News & World Report* got a purloined copy of the galleys, forcing the *Post* into a last-minute scramble. A publisher's nightmare? Hardly. The *Post* quickly assigned a reporter to write a Saturday story stripped across the front page, outlining the book's highlights and, in effect, creating even more interest in Sunday's edition, which ran the magazine piece *and* a front-page excerpt initially slotted for Monday. *U.S. News*'s early analysis got picked up by the three TV networks, the wire services, and some newspapers. The weekly magazine's two-page synopsis in the end proved to be just the kind of teaser that *Newsweek* knew would draw more readers to its pages.

Woodward called the book *Veil*, after the code word the Reagan administration used for covert operations aimed at influencing events overseas. Bernstein, along with a handful of other *Post* editors, helped Woodward shape the initial unwieldy manuscript into its final form. "I know when I was doing the CIA book, *Veil*, Carl came down here, spent a day or two, read it," Woodward said. "Provided some wonderful editing ideas. Asked some questions. I remember I just had this image of, there he is. He knows how to do this. He's remarkable." In some ways, the book expanded on stories that Woodward had already broken in the *Post*. In others, it broke new ground. In 1985, for example, Woodward did a story about a CIA-trained "hit squad" that unsuccessfully attempted to assassinate a major terrorist leader in Beirut that year by setting off a car bomb. It missed the target but killed eighty innocent bystanders. When Woodward wrote the story, he said that the hit squad was operating without CIA authorization. In *Veil*, however, Woodward nailed down that Casey had secretly worked with the Saudi Arabian intelligence service and had personally arranged the covert assassination attempt. Woodward also detailed two other "off-the-books" covert actions that Casey had directed.

Like all of Woodward's previous books, *Veil* caused a stir. It made news. It was attacked and glorified, depending on one's political viewpoint. President Reagan denounced the book as "an awful lot of fiction." He wasn't talking about the entire book, but instead the last four pages that dealt with Woodward's clandestine visit to Casey when he was in the hospital.

In December 1986, Casey, seventy-three, suffered a seizure and was rushed to the hospital, where doctors removed a brain tumor. The following month, Woodward snuck into room C6316 of Georgetown Hospital for what would be his last interview with Casey, although he didn't know it at the time. (Casey died in May 1987.) Woodward had tried a few days earlier to get in, but a CIA security guard blocked him. This time Woodward eluded the guards. He had carefully written out his questions on yellow legal paper. There were many, but he boiled them down to one page, given the gravity of Casey's illness.

Casey could communicate, although not well. Woodward was able to ask only one question.

> "You knew, didn't you?" I said. The contra diversion had to be the first question: you knew all along.
> His head jerked up hard. He stared, and finally nodded yes.
> Why? I asked
> "I believed."
> What?
> "I believed."
> Then he was asleep, and I didn't get to ask another question.

Casey's wife, Sophia, publicly and vehemently denied that Woodward had ever set foot inside her husband's hospital room. It wasn't possible; there were four security guards. She was livid with Woodward. When he sent the book to Mrs. Casey, she returned it. Other medical experts weighed in that such a conversation was not possible. Woodward was respectful of Mrs. Casey's denial but insisted that he had spoken briefly with her husband. "Use common sense," he told the *Los Angeles Times*. Casey "was in the hospital three months. Did they go to the bathroom? Did they go to lunch? Did they go to sleep? . . . I talked to him. No one from the family was there."

Steve Luxenberg, who ran Woodward's investigative unit, was there when Woodward returned from the hospital visit. "I remember him going to do it and coming back and saying I just had this really weird experience with Casey," said Luxenberg, who as Woodward's deputy had helped to excerpt the book in the *Post*. "I took it on face value: 'I just went to this hospital room. I needed to sneak in for this reason. Here's what happened.'"

Reams were written about the hospital scene. More attention was given to questioning whether it had occurred than to parsing Woodward's other newsworthy revelations about how the powerful Casey had influenced Reagan's foreign policy and the different ways Casey had used the CIA to skirt the law.

"The public and the news media have fastened onto Bob Woodward's visit to Bill Casey in the hospital, making it the focal point of scrutiny of the entire three-year project. Unfortunately, Mr. Woodward bears some of the responsibility for this distortion," wrote the *Post* ombudsman at the time, Joseph Laitin. "While the final meeting provided a dramatic flourish to the book's ending, it has also made him fair game for critics. To have included this four-minute interlude may have been irresistible—the controversy aroused is a publisher's dream—but it has served to distract from what should be a more primary concern. . . . It would be far more profitable to speculate on why Bill Casey, confidant of the president and engaging in roguish intelligence operations when the White House was calling for lie detector tests, opened his door to the country's best-known investigative reporter."

While the rest of the news media (even *Newsweek*) led with Casey's hospital-bed nod, the *Washington Post* did not. The paper ran it deep on the page of the series' last day, not considering it as earth-shattering as the rest of the world did. The hospital death-bed scene worked as a dramatic ending for Woodward's book, but it was not a news story, said then assistant managing editor Robert Kaiser, backed up by Bradlee. Woodward had told his editors about the clandestine visit after it occurred, but they all considered Casey's nod ambiguous. Woodward was convinced that Casey was well aware of the illegal diversion to the contras. "On a personal level, Casey's nod meant a lot. But as a reporter, it's not a word. It's only a nod and I got to ask no follow-up questions," Woodward told the *New York Times* on September 29, 1987. "What do you write? A story saying that Casey nodded?"

As with some scenes in *The Final Days*, critics accused Woodward of making the scene up, putting words into his mouth that Casey could not speak. Yet no one who knows the Midwestern, highly disciplined, exceedingly professional former naval man Bob Woodward well would ever believe that. Woodward has invested his whole career in perfecting the brand Bob Woodward; he would not risk it all for one sensational anecdote. "Bob Woodward mastered the art of playing the role of Bob Woodward; this is a crucial ingredient," said a knowledgeable source. "He understood that if he ever made a bad mistake, the whole thing would collapse." Just as Woodward would never have made up his legendary Watergate source Deep Throat, although scores of people were certain he did. If he had done so, he would have been basing his career—the career that he has carefully and successfully built into a multimillion-dollar industry—on a lie. "I don't think that [Casey scene] should dog Woodward's career," said Kaiser. "I can't imagine that he made it up. I think it's a critical fact about Woodward's career that he's never made a serious mistake. I just don't think Woodward makes stuff up."

It is possible, however, that Casey snookered Woodward. He knew that Woodward, the country's premier investigative reporter, was going to do a book on his agency, and he thought he could have more control over the outcome if he played a hand in shaping it by talking with Woodward. Admiral Stansfield Turner, the CIA director during the Carter administration, believes that Casey did fool Woodward, and he said so in the *Washington Post*. Turner, no fan of Casey's, told the *Post*: "It was a case of the biggest con man in the country taking on the best reporter and I think the con man won. Bob very faithfully reprints Casey's views on these matters and I think that's what Casey wanted." Casey "came off a lot better than he deserved."

When I sought advice from someone who has known Woodward for decades and worked with him, he suggested that I look into whether Woodward outsmarts sources or sources outsmart him. "I think there are a number of cases where smart, smooth operators have fooled him and have figured out his appetite for the detail that he loves—the quotations, the atmosphere, the color, the dress, and so on, and they get the best of him," said the knowledgeable source. "People learn that if 'I give him that stuff, then I can give him my personal spin.' I think it did happen with Casey. Casey told him just what he wanted to tell him." With *Veil*, some say, Woodward had cut the Faustian deal and moved from being the outsider who once diligently pursued government transgressions to being a careful chronicler of powerful institutions. The mythological slayer of giants had crossed over.

"I think the theory is true in the sense that he once was an outsider and now he's an insider," said Luxenberg, who worked directly for Woodward from September 1985 to 1991. "But I don't know what that means. You can't be an outsider forever. Bob has chosen to be a certain kind of history journalist. He's chronicling. The insider access is a route to that. I don't think he's an insider so he can say I went to this dinner or that. It is in service to his goals as a journalist."

Woodward, after the Belushi book, tended to write, though not always, from the point of view of the man or men at the top.

Some critics question whether he relied too heavily on the perspectives of the people who would let him in, such as Casey. "Think of the number of unflattering stories you get in *The Final Days*, *The Brethren*, or *All the President's Men*," said someone who has known Woodward since his early days at the *Post*. "The stories that are told are from the perspective of the people who work for people in power. The people who say, in effect, my boss or these other guys did this really unflattering thing. That's what I call the clerk's perspective. They have a perspective that is less than heroic for the people they work for. That perspective is what infused books like *Final Days* and *The Brethren*, and it's utterly lacking in the late books."

Woodward still sees himself as a simple gatherer of facts. Some reporters gather facts in the public gardens; Woodward is now allowed inside the secret gardens that few other journalists ever visit. People who are critical of Woodward, for the most part, refuse to go on the record because they fear Woodward, who has occasionally called bosses when he hasn't liked a story about him.

What Woodward did in *Veil* and his other books is what few other journalists can do. He gets the inside story. Over the years, the criticism that he is an amanuensis to power has grown, but the fact is that he often gets beyond the official version of events, and he gets it right. "The thing about Woodward's books is he's not wrong," said *CBS News* correspondent Bob Schieffer. "He can get stuff that other people just can't get. He has this tremendous ability to find sources. Sy Hersh [the closest to a true Woodward competitor] goes at it with a real passion. Bob is just a great reporter. I think he is the best reporter, frankly. But he's not passion or issue-driven. He's just trying to figure out what's going on. I do believe that is the secret to his success." No other reporter gets the kind of varied access at all levels of government—Woodward calls it good reporting—that Woodward does.

"He's become a phenomenon," said retired *New York Times* reporter Anthony Lewis, who covered the Supreme Court and wrote what was the most devastating critique of *The Brethren*. "He's found a métier, a way of doing things that people like to read. He writes a book, and you know it's going to be number 1 on the best-seller list. He does something no one else does."

What he does not do, however, is analyze the stories he col-
lects, and for that he is roundly assailed routinely with each book.
Yet that's not who Bob Woodward is. While people criticize Woodward for not interpreting the facts, it is imperative to recognize
and accept that Woodward is a reporter, a fact gatherer, and, even
if people wish differently, he does not pass himself off as anything
more. He prefers to leave the analysis for historians.

In reporting on a playing field that is virtually empty, Woodward comes up with stories time and again that other reporters
either miss or could not get. "Woodward has since carved out a
personal niche for super access journalism, in which he gets access
to very important people and uses that access to tell stories that
would almost certainly otherwise not be told," said Alex Jones,
the director of the Joan Shorenstein Center on the Press, Politics and Public Policy. "But they are told without attribution, and
you basically have to trust Bob Woodward, and an awful lot of
people do."

Woodward, unlike the traditional investigative reporter, does
not spend hours pawing through paper records. He likes to talk to
people, and he's surprisingly skilled at it, considering that he's
socially awkward. "Bob is Bob," said Sally Quinn, who has known
him for over three decades. "He's very much what he seems. I don't
ever think of him as uptight. But he is a serious, quiet person. He's
much more interested in a conversation on what he's working on
than he is with small talk. He really isn't that comfortable with
small talk. He really believes that he is not that interesting. I don't
know why. It's just who he is."

Because that is Woodward's reality, he continually tries to talk
reporters out of writing about him; the stories are legion among
journalists. "Being interviewed doesn't interest me," Woodward
told me in the flat, nasal Midwestern accent that he's never lost.
"I am just a ra-por-ter. The only interesting thing about me is the
sources I get or the information I have, and I don't talk about
those. The rest is pretty uninteresting. These aren't just words to
fill the space. That's really how I feel." Disingenuous as that
sounds, he believes it.

His former assistant, David Greenberg, now a history professor at Rutgers University, worked with Woodward from mid-1991

to summer 1994. "Bob really doesn't think his opinions are that interesting," said Greenberg. "He believes it is his job to bring to light secrets that would otherwise not be told, not give his opinions." His approach has always been to present the facts and let the reader be the judge.

The belief that his opinions don't matter is part of what makes him an amazing listener. He is the interviewer par excellence, which helps him tremendously in his chosen business of exposing secrets. He thinks other people, those who might advance his reporting, are fascinating. As he is endlessly inquisitive, he has earned the nickname "The Question Man."

"Bob was always infinitely curious about people," said Scott Armstrong. "What do they believe and why do they believe it; who are the people most influential on their worldview. Bob would never use the terms but he was the master of the weltanschauung, the worldview. He wanted to know what formative influences had made them unique."

"Certainly, I've been subjected," said Carl Feldbaum, a life-long friend, who first got the Woodward treatment when he was on the Watergate prosecution team. "He comes off as this nice Midwestern guy from Wheaton, Illinois, and has the insight to know that people have the need to talk about who they are, what they do, and what they've accomplished. Bob has the gift of not asserting himself in those conversations but frankly of being rather passive, with long silences that the interviewees find they have to fill in. It's quite a remarkable talent." It's also served him well. Woodward is able to pry secrets out of reticent government sources that other people think would be possible only under means of torture.

"His greatest gift in a personal contact," noted his longtime colleague Kaiser, "is his Cheneyesque [referring to Vice President Dick Cheney] sense of absolute authority and calm. He just conveys when he's talking to you that he's totally relaxed about whatever it is, and he knows about it, and there's no doubt in his personality. There's no uncertainty." Woodward learned the art of interviewing long ago, realizing that being a good listener is like administering a drug to a person being interviewed. Most journalists know that people in general are hungry to talk, and that few are asked questions by someone who genuinely wants to know what they think. Woodward does. It can be intoxicating, say those who have sat down for a Woodward interview.

"There's both a psychological quality and an empathic quality to him," said David Gergen, who has known Woodward since Watergate and has fallen under his spell while working for the Nixon and Clinton administrations. "He provides people with this sense of safety, that somehow, if you tell him, it will be reported straight, straighter than anyone else. He is able to bond with people in a way that most journalists can't. There's a psychological bonding that goes on. He's very good at putting himself in the minds or shoes of others. But you've got to know before you sit down with Bob Woodward how far you are willing to go with the information. He's very seductive."

Here's how Woodward works, said Gergen. "Let's say there are four people in a room. And Bob comes to you and he already has everything that was said, and the two things you said are slightly off. You face a dilemma. Do I stay mum, or do I correct him? So there is a temptation to talk to him."

There is also another side, however—a more ruthless Bob Woodward. Although he's known to be fiercely loyal, he can put a story in front of a friendship, as happened with Richard Darman. Darman has known Woodward since Watergate, when Darman was a trusted aide for Attorney General Elliot Richardson. Woodward and Darman grew to be close friends, and Darman was among a select group invited to the Woodward-Walsh wedding in 1989. In late 1991, Woodward talked to Darman, then the budget director under the first President Bush, about doing a book on Bush's economic policy. Darman talked freely to Woodward, believing that the information would appear after the November 1992 election, when Bush was running for reelection—but then things changed. Woodward called Darman a few weeks before the election. Instead of a book, the *Post* was going to run a series on Bush's economic policy. Woodward wanted to give Darman a heads up. Darman was furious; that wasn't the plan. Katharine Graham confirmed this in a 1995 *Vanity Fair* piece about Woodward and Walsh, demonstrating that a source cannot co-opt Woodward; the story comes first.

"Look what he did to Dick Darman, who was a great friend," said Graham. "[Bob] ran some very sensitive pieces about him. He interviewed Dick, who I believe said he didn't quite believe in Bush's economic plan. [Bob] did in his great friend and lost him."

In Darman's 1996 book, he wrote about the experience. "A longtime reporter-friend violated both a specific promise and a basic trust with a regrettable public account of the [Bush] administration's trial," according to Darman's 1996 book *Who's in Control?* "I wondered if journalists thought to imagine what it might be like, for example, to be a child and find that a gratuitously critical article on one's father was the subject of a classmate's show-and-tell project."

Others have Woodward stories, but often their criticism comes from not liking how they were portrayed, rather than from a feeling that Woodward was inaccurate.

Nowadays, it is easy for Woodward to reach high-level people. "But it wasn't always like that," said Armstrong, who wrote *The Brethren* with him. "You build relationships over years and years. It's not a relationship that arises from one significant interview for Woodward. It has to do with cultivating a deeper relationship by going back and back. It's the durability of the relationship that you are developing with a human being."

Woodward's thoroughness also gives him an insight into the source's worldview, which allows him to write so authoritatively about what a person thought and why, said Armstrong. Woodward interviewed one Supreme Court clerk sixteen times. He works tirelessly at it.

No one knows this better than his assistants. Greenberg worked for Woodward on *The Agenda: Inside the Clinton White House* (1994), about Clinton's first budget. Greenberg had about seven conversations with Woodward before Woodward decided that the chemistry was right. He hired Greenberg in 1991. "I worked out of Bob's house for almost three years," said Greenberg, today a historian and a journalist. "It is a very close relationship, especially the way Bob uses his assistant."

Greenberg witnessed Woodward in action. "Being Bob Woodward helps you to get calls returned," said Greenberg. "But Woodward works as hard as anyone I've seen. He's working the phone.

If there's a meeting with four people, and he's talked to two, he's going to try to talk to the other two. He's relentless, persistent; works all the time and loves it. There is no stopping him." He has no agenda other than to get to the bottom of things (and to write a best-selling book about it). He is motivated by a strong conviction that the more information the public has, the better our democratic system will function.

"I said this in the beginning of the book I did on the Gulf War, *The Commanders* [1991]," Woodward told me in 2003. "The decision to go to war is the biggest decision a president makes, the country makes. It tells the world, when we say these are our enemies: This is what we are doing. This is what we are going to fight for. That tells the world who we are. In a more interesting way, it tells us who we are. So it's not just on this strategic foreign-policy level. It is on a very human level. It is all about human motivation and decision. Whether you like the war in Iraq or don't like the war in Iraq, how we got there is . . . that's a big call by the president." Woodward's obsession is to get to the bottom of why that call was made.

In 1996, Woodward described his technique to *Writers Digest* while he was working on his eighth book, *The Choice*, about Bill Clinton's reelection bid. His trademarks are careful preparation and repeated interviewing of crucial sources. He says he starts at the bottom with peripheral but valuable people and works up, something he still does, although more and more critics believe that he now goes right to the high-level source. "Woodward and I were writing a story," said Richard Cohen, who has known Woodward since 1971. "I said, 'Are you ready to go?' He said, 'I only have these many calls to make yet.' He had a legal pad with about thirty names on it. I thought to myself: 'I haven't called that many people in my entire career.' Woodward just keeps coming at you."

His work ethic and meticulous research do not inoculate him from criticism, however. And it's not just the material in his book that generates criticism; it's the unique treatment his books get from the *Washington Post*. When one of his books comes out, the *Post* typically treats it like a major news event, often running an excerpt on the left side of the front page and a news story on the book on the right—the side typically reserved for Big News.

With *Veil*, there were two stories, and both played prominently above the fold. When Woodward's 1996 work *The Choice*, about the 1996 presidential election, came out, the *Post* was inundated with criticism about the play it gave Woodward. A reader called it "Woodward's infomercial," and others suggested that the paper should have printed "Advertisement" over the news story.

"We used to do a news account, and then the excerpts would begin," said the *Post*'s Steve Luxenberg. "I always felt queasy about that. We should do one or the other. If we are treating him as a staff member, which I think we do, and treating the book as his labor, then it should just be the excerpts. If we are treating him as an author and saying here are the highlights of Woodward's book, then why are we running the excerpts? The answer is, because both help readers. I always felt that the charge we are always promoting Woodward's books was bogus except on this score."

Geneva Overholser was the *Post*'s ombudsman when the paper turned the front page over to *The Choice*. She, too, agreed that the coverage was excessive and wrote her thoughts. When she was leaving the three-year contractual ombudsman job in 1998 as planned, Donald Graham, then the paper's publisher, told her that the only column he was unhappy about was the one criticizing *The Choice*'s story play. "It speaks to the importance of Woodward's role at the paper and the pain of having negative things associated with Woodward's name for Don," said Overholser. Her column and others' criticisms did not make a difference. When *Plan of Attack*, about Bush's decision to invade Iraq, came out in April 2004, the *Post* ran excerpts of Woodward's twelfth book for five days and included a 2,500-word staff-written story on the first day—on the front page.

The other concern is how much Woodward learned while reporting for the *Post* and how much he holds back to use for his book. In 1987, with *Veil*, it became common to see Woodward identified as the most influential investigative journalist alive. He could do whatever he wanted. During the three years that he reported on *Veil*, several stories he uncovered along the way made it into the *Post*—but not all of them. By the time he wrote *Veil*, Woodward, at forty-four, was so firmly established at the *Post* as sui generis that he could call the shots about what the paper could have and what would be held for his next book. It was the beginning of a delicate balance between Woodward, the loyal *Washington Post* employee, and Woodward, Simon & Schuster's blockbuster author. He wasn't willing to give up either identity, and neither institution wanted him to in 1987 or for his next eight books.

The dichotomy between author and reporter became a problem with *Veil* that required the *Post*'s response. *New York Times* columnist Flora Lewis attacked Woodward after the *Veil* excerpts appeared, basically asking the well-worn Watergate question in a new way: What did the editors of the *Post* know and when did they know it? Never before had the issue of what a journalist saves for his book become such a public debate. "So it comes as a shock to read that Bob Woodward of the *Washington Post* hoarded information from the late CIA director William Casey that could have made an important contribution to the recent congressional Iran-contra hearings," wrote Lewis on September 29, 1987, two days after the first *Post* excerpt. Although she found it unpleasant to criticize a competitor, she felt compelled to say that the issue jeopardized the press's First Amendment freedom. Lewis was offended that information a reporter gathered for a daily newspaper would be held back for a book. "It will not make it easier to assert the public's right to know and to know in a timely way the next time there is a delicate matter of public policy. . . . It is remarkable that Mr. Woodward pried so much sensitive information out of Mr. Casey. It is even more surprising that such a good reporter, who works for a vigorously enterprising newspaper, would sit on such an explosive story for such a long time." It would not be the last time this criticism was leveled.

The next day, the *Washington Post*'s media writer had a story outlining the controversy, even documenting that Woodward had not held stories back. In fact, he'd written seventy-five stories since January 1986. Yet many critics questioned why, if Woodward believed that Casey knew about Iran-contra, the *Post* didn't publish that—or publish that Casey had been directly involved in the 1985 failed Beirut assassination attempt. Several newspaper editors were quick to say publicly that they would not stand for that. Bill Kovach, then the editor of the *Atlanta Journal-Constitution*, said that Woodward's book highlighted a "confusion of roles" for

reporters who also author books. "The relationship for a daily reporter is with the reader of a daily paper, and when the daily journalist has information that is of use and interest to the daily
reader, it seems to me there is an obligation to get that information out." Kovach and other editors, however, didn't have *the* Bob
Woodward, the most famous reporter in the country, on their
staff. Exceptions can be made. There would always be exceptions
made for Woodward not afforded to other *Post* reporters.

Woodward responded to Lewis's attack by saying that a reporter holds back information with the hope that a source will
offer more. It's also true that many Woodward sources will talk to
him for a book that has a publication date months or years in the
future but not if the story is going in the next day's paper. Bradlee,
somewhat defensively, wondered what all the fuss was about. He
knew he had a good deal; that life is full of trade-offs. He was willing to continue to reap the fruits of Woodward's reporting instead
of lose him to the book world. "Bob is going to write books,"
Bradlee told the *Washingtonian* in September 1987. "That's a fact.
The failure to accommodate him would be idiotic. We can never
give him back as much as he has given us."

Nearly two decades later, when Luxenberg was asked about
the conflict, he said that most people missed the point. The *Post*
gets a lot more from Woodward than Woodward gets from the
Post. "When people ask me, 'Don't you think that Bob and the
Post's interests aren't the same?' I say, 'You are asking the wrong
question,'" said Luxenberg. "The right question is: Do both parties understand the agreement and what are the benefits and costs?
The answer is absolutely. The *Post* is not fooled. There are no surprises here."

Bradlee and other *Post* editors all know it is to the paper's benefit to have Bob Woodward connected to the *Post*. What, however, does Woodward gain by this arrangement that is unique in
the annals of daily journalism? First of all, Woodward is a crea-
ture of habit. He started working at the *Post* thirty-five years ago.
It is home. Ben Bradlee, age eighty-four, who retired as executive
editor in 1991, still goes to the *Post* every day. "The Ben factor is
important," said Kaiser. "Woodward still just worships Ben." It
also helps Woodward to have the emotional connection to the

Post; it's a bit like never leaving home, especially since Bradlee, twenty-one years his senior, and Katharine Graham may be the parents he always wanted.

"Bradlee is a like a father," Woodward told me. "Mrs. Graham was like a mother, to be direct with you. It was home. It was obvious that the kind of stories and work they wanted done were the kinds of stories I wanted to do. I have this enduring relationship with Bradlee. Still see him all the time. They live a few blocks away. We see them, visit them, go on trips with them, spend Christmas with them. It is a real family. And Katharine Graham lived two blocks away. She'd come down here for dinner with Elsa and myself. Or she'd go to our place in Maryland. Or we'd go up there for dinner, talk to her."

Bob Woodward became *the* Bob Woodward because of the work he did three decades ago with the *Post*'s unalloyed support. Plus, it's a sweet deal for Woodward. He is in effect paid a salary while he researches his books, for which Simon & Schuster is said to give him seven-figure advances. In return, Woodward sells the paper the first serial rights for $1. About the most disloyal thing Woodward has done to the *Post* was to renounce a book that he once wrote with *Post* reporter David Broder, the dean of political columnists, on former vice president Dan Quayle. "You'll notice he took that off his list of all the books he's written," said Broder. *The Man Who Would Be President: Dan Quayle*, published by Simon & Schuster, evolved out of a January 1992 *Post* seven-part series that Woodward and Broder wrote, exploring Quayle's qualifications to be president, which was, uncharacteristically for Woodward, largely on the record. Because it was somewhat favorable—though not by any means fawning—critics accused Woodward of going soft.

"I remember him saying, 'I want to try seeing how much I can get on the record because it's not the kind of reporting that I usually do,'" said Luxenberg. "Then when they got criticized for being so credulous, being too willing to accept the Quayle version of things, he wondered, 'Hey, I do it on the record, and I get criticized for being a worse reporter.' I think Bob was experimenting."

Woodward's intense loyalty also extends to his lifelong publisher, Simon & Schuster, and its ubereditor Alice Mayhew. For each new book, Woodward dutifully returns to the publishing house that first took a chance on him and Bernstein in 1972. If Woodward wanted to, he could command even more staggering book advances by getting into a competitive bidding situation with publishing houses, but he doesn't. He does not need the money, and he prefers the comfort of Simon & Schuster, which is another home to him.

Unlike his former Watergate partner, who has careered through his life with different jobs, different homes, and different women, Woodward has lived in the same house and worked for the same newspaper most of his adult life. He has also been in a committed relationship with the same woman, Elsa Walsh, for a quarter of a century. In 1989, a few months after Woodward's mother died that June, he asked Walsh, who had lived with him for seven years, to marry him. Walsh told the *New York Times* in 1990 that her husband had gotten closer to his mother before she died but that he was "devastated by her death, out of a sense that it was too late to resolve their difficult relationship." At forty-six, Woodward married for the third time on November 25, 1989, in a private ceremony at a hotel in Washington, D.C., with his father, an Illinois Appellate Court judge, officiating and his daughter, Tali, thirteen, as maid of honor. Bernstein spoke touchingly. Walsh, thirty-two, quipped that the marriage was "her only, his last." The *Post*, which rarely writes about its staff nuptials, noted the marriage in its pages.

Again, a Woodward honeymoon was delayed for work—but hers, not his. "The couple delayed a honeymoon because Walsh, a *Washington Post* reporter who is covering the Rayful Edmond III trial, wants to see the case to its conclusion. A wedding trip to Venice is planned for the Christmas holidays," reported the *Post*. In August 1996, Walsh and Woodward had a daughter, Diana, named after Walsh's sister. Walsh is unquestionably the love of Woodward's life. "I do know that he has got a very deep, rewarding, loving relationship with Elsa, and vice versa," said Richard Cohen. "When my marriage broke up [in the late 1980s], I stayed with them and I saw firsthand. I think that is the true reason for his feeling content. Bob has no necessity to go out because he has everything he wants at home. He has a wife he truly and intensely loves, and she feels the same way about him. I just love being with them. They are very at ease with each other. There's no tension. No barbs. I think that was a change, and then Diana made it even more."

Walsh has succeeded in reining in the work machine in a way no one before her could. In the process, she freed a more human side of Woodward that may have always been there but had been sublimated by an unparalleled Calvinist work ethic. "Bob has a sort of a Puritan streak in him, which is the antithesis of Carl," said Bradlee. "Bob is so incredibly focused and motivated; I never saw anybody like that. He's up at 5 a.m. and working off a schedule that goes from there to eternity." Walsh has the capacity to alter that schedule. "Elsa will say, 'We are going on vacation now, Bob. Vacation,'" said Sally Quinn. "He'll do it. He can't do it for long periods of time. He can do it for a weekend here, a long weekend there. Elsa just knows that he needs a break even though he doesn't know it. Elsa's a lot of fun. She likes to have a good time. She makes sure he's not all work and no play." Bradlee added that with Walsh, Woodward, after two failed attempts, finally learned how to tend and care for a marriage. "My wife, Elsa, has written a book called *Divided Lives*, about balancing. You need to have time for yourself," said Woodward. "Time for family. Time for work. A place to go. If it's a room or a house or a walk. I think there's an awful lot of wisdom in that. She's a balanced person and has helped me over the last twenty plus years that we've been together, helped me balance."

Walsh is the key, said Alex Jones, who wrote about Woodward in 1990 for the *New York Times*. "When I did a story on him, she wanted me to understand Bob from her perspective. She hero worships him. She understands him in a maternal way in terms of his needs and vulnerabilities." In 1995, Walsh's sister Diana told *Vanity Fair* that Walsh was looking for a mentor, and she found that in Woodward. Not only do they share a profession, but they share a more-than-comfortable life in Georgetown with a cook and a second home near Maryland's Chesapeake Bay that was featured in an eight-page spread in *House Beautiful*. Although the owners were referred to anonymously, everyone knew it was Woodward and Walsh's spread. "Is there no privacy?" Woodward asked, laughing, when *USA Today* inquired. "You do whatever you want. I'm just not going to say anything."

12

The Revelation

Finally, I will be forever grateful to W. Mark Felt. It was a tug of war at times, but he came through, providing the kind of guidance, information and understanding that were essential to the story of Watergate.

—Bob Woodward, *The Secret Man*, July 2005

At 9:30 a.m. on the last day of May in 2005, Bob Woodward's phone rang in his Washington, D.C., home office. It was the call he'd been waiting 33 years to get.

Who it came from, though, was a bit of a shock. It was an editor from *Vanity Fair* magazine, a publication that in August 1995 wrote the kind of flattering piece about Woodward, his wife, Elsa Walsh, and their love story that one couldn't pay a publicist enough to get written. About ten minutes later, Carl Bernstein, who appears on *Vanity Fair*'s masthead as a contributing writer, got a similar call in New York, where he lives.

On the phone to Woodward was *Vanity Fair* editor David Friend. He had some surprising news. His magazine was about to expose the name of the most famous confidential source in American journalism. Within an hour, *Vanity Fair* would go public and name W. Mark Felt, the number-two man in the FBI during Watergate, as Woodward and Bernstein's top-secret source, Deep Throat. The high-circulation glossy that dances between glitz and gritty investigative reporting was going to put an end to Washington's three-decade-long parlor game. The guessing would be over, and neither Woodward, sixty-two, who had a filial devotion to Felt, nor Bernstein, sixty-one, had any say in the matter.

Vanity Fair had scooped them.

Friend was calling Woodward and Bernstein out of respect, to give them a heads up and some quiet time to read the piece. "Look, we've got a story," Friend said. "We are printing it today. I want to get it to you. We didn't call in advance. It's about Deep Throat. I'm going to e-mail it to you."

Bernstein asked how soon he could get back to them with a comment. Friend said it was too late. The magazine had gone to print a week and a half ago. *Vanity Fair* was going to release it on the Internet momentarily. "We broke it before the story was published because we knew our British edition was going to the printing plants," said Friend. "We trusted our U.S. printers to keep quiet. But with the British tabloids, we didn't know how to keep a lid on it. So we broke it early."

Vanity Fair had kept its own secret for two years, ever since San Francisco lawyer John D. O'Connor, who represented Felt and his family, first contacted the magazine in early 2003. At the time, *Vanity Fair* top editor Graydon Carter, Friend, and the magazine's lawyer signed nondisclosure agreements before O'Connor would talk, but a deal could not be worked out. The editors told O'Connor that the magazine wouldn't pay Felt for his story, but it could offer the family the best platform for attracting Hollywood and book agents. Friend tried to convince O'Connor that *Vanity Fair* could be an insurance policy. Run the story in that magazine, and an agent would surely want to buy Felt's life rights. He encouraged them to get the story out. What if they did a book and Felt died before the book was published?

O'Connor had other irons in the fire, however. The family, working with a former *People* magazine contributor named J. Todd Foster, also tried to work out a book and magazine deal with Time Warner, which would have meant access to *People* and *Time* magazine.

Foster had worked on *People*'s thirtieth anniversary Watergate issue in 2002 and was convinced that Felt was Deep Throat after interviewing Felt's son, Mark Jr., but the family wasn't ready to go public. So Foster kept in touch with Mark Jr. In early 2003, after taking another job and getting the family's permission, Foster pitched the story to his former editors at *People*. They were interested. Furthering the intrigue, *People* editors code-named the story "Project Green Door" and tightly limited who could know the story's subject. Eventually the magazine decided not to do the story because the family wanted money, and *People* doesn't pay for news. *People*'s parent, Time Warner, and another publisher, HarperCollins, also got nervous. For them, the problem wasn't money but one of identity. Was Felt *really* the legendary Watergate source?

Foster, a reporter with more than twenty-five years' experience, had teamed up with author-friend Jess Walter, but in the end, after Walter had talked with Felt three times in late 2003, neither was comfortable outing the ninety-one-year-old man. Not because they wanted to protect his identity, but because they believed that Felt, the victim of several strokes, was not mentally competent. He kept changing the story, corroborating and then denying certain facts. Felt himself would not absolutely confirm that he was Deep Throat.

Walter and Foster would love to have broken the Deep Throat story. "But what would have happened if we had come out with a big book saying Mark Felt is Deep Throat and we were wrong?" said Foster. "We just couldn't provide one hundred percent assurance. As hard as it was, I know I did the right thing."

But O'Connor was certain and would not give up. He eventually returned to *Vanity Fair*. "I had no intention of writing this," said O'Connor, "but things didn't work out. I felt that time was getting short, having gone up to the altar with a couple of publications and them getting cold feet. It scared people that Mark could not tell his own story. What we had was circumstantial."

Vanity Fair editors decided that the best way to handle it was for O'Connor to write the story of how he and Felt's family had come to believe he was Deep Throat. The magazine would pay O'Connor—in this case, $15,000—for the story just as it does other authors.

From the beginning, the project was cloaked in secrecy. It was given a code name, "Wig," a play on Watergate. Woodward was known as "W," and Felt was referred to as "The Guy." Felt's daughter, Joan, called her father "Joe Camel." Staffers working on the story had to sign nondisclosure agreements. (By the time the story appeared, nineteen people, including printers, had signed.) Friend flew to San Francisco to meet Felt and watched him sign a document waiving his attorney-client privilege. To throw off *Vanity Fair* staff members, the editors invented a fake story about steroids that Friend was supposedly checking out in San Francisco. Once O'Connor's story was turned in, only five people were given the secret access code to get into a dedicated section of the computer server. The dummy issue ran a fake cover line that read: THE CAR DOOR SLAMS SHUT.

"As we got close to publication, we faced a conundrum," wrote editor in chief Graydon Carter for the magazine's July 2005 issue. "If we called Woodward, assistant managing editor of the *Post*, to verify the identity of Deep Throat, he could rush into print his own article about the source's identity, well in advance of our own. Checking the story with his former partner Carl Bernstein (a *Vanity Fair* contributing editor) posed a similar problem. We didn't call either of them . . . and we chose, instead, to verify the facts surrounding this amazing tale of intrigue and courage as best we could, using alternative and overlapping sources."

By the time Friend called Woodward and Bernstein, it was a done deal. "Though we were elated at the way the story was taking off across the media, our stomachs were in knots," said Friend of that day. "We were only 90 to 95 percent sure once we got the piece together."

The weekend before the release, Friend panicked. His fact checkers had independently corroborated Felt's tale, but still. One bit of key corroborating evidence was that Woodward had gone to visit Felt in 2000 at his Santa Rosa, California, home. "The weekend it breaks, we are tossing and turning," said Friend. "I am convinced that maybe I am wrong. Maybe Woodward went to visit Felt because Woodward was doing his memoir. Maybe Felt's daughter was exaggerating or misperceiving her father's role."

Friend wasn't the only one having last-minute doubts. Felt's family was nervous, too. While Joan Felt and O'Connor had had several conversations with Woodward and had tried to work with him, the famous author had never positively confirmed that Mark

Felt was indeed the celebrated Watergate source. In fact, at one point, Woodward had tried to warn them off when they said they would pursue the story without his help.

"Be careful," said Woodward. "You might be surprised."

That threw the family. "They really started doubting Mark was Deep Throat," said O'Connor. "Maybe he was just a confused old man. Maybe he really wasn't. Maybe it was just the power of suggestion."

The day before the story was released, Friend, employing gallows humor, joked to O'Connor, "Am I going to have a job tomorrow?" O'Connor never thought for a minute his story would be wrong.

What Carter, Friend, and others at *Vanity Fair* really wanted was confirmation from Woodward, Bernstein, or Ben Bradlee. Bradlee, the *Post*'s executive editor during Watergate, also was sent the story. Though he'd "retired" fourteen years earlier, Bradlee's vote on how to handle this situation would still matter. "Holy moly," said Bradlee. Then he went to talk to Woodward.

Friend, who had edited the story, told Woodward and Bernstein that the magazine was going to name Felt. They both said something to the effect of, "Great. Send the story," and gave away nothing.

This had happened before. Many times. Other authors had come out with books naming Deep Throat, but the books always lacked the essential confirmation from either Woodward or Deep Throat—the only two people with firsthand knowledge. Bernstein knew, but he had never met the man. As mentioned before, a class at the University of Illinois had spent four years on a project reading every tea leaf in the Woodward-Bernstein oeuvre and confidently concluded in April 2003 that Deep Throat was Fred Fielding, a former Nixon White House lawyer. Each time this happened, Woodward and Bernstein remained mum. Without their confirmation, the mystery continued. Why should this article be any different?

In fact, even Felt had denied that he was Deep Throat in the pages of his 1979 memoir, *The FBI Pyramid*. He wrote that he had met with Woodward only once during the Watergate investigation. "He wanted to check out the information that he and

Bernstein had collected and he asked me to tell him which was accurate and which was not. I declined to cooperate with him in this manner," lied Felt, "and that was that."

As Bernstein read *Vanity Fair*'s story, which was titled, "I'm the Guy They Called Deep Throat," he knew the magazine had the right man. He immediately dialed Woodward. Bernstein was worried. They were losing control of the story. When reporter Joe Strupp from *Editor & Publisher* called, Bernstein wasn't forthcoming. He stuck to what he had said ever since Deep Throat's existence came out when *All the President's Men* was published in 1974. In fact, since more Watergate figures had been dying and narrowing the field, Woodward and Bernstein had taken to refusing to comment altogether.

"We'll tell you when Deep Throat dies," is what both men steadfastly replied. Over the years, rarely did either man speak publicly without being quizzed about Deep Throat.

Initially, only Woodward, Bernstein, and Bradlee knew the source's identity. Another person joined the exclusive club in the early 1980s, when Woodward shared the secret with Elsa Walsh, whom he began dating in 1980. In a way, it was the ultimate romantic gesture and sign of love. "We have a relationship of total trust," Woodward later told CNN's Larry King. "And this was such a part of my life, I just shared, and she obviously kept the secret also." *Washington Post* writer Sally Quinn, who married Ben Bradlee in 1978, later wrote a *Post* column after Deep Throat's revelation that exposed tinges of hurt that Bradlee had never shared that information with her. "I've never told anyone," Bradlee said to me in March 1995. "And Sally is permanently pissed that I never told her."

Over three decades, only five people—Woodward, Bernstein, Bradlee, Walsh, and Felt—knew the secret. Six people really. A Justice Department lawyer, Stanley Pottinger, accidentally learned it in 1976. Pottinger had been in charge of the grand jury investigation into the FBI break-ins years earlier that had involved Mark Felt. On the witness stand Felt said that he went to the White House so often some suspected he might be Deep Throat. Out of the blue, a juror asked Felt if he was. Pottinger could tell by Felt's stricken look that he was and rescued Felt, telling Felt he could withdraw the question since it was not relevant to the case at hand. Felt did. Pottinger told Woodward about this in 1976, and though Woodward did not confirm Pottinger was right, he was never certain that Pottinger would not tell.

In retrospect, it's possible that Bernstein's son Jacob also knew by osmosis. "I knew that Deep Throat was Mark Felt because I figured it out," wrote Jacob's mother, Nora Ephron, in 2005. "Carl Bernstein, to whom I was married for a brief time, certainly would never have told me; he was far too intelligent to tell me a secret like that. He refused to tell his children, too, who are also my children, so I told them, and they told others." Jacob Bernstein did tell a camp friend, Chase Culeman-Beckman, in 1988, and that friend believed him. Later, as a college student, Culeman-Beckman wrote a research paper on why Felt was Deep Throat and gave the story to a tabloid in April 2002. "Very nonchalantly, [Jacob] said his dad had told him that Deep Throat was an FBI employee named Mark Felt," Culeman-Beckman told the *Globe*. "It didn't mean much to me because I was so young. But I mentioned it to my mother when she picked me up—and she nearly drove off the road."

On March 3, 2005, a seventh person would know. *Washington Post* executive editor Leonard Downie Jr., sixty-two, became concerned as the *Post* had no plans to handle Deep Throat's death. "I wanted to make sure we had a contingency plan," said Downie. He approached Woodward, and Woodward invited Downie to his Georgetown house that March day to read the manuscript of what would later become *The Secret Man: The Story of Watergate's Deep Throat*, published in July 2005.

Now *Vanity Fair* was making a pretty strong claim. Bernstein, though, was not ready to give it up, although it wasn't really his to give. Felt had always been Woodward's source. It was Woodward who had taken multiple taxis to meet him at 2 a.m. in a desolate underground parking garage in Arlington, Virginia, during the early frightening days of Watergate. It was Woodward who as a young man had befriended Felt and cultivated a relationship that helped keep the *Washington Post* way out front on the Watergate story. It was Woodward whom Felt trusted.

"I think people are jumping up and down about this, but we have nothing to say other than what we have said, which is when the individual dies, we will disclose his identity," Bernstein told

Editor & Publisher, which posted his quotes on its Web site at 12:15 p.m. "Other sources have released us from pledges, but nothing has happened that could change that in these circumstances."

After reading the story, though, Woodward concluded that Felt's family and his lawyer, John D. O'Connor, had clearly decided to expose Felt's identity as the high-level source whose nudging and confirmations helped to keep Woodstein on the story and had reassured Bradlee.

Vanity Fair may have correctly identified Deep Throat, but so what? Author James Mann, a former *Washington Post* reporter who had worked with Woodward in the early 1970s, had made a convincing case for Felt in a 1992 piece in the *Atlantic Monthly*. This privately infuriated Woodward, although he said nothing at the time.

So had another former *Post* reporter, Ronald Kessler, in his 2002 book *The Bureau: The Secret History of the FBI*. Kessler reported that Woodward had unexpectedly visited Felt at his Santa Rosa, California, home where he lived with his daughter and took him to lunch in 1999. Though Kessler was off by a year, the rest of his details about the 2000 visit jibed with what Woodward later revealed. *Washingtonian* magazine editor Jack Limpert outright fingered Felt in August 1974. When he confronted Felt, we now know the former G-man barefacedly lied to Limpert. "I can tell you that it was not I and it is not I," said Felt.

None of those highly credible guesses resulted in a bona fide confirmation. Why shouldn't the *Vanity Fair* piece wind up on a growing pile of speculative articles and books?

For a while, Woodward had been talking with the Felt family, especially to Felt's daughter, Joan, who is Woodward's contemporary, about a collaboration. Yet Woodward never specifically confirmed to Felt's family that their father, ninety-two at the time of this writing, was the mythical man in the parking garage whom Woodward and Bernstein had relied on to confirm information during the twenty-six months that Watergate had played out.

Woodward knew that Joan Felt strongly suspected that her father was much more than just a long-serving FBI man, and that Felt's family was considering going public, but he didn't realize it would be so soon, so sudden. Over Memorial Day weekend in

2005, Woodward received an e-mail from the family that was typical of earlier communications, indicating that they would disclose the secret together. Woodward and the family had discussed jointly writing a book, but something held Woodward back. It wasn't money. It wasn't a reluctance to share the limelight. He had grave doubts about his former source's mental acuity. Since Felt's first stroke in 1999, he had suffered another mild stroke in 2001. Some days he was lucid; many days he was not.

In February 2000, Woodward had flown to California to give a speech and arranged to visit Felt and take him out for lunch. Woodward was fifty-six; Felt, eighty-six—the same age as Woodward's father. Woodward brought along a tape recorder, and, after Felt had fish and a glass of wine, he and Felt retired to his garage apartment for an interview. It was pointless. Felt suffered from dementia. He couldn't even remember that Nixon had resigned or any details about Watergate. Nor did he remember Woodward nagging him for information. To many of Woodward's questions, he simply replied, "I don't remember."

"I left in a tangle of emotions," Woodward later wrote about the visit. "I did not want to become confrontational or accusatory or reckless. I hoped I had not stepped over that line. But there were still those ultimate questions, the ones I could not bring myself to ask or had not asked 28 years earlier, and that I could not seem to reach now: Why were you Deep Throat? What was your motive? Who are you? Who were you? Worse, I had to consider whether the man I had dealt with in this visit was the same man I had made the pledge of confidentiality to. What was my responsibility? To whom?"

Soon Woodward, provoked by his mentor Bradlee and his wife, Elsa, sat down to write the story. Woodward is by nature secretive. In fact, he keeps his files and home office locked when he's not there. To write about Deep Throat, he worked at a computer that was not connected to the Internet. He wanted to make sure that no one, absolutely no one, could hack their way into his computer and discover Deep Throat's identity. He began to write his personal story chronologically, about how he'd accidentally met Mark Felt in about 1970 and the role that Felt—an FBI agent straight out of central casting—had played in his life. It wasn't a story he intended to publish until Felt died or personally released him from their decades-old confidentiality agreement, but he wanted to be ready.

In spring 2002, Woodward showed the first draft to Bradlee and Elsa. He did not give Bradlee a copy; his former editor had to come to Woodward's Georgetown home in May to read it. When talking with Elsa after she read it, she made a daunting suggestion. "My wife, Elsa, posed—and I think quite wisely—she said, 'Maybe this is just a secret that should never be told,'" Woodward told NPR's Terry Gross on July 7, 2005, "'and that when Mark Felt dies you shouldn't say anything and the book should not be published,' or at least, you know, maybe until I'm gone or something like that." It didn't sit well with Woodward as he struggled to figure out what was the right thing to do by the man for whom he had nothing but gratitude.

Woodward disagreed, though—especially after George W. Bush had begun an era of government secrecy under the guise of national security. Woodward has always felt that the government should be more open. He also believes it is imperative for sources to know they can talk to reporters off the record, can speak the truth, and can be confident that under no circumstances will their trust ever be betrayed. This was Mark Felt's legacy to Woodward. Their extraordinary unbroken promise over three decades, Woodward knew, was why so many high-ranking officials, with so much to lose, do in fact speak with Woodward. They believe—because of his track record—that he will never betray them. Bernstein believes that he's benefited equally as well.

Yet it no longer mattered whether Woodward might tell the story of his complicated relationship with Mark Felt. Here it was. But he was also not ready to confirm the story. Woodward had given Felt his word. That morning, despite the *Vanity Fair* story and the barrage of media phone calls, Woodward was not convinced that Felt's words in the *Vanity Fair* piece effectively released him.

The problem was Felt's competence. Woodward did not believe Felt was mentally able to end their agreement. The question became—to Woodward and Bernstein—whether Felt's family or the family's lawyer was in a position to act on Felt's behalf. Woodward did not think so. He argued that silence was the best and most honorable response. Bradlee disagreed. He was certain that

Vanity Fair nailed it. To him, the daughter's and the lawyer's words effectively unchained Woodward and Bernstein. "They've got it," said Bradlee.

"Woodward's first tendency is he was bound by having given his word," said Bradlee. "I said that was academic. That the effect of the *Vanity Fair* story with the authenticity of Felt's words in the story in effect freed him."

Whatever plans either Woodward or Bernstein had made for the day evaporated. Bernstein quickly made arrangements to fly to Washington to confer with Woodward, Bradlee, and Downie. With Woodward's permission, Bernstein released a statement around noon to CNN, neither confirming nor denying anything. He was buying time.

While outside the *Post*, the news media was in a frenzy to discover the truth, life inside the *Post* ground to a standstill, especially after an electronic message was sent with a link to *Vanity Fair*'s story. The electricity in the air was palpable. Something really exciting was going on, and everyone could feel it, said Tom Wilkinson, who had been Bernstein's editor just before Watergate. "All work stopped," said metro reporter Karlyn Barker, who had joined the paper the same day as Woodward in September 1971. "Almost everyone in the newsroom was online reading the *Vanity Fair* article or talking about it in the cafeteria." Even Barker's mother, Mary Joy Barker, was mesmerized. "I hope it's true," she wrote in an e-mail to her daughter from her home in El Cerrito, California. "I was afraid I would die without knowing."

Downie, as it happened, was out of the office at a company retreat in St. Michael's, Maryland, about two hours east of the office. In the midst of a scheduled 10:30 to noon presentation on coming changes at the newspaper, Downie's cell phone started ringing repeatedly around 11:30 a.m. Each time he hit the end button, there would be another call. Finally, he turned the phone off. Then hotel staffers interrupted with written notes. His assistant, Pat O'Shea, was desperate to reach him. Other senior editors wanted him to call immediately. He put the messages in a pile. He would deal with them later.

Sitting in the audience was Downie's boss and friend, Donald E. Graham, the chairman and CEO of the Washington Post Company. Graham's cell phone rang, and he went outside through a pair of French doors to take the call and learned about *Vanity Fair*. Just as Downie was finishing his talk, Graham interrupted. "You'd better call Woodward," advised Graham.

Minutes later, Downie was on the phone to Woodward. Then he jumped into his BMW 330, breaking the speed limit as he raced to Washington to read the story and decide what to do. This wasn't the *National Enquirer* revealing Deep Throat; it was *Vanity Fair*, a magazine with some of the most respected journalists in the country. He ordered his senior editors to put together a package of stories but was willing to talk about it with the Watergate players when they converged at the *Post*. Driving back, he made it clear that he wanted David Von Drehle, one of the *Post*'s best writers, to start working on the story. They budgeted him seventy to eighty inches of copy, although Von Drehle was clearly nonplussed about how to handle writing the story. He had long known it would fall to him to write the Deep Throat story, but he'd never been told the man's identity. Now he still had no confirmation from Woodward and had not written any advance copy.

"Assume it is Mark Felt," Downie told editors over a speaker phone. "We are going to announce it." Sometime later that afternoon, a *Post* copy aide sent out an e-mail to the staff: "If you snagged the 'All the President's Men' file from the fourth-floor photo archive today, can you phone me?"

This time, it was Downie's decision how to handle the story. "The big question," said Downie,"was whether the family's revelation of Mark Felt as Deep Throat was sufficient reason for us to no longer have this confidentiality agreement that Bob had observed now for more than thirty-three years."

Downie reached the paper at 2:15 p.m. Television crews were clamoring outside the *Post*. They were also staked out in front of Woodward's Georgetown home. Downie quickly read the piece, which reinforced his sense that the final chapter of Watergate was over. The paper had to confirm the story. It was an awkward situation. Woodward and Bernstein had always thought of themselves as reporters, but in this instance they were The News, and the *Post* had The Story. Downie, a newsman with ink in his blood, could not in good conscience withhold the truth. It was not in his nature.

Woodward walked into the newsroom around 2:30 p.m. with a trenchcoat thrown over his shoulder. Bradlee was already in the building. Woodward walked into Downie's office, the same office that, long ago, he and Carl had sat in, talking so often with Bradlee about Watergate. "Exact same office but newer furniture," joked Downie.

"I read the story when I first got into the office," said Downie. "My first reaction after reading it was, it enforced my sense that this was over. Otherwise, it was kind of an odd piece. It was unusual for the family lawyer to write it, as opposed to a journalist."

Woodward and Downie talked for only about ten to fifteen minutes. They'd been having an ongoing conversation about how to handle Deep Throat after Downie had read the manuscript months earlier, but Woodward was resistant. This was clearly not how Woodward saw the story playing out. He wanted more control. Woodward had initially talked about revealing Deep Throat's name several weeks after Felt's death, when the paper could run a prepublication excerpt from his new book on Felt and break the news, as the *Post* had done with other Woodward books. Downie, however, said that was not going to happen in this case. "We had to let it hang out as soon as possible," he said. Before *Vanity Fair* even became an issue, Woodward had agreed.

"Bob is a manipulative person," said Downie, of the man he first met in July 1972. "That's one of his great strengths and one of his weaknesses. He tries to control everything. When he comes to see me, he has an agenda. He doesn't have a conversation with me unless he's got an agenda. If he calls or comes to see me, he's got an agenda. Something he wants to accomplish. I need to figure out what it is. Quite often, he's not going to tell me outright."

In this case, Woodward did have an agenda. He had planned for the story to be revealed either by Felt's death or in agreement with Felt. Not this. He wasn't comfortable with the ambivalence.

"I think Bob was really thrown by this happening," said Downie. "He had no idea this was going to happen. That's unusual for Bob. He's normally in control. He has all the angles figured out. In this case, he was completely surprised."

As far as Downie was concerned, the jig was up. There was no ambivalence. Woodward wasn't so sure. He proceeded to tease through all the reasons not to confirm the story. He was very uneasy. He told Downie that his confidential source arrangement was with Felt—not with Felt's daughter or his lawyer. Woodward had made a promise; Felt was feeble. Woodward questioned whether the family could make this decision for Felt. It was Felt's decision, not theirs.

Downie listened. He was sympathetic. "These were understandable worries," said Downie. "They were laudable. I understood his discomfort." Downie knew that when you hold on to a secret for decades, it would be extraordinarily difficult to let it go. He said as much to Woodward, although he knew that this sentiment was not one that Woodward would share. "He doesn't talk about things like that," Downie said later. "He keeps things to himself. He's very guarded."

Downie explained that revealing Deep Throat's identity now could only be good for the *Post*. Bradlee agreed. "One of the things that editors do is nudge," said Bradlee of dealing with Woodward. "Say, 'C'mon, that's not realistic.' We don't want to lose control of the story." If the *Post* waited until Felt died, then only the *Post* and Woodward would be heard from. There'd be no chance for Felt to weigh in, and the questioning, the doubting, would continue.

There really was not a lot of time for thumb-sucking. Downie and Woodward had known each other for thirty-three years. Downie had edited Woodward and Bernstein's Watergate copy in 1973. The two men had had this conversation before. It was getting near deadline—especially for the *Post*'s Web page, the editors of which were pressuring Downie for a decision. "I knew the entire manuscript," said Downie. "We had talked a lot. There wasn't a lot of preamble necessary. And we didn't have much time. We were on deadline, literally on deadline with the Web, with people wanting to know."

Was the *Post* going to confirm it or not?

Finally, Downie ended the conversation. The story was out. "Bob, it's over," he said.

Yet Bernstein hadn't arrived from New York yet. Woodward wanted to talk it over with him before anything final happened. The pair had shared this secret like Huck Finn and Tom Sawyer, who had witnessed a murder, then ran away and swore an oath in blood not to ever tell anyone what they had seen. Despite decades of badgering about Deep Throat's identity, Woodward and Bernstein, too, had made an oath.

Now, however, it was time to tell. On his way to the *Post*, Bernstein called Woodward, and they talked some more. Bernstein thought the story was out of their hands at this point. They agreed that it was over. Bernstein asked that they wait until he got to the paper and then to let Woodward and Bernstein—not the *Washington Post*—give final confirmation. Around 5 p.m., Bernstein arrived carrying an overnight bag, and the newsroom fell silent. Woodward and Bernstein hugged. It had been a while since Bernstein had been inside this newsroom, which was once home to him. He noticed the quiet. It wasn't just that people were watching; the clacking of typewriters—once such a familiar sound before the era of computers—was gone. Only a handful of people inside the newsroom that day were familiar faces from Watergate.

"Carl came waltzing in. Bob was here, and people were paying rapt attention," said Wilkinson. "It was a wow moment."

There was more conferring, and then it was over. A thirty-three-year-old secret ended with the push of a "send" button from WashingtonPost.com. At 5:12 p.m. on May 31, 2005, the *Post* ran this news alert:

WOODWARD CONFIRMS IDENTITY OF "DEEP THROAT"

Former FBI official W. Mark Felt was the source for leaked secrets about Nixon's Watergate coverup, the *Washington Post* confirms after Felt's admission.

The last secret of the story was revealed. "W. Mark Felt was 'Deep Throat' and helped us immeasurably in our Watergate coverage," Woodward and Bernstein said in a statement on the *Post*'s Web site. "However, as the record shows, many other sources and officials assisted us and other reporters for the hundreds of stories that were written in the *Washington Post* about Watergate."

Seventeen minutes later, the *Post*'s Web site ran a long, detailed story by David Von Drehle and another reporter, filling in details that had been left out in the news alert. The newsroom then went into overdrive to get out more Deep Throat stories for the next day's paper. While this was clearly a national story, the metro section decided to do a piece on the underground parking garage where Woodward and Felt met long ago. Woodward wrote in *The Secret Man* that it was at their first garage meeting on October 9, 1972, that Felt said, "There is a way to untie the Watergate knot." But Woodward wouldn't give the address to the metro section. He said he needed to check something. (Later, in July, he would reveal the location on an NBC special with Tom Brokaw when his Deep Throat book was published.) Here again was the difficult balance Woodward had to negotiate between pleasing his book publisher and his employer. "If there was any kind of resentment it was that Bob was doing too much for the book and not enough for the newspaper," said a longtime *Post* editor who did not want to be identified because of Woodward's power at the paper. But the tension was short-lived. He was Mr. Carte Blanche. No one could force Woodward to give up the location.

That night the revelation led the evening newscasts. At 6:30 p.m., while the Watergate duo watched on a TV in Woodward's *Post* office, NBC anchor Brian Williams began:

> One of the great mysteries of our time is no more. Tonight we know the identity of the secret Washington source known as Deep Throat, the man who gave the information to two young reporters for the *Washington Post* in the scandal called Watergate that ended with the first ever resignation of an American president. Deep Throat, it turns out, was Mark Felt. Back then he was the number two official in the FBI. He is now ninety-one years old and going public because of his family's deep belief that what he did was heroic. In a town where leaks are a daily event, it stayed a secret for over thirty years and bordered on obsession. In the end, late today, the same paper that broke Watergate was forced to admit the secret to Watergate was out.

The next morning, June 1, anyone picking up a daily newspaper was treated to news that a nonagenarian former lifelong FBI agent was Deep Throat. Editorials hailed Felt as a hero who had played a key role in bringing down a corrupt president and many people in his administration. Nixon loyalists, although they were few, took to the airwaves condemning Felt as a traitor who had ignominiously betrayed his country by sharing confidential information with a pair of reporters who they said were out to get a sitting president.

"The next day it was on the front pages of every newspaper in the world," said *Vanity Fair*'s David Friend, who breathed a sigh of relief when Woodward and Bernstein confirmed the magazine's story. "Within thirty-six hours, it was on twelve thousand blogs, according to Technorati, which monitors blog traffic. We never expected this colossal secret to disintegrate so fast. Forget the proverbial twenty-four-hour news cycle, which is no longer relevant in the digital age. Instead, decades of secrecy and denial evaporated in a mere seven hours and forty-two minutes—from the time I called Woodward until they revealed it on the *Post* Web site."

The secret was out. Downie was right. It was over. Now the pair would trot around to TV interviews and answer a barrage of questions from print and radio reporters. For about a week, they would be everywhere, mostly together, taking a victory lap just as they'd done after writing *All the President's Men* thirty-one years earlier.

On the June 2 pages of the *Washington Post*, Woodward shared the story of how he had met Deep Throat; then the Watergate reporters hit the New York circuit, checking in early that morning with radio personality Don Imus. Wherever they went, they could not stay long before they would be late for the next interview.

When *Today Show* cohost Matt Lauer asked how it felt to let go of a secret they had harbored for thirty-three years, Woodward began to answer. After all, Felt was his source. Yet in a tableau that perfectly captured their relationship, Bernstein interrupted and got in the last word. "I think it's like having tried to protect something precious for all these years that you carry around, and for the first time it's not there to protect in your pocket anymore. It's a very strange feeling."

More than three decades have passed since the Watergate break-in and President Nixon's resignation on August 9, 1974. Woodward and Bernstein have become historical figures, as much a part of the Watergate story and the historical record as any of the people they reported on. Woodward has gone on to write eleven more books after the two on Watergate, and Bernstein has garnered his own distinction with books on a pope and one on his parents. The reality, however, is this: no matter how much they accomplish, no matter how far they have traveled beyond the destructive political days of the early 1970s, Woodward and Bernstein will *always* be introduced—and the first paragraph of their obituaries will note them—as two of the most famous journalists in the world, whose systematic Watergate reporting for the *Washington Post* between 1972 and 1974 set the stage for the downfall of an American president.

Acknowledgments

I once saw an op-ed piece by someone who had done a good deal of work on a friend's book and then was left out of the acknowledgments. They no longer speak. That tale terrifies me. Writing a book is a long, lonely experience. You lose your mind, you lose your way. But then friends, family, and editors pull you back. The reality is that while it is a solo experience, you do not do it alone. There are many people to thank.

This book would not have been possible without the help of Lorraine Branham, director of the University of Texas's journalism department, who gave me a visiting professor fellowship that allowed me to teach while I pawed through the Woodward-Bernstein Watergate archives on campus. I am also grateful to Gene Roberts, my friend and mentor, and to the Fund for Investigative Journalism, which padded my pocket with extra money for travel. Whenever I flew to Austin, my good pals Denise Gamino and Jay Godwin generously opened their home and always had a bed for me. I don't know what I would have done without their support.

This book grew out of an oral history I did on what happened to Woodward and Bernstein after Watergate for *Washingtonian* magazine in September 2003, which was deftly edited by Bill O'Sullivan and done with the encouragement of Jack Limpert.

I am indebted to my old friend Mike Isikoff, who pushed me to write the book and introduced me to my superswell agent, Gail Ross, who led me to John Wiley & Sons, where my editor, Eric Nelson, made sure the book got done. Had he not set a deadline, I'd still be picking through the thirty-one feet of Watergate documents in Texas. I could not have had a better editor and team, including production editor Lisa Burstiner, than the one I had at Wiley. Eric Nelson is not only intelligent and insightful but also supportive, encouraging, and easy to work for. Thanks also to my fabulous fact-checker, Elizabeth Gardner, who worked tirelessly.

Thanks to Bob Kaiser for alerting me to the existence of David Halberstam's and Alan J. Pakula's archives, rich with contemporaneous interviews from the 1970s with Woodward, Bernstein, and others. Thank you especially to David Halberstam who generously gave me permission to explore his still unopened archives at Boston University of interviews he conducted in the mid-1970s for his book *The Powers That Be*, and to Hannah Pakula who steered me to her husband Alan's notes compiled in 1975 while making the film *All the President's Men*. Pakula died in a freak accident in 1998, but I would still like to thank him for being the kind of filmmaker who conducted such detailed, analytical interviews before making a movie. Thank you to Barbara Hall, the research archivist, who specially opened the never-before-seen Pakula papers for me in the Margaret Herrick Library of the Academy of Motion Picture Arts and Sciences in Los Angeles.

I must also mention all the help and guidance I received from Steve Mielke, the University of Texas at Austin archivist who organized the Woodward-Bernstein Watergate papers; Scott Armstrong; Steve Luxenberg; Geneva Overholser; Leonard Downie Jr.; Ben Bradlee; Sally Quinn; Richard Cohen; David Friend; Harry Rosenfeld; David Greenberg; Peter Osnos; Karlyn Barker; Mark Feldstein; Jack Nelson; David Von Drehle; Mildred Marmur; Robert Redford; Dustin Hoffman; and my friends at American University. And to Rem Rieder, editor of the *American Journalism Review*, to whom I am forever grateful for launching me into the intriguing world of media writing.

The enthusiastic support of my friends and family has been an unending source of encouragement. To all of them, especially Judy Belk, Kelly Degnan, Sally Gabler, Cina Radler, Celeste Szewczyk, and my sister, Judy Long, I am most grateful. More thanks to Randy and Judy McKnight for generously helping me get started, to the Slovers for providing a home away from home in Austin, to my J315 class for making me laugh, and to my other "son," Othman Bouchareb, for keeping me sane. I owe special gratitude to Robert Hodierne, who has always been one of my biggest fans, for his perceptive comments, his homemade cookies, and especially his willingness to drop everything to help when I was in Austin.

To write this book, I relied on the Woodward and Bernstein, Halberstam, and Pakula archives, plus research, reporting, and interviews with Woodward, Bernstein, and more than 175 people. It was never my intent to do a definitive biography on either man but rather to tell the fascinating story of what happened to both of them during Watergate and beyond. When Deep Throat was revealed in May 2005 in the midst of my research, I realized I was blessed with the perfect, natural ending for a book about two men who are still very much alive.

The good things about this book owe a great deal to others, while the errors and omissions are solely mine.

Works Cited

Archives

Halberstam, David. Special Collections. Howard Gotlieb Archival Research Center, Boston University.

Pakula, Alan J. Papers, Special Collections. Margaret Herrick Library, Academy of Motion Picture Arts and Sciences, Los Angeles.

The Bob Woodward and Carl Bernstein Watergate Papers. Harry Ransom Humanities Research Center, University of Texas at Austin.

Books

Arledge, Roone. *Roone: A Memoir*. New York: HarperCollins, 2003.

Bernstein, Carl. *Loyalties: A Son's Memoir*. New York: Simon & Schuster, 1989.

————, and Marco Politi. *His Holiness: John Paul II and the Hidden History of Our Time*. New York: Doubleday, 1996.

————, and Bob Woodward. *All the President's Men*. New York: Simon & Schuster, 1974.

Bradlee, Benjamin. *A Good Life: Newspapering and Other Adventures*. New York: Simon & Schuster, 1995.

Brown, Jared. *Alan J. Pakula: His Films and His Life*. New York: Backstage Books, 2005.

Colodny, Len, and Gettlin Colodny. *Silent Coup: The Removal of a President*. New York: St. Martin's Press, 1991.

Crouse, Timothy. *The Boys on the Bus*. New York: Ballantine Books, 1974.

Darman, Richard. *Who's in Control? Polar Politics and the Sensible Center*. New York: Simon & Schuster, 1996.

Downie, Leonard, Jr. *The New Muckrakers*. Washington, DC: New Republic Book Co., 1976.

Emery, Fred. *Watergate: The Corruption of American Politics and the Fall of Richard Nixon.* New York: Simon & Schuster, 1994.

Ephron, Nora. *Heartburn.* New York: Alfred A. Knopf, 1983.

Felt, W. Mark. *The FBI Pyramid from the Inside.* New York: Putnam, 1979.

Frankel, Max. *The Times of My Life and My Life with the Times.* New York: Random House, 1999.

Garment, Leonard. *Crazy Rhythm: My Journey from Brooklyn, Jazz, and Wall Street to Nixon's White House, Watergate, and Beyond.* New York: Times Books, 1997.

————. *In Search of Deep Throat: The Greatest Political Mystery of Our Time.* New York: Basic Books, 2000.

Gelb, Arthur. *City Room.* New York: Putnam, 2003.

Goldman, William. *Adventures in the Screen Trade: A Personal View of Hollywood and Screenwriting.* New York: Warner Books, 1983.

Greenberg, David. *Nixon's Shadow: The History of the Image.* New York: W.W. Norton, 2003.

Graham, Katharine. *Personal History.* New York: Alfred A. Knopf, 2002.

Havill, Adrian. *Deep Truth: The Lives of Bob Woodward and Carl Bernstein.* Secaucus, NJ: Carol Publishing Group, 1993.

Hougan, Jim. *Secret Agenda: Watergate, Deep Throat and the CIA.* New York: Random House, 1984.

Halberstam, David. *The Powers That Be.* New York: Alfred A. Knopf, 1979.

Hirshberg, Jack. *Redford/Hoffman: A Portrait of All the President's Men.* New York: Warner Books, 1976.

Kutler, Stanley I. *Wars of Watergate: The Last Crisis of Richard Nixon.* New York: Random House, 1990.

Liebovich, Louis W. *Richard Nixon, Watergate and the Press: A Historical Retrospective.* Westport, CT: Praeger Publishers, 2003.

Lukas, J. Anthony. *Nightmare: The Underside of the Nixon Years.* Athens: Ohio University Press, 1999.

Obst, David. *Too Good to Be Forgotten: Changing America in the '60s and '70s.* New York: John Wiley & Sons, 1998.

Smith, Liz. *Natural Blonde: A Memoir.* New York: Hyperion, 2000.

Streitmatter, Rodger. *Mightier Than the Sword: How the News Media Have Shaped American History.* Boulder, CO: Westview Press, 1997.

Sussman, Barry. *The Great Cover-Up: Nixon and the Scandal of Watergate.* New York: New American Library, 1974.

Woodward, Bob, *Plan of Attack.* New York: Simon & Schuster, 2004.

————. *The Secret Man: The Story of Watergate's Deep Throat.* New York: Simon & Schuster, 2005.

————. *Veil: The Secret Wars of the CIA.* New York: Simon & Schuster, 1987.

————. *Wired: The Short Life and Fast Times of John Belushi.* New York: Simon & Schuster, 1984.

————, and Scott Armstrong. *The Brethren.* New York: Simon & Schuster, 1979.

————, and Carl Bernstein. *The Final Days.* New York: Simon & Schuster, 1976.

Index